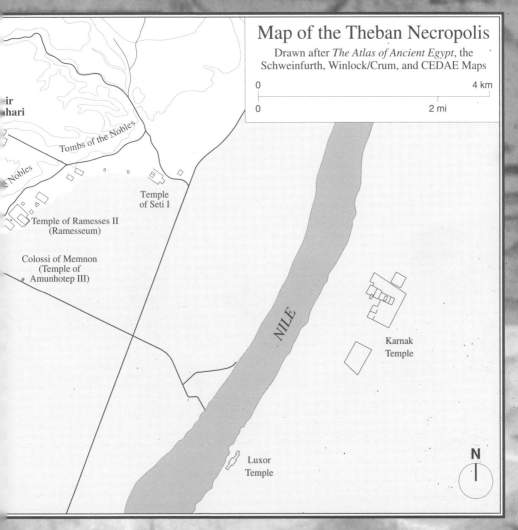

Map of the Theban Necropolis

Drawn after *The Atlas of Ancient Egypt*, the
Schweinfurth, Winlock/Crum, and CEDAE Maps

0	4 km
0	2 mi

ir
hari

Tombs of the Nobles

Nobles

e Nobles

Temple
of Seti I

Temple of Ramesses II
(Ramesseum)

Colossi of Memnon
(Temple of
Amunhotep III)

NILE

Karnak
Temple

Luxor
Temple

N

THE LOST TOMB

ALSO BY KENT R. WEEKS

X-raying the Pharaohs (with James Harris)

In 1995, an American Egyptologist

Discovered the Burial Site of the

Sons of Ramesses II

THE LOST TOMB

This Is His Incredible Story of KV 5

and Its Excavation

KENT R. WEEKS

WILLIAM MORROW AND COMPANY, INC. / NEW YORK

Copyright © 1998 by Kent R. Weeks

Chapter openings drawn by Susan Weeks
Figures and maps drawn by Walton Chan, copyright © 1997
by The Theban Mapping Project
Photographs, unless otherwise credited, by Francis Dzikowski,
copyright © 1997 by The Theban Mapping Project

All rights reserved. No part of this book may be reproduced or utilized in any form
or by any means, electronic or mechanical, including photocopying, recording, or by
any information storage or retrieval system, without permission in writing from the
Publisher. Inquiries should be addressed to Permissions Department, William Morrow
and Company, Inc., 1350 Avenue of the Americas, New York, N.Y. 10019.

It is the policy of William Morrow and Company, Inc., and its imprints and affiliates,
recognizing the importance of preserving what has been written, to print the books we
publish on acid-free paper, and we exert our best efforts to that end.

Library of Congress Cataloging-in-Publication Data

Weeks, Kent R.
   The lost tomb / Kent R. Weeks. — 1st ed.
      p.   cm.
   "In 1995, an American Egyptologist discovered the burial site of
the sons of Ramesses II : this is his incredible story of KV 5 and its
excavation."
   ISBN 0-688-15087-X
   1. Tombs—Egypt—Valley of the Kings. 2. Excavations
(Archaeology)—Egypt—Valley of the Kings. 3. Princes—Egypt—
Tombs. 4. Ramses II, King of Egypt. 5. Weeks, Kent R. I. Title.
DT73.B44W43 1998
932' 014' 092—dc21   98-21769
                                                              CIP

Printed in the United States of America

First Edition

1 2 3 4 5 6 7 8 9 10

BOOK DESIGN BY JO ANNE METSCH

www.williammorrow.com

For Susan, Christopher, and Emily

PROLOGUE

"WE have finished, Doctor. Do you want to go inside?"

Mohammed, one of our senior workmen, stood at the top of the deep pit we had exposed at the entrance to the Valley of the Kings. He pointed down into a doorway cut through the bedrock on its eastern end, clearly the entrance to a tomb. For several weeks, we had been digging a trench along the base of the hillside here, searching for KV 5, a tomb that had been seen 170 years earlier, then forgotten.

"Absolutely! Bruce, do you want to come with us?" I turned to Bruce Ludwig, a longtime benefactor of our project. "Be the first in over 160 years to see what's inside?" A British explorer, James Burton, had seen the entrance to KV 5 in 1825, but there was no evidence that anyone else had crawled inside since then.

"No thanks. I'll wait until there's more room to maneuver." Bruce is over six feet tall, and the trench through the doorway was extremely narrow.

"But I'm going," said Catharine Roehrig, the assistant director of our Theban Mapping Project since 1980. "I've been in every tomb we've ever mapped on this project—more Theban tombs than anybody else in history, I think—and I don't want to ruin my record now. Wait a second." She rushed off to get another flash-light. A few minutes later, we started crawling into Burton's trench, first Mohammed, then Catharine, then me.

Crawling into the tomb was difficult. Burton's channel was only about fifty centimeters (twenty inches) wide, not even that in height, cut through debris that consisted of thousands of razor-sharp fragments of limestone. Burton had hired two or three work-men to dig this channel and it had been done quickly and rather sloppily. We slithered forward, using our fingers and toes to pull and push ourselves farther into the tomb's first chamber. To our left and right and beneath us, the chamber was packed with dense layers of silt and stone chips. Above us was broken and undeco-rated bedrock, which formed the tomb's ceiling. Burton's remarks about the tomb had been brief, and no wonder: practically noth-ing could be seen of the tomb itself.

The air was hot and humid and the smell was foul. In a matter of minutes, our clothes were soaking and we were covered with a thick layer of dirt and mud and things that didn't bear thinking about. My glasses kept slipping down my nose; the lenses fogged and I had to peer over the top of the frames. Ahead of us, Mohammed stopped, then handed back a broken champagne glass he had found lying in the trench. I turned it over in my hand, then set it down beside the trench.

"This may have washed in after one of Howard Carter's fabled luncheons," I suggested to Catharine. In several photographs taken after his 1922 discovery of Tutankhamun's tomb, Carter is shown toasting new finds with colleagues at a lunch table he'd set up in a nearby tomb.

As we continued farther into KV 5, through a broken doorway and a second chamber that seemed to be about the same small size as the first, I remembered that, according to Burton's sketch plan, the tomb's third chamber was a huge pillared hall. Almost on cue, as we crawled through another doorway, the tops of broken pillars could be dimly seen jutting up through the debris, just visible in the few centimeters of open space below the ceiling. Things began to get dicey almost the moment we crawled into the room: Burton's channel made a sharp turn to the right to avoid a pillar, then began weaving between huge blocks of limestone that had fallen from the ceiling. We had to crawl over and around two- and three-ton slabs lying at the top of the debris. The blocks had obviously fallen before Burton crawled through here because no part of the ceiling appeared to have collapsed more recently than his visit in 1825. Even so, these fallen blocks were unnerving, and a headline flashed through my mind: EGYPTOLOGISTS FLATTENED AS TOMB COLLAPSES: PHARAOH'S CURSE RETURNS.

Along the sides of the pillared hall, we could see the tops of several doorways cut through its walls. Catharine crawled ahead to peer into one of the side chambers. "There's a huge room over here," she called back. "It has six pillars." That, too, squared with Burton's sketch plan.

After another ten minutes of exploration, Catharine crawled back into the sixteen-pillared hall, and the three of us decided it was time to leave. Fascinating though it was inside the tomb, we were all ready to get out of the uncomfortable and claustrophobic surroundings. It was eerily silent and dark, the air was bad, and it was extremely hot and humid.

Soaking wet, sweat streaking my glasses, covered in mud, flashlight almost dead, I turned to Mohammed. "Do you remember where the entrance is?"

"No."

Catharine said she wasn't sure either. The pillared hall was so filled with debris that it was impossible to see more than a few centimeters in any direction. Mohammed, who was in the lead, paused after a few moments to reconnoiter. He decided we'd made a wrong turn after rounding one of the pillars, and he told us to turn back and retrace our path.

"I think we came in from over there," he said. "Wait. I will check." He crawled forward, looking for a recognizable pillar or a scrape in the debris that might show where we'd been. Shining his flashlight around the chamber, he looked up at the ceiling for a moment, stopped, then called us over.

"Look," he said, and pointed to the ceiling with his light. Directly above him, written on the ceiling, were the words BURTON 1825. They had been written in the smoke of a candle, in letters about forty centimeters (sixteen inches) tall. I could imagine Burton lying here on the debris, as we were doing, anxious to leave but wanting to leave a record of his visit into this unpleasant and rather unnerving chamber, writing his name slowly, the letters becoming fatter as the candle approached the ceiling, the date hastily written as he tired and longed to return to fresh air.

"We're probably the first to see this since Burton wrote it," Catharine remarked, and she was almost certainly correct. Neither Howard Carter nor any other explorer or archaeologist had come this far into the tomb in modern times.

After a few minutes, we began moving again and, finally, after a few more wrong turns, Mohammed led us into welcome daylight. Happily, we clambered out of the tomb into the open air. It was 35 degrees Celsius (95 degrees Fahrenheit) outside, but after being in the tomb it seemed wonderfully fresh and comfortable.

"What'd you see?" Bruce asked.

"Burton's plan is right on," I replied. "The tomb seems huge. It's at least forty meters from the entrance to the back of the pillared hall. The whole place is fascinating. Burton's sketch was correctly drawn—as far as it goes. But I'll bet there's more to KV 5 than the seven or eight chambers Burton saw. Almost every tomb in the Valley of the Kings is a series of long corridors cut into the hillside, and almost every noble's tomb has just two or three simple, rectangular chambers. But this tomb is nothing like that. Doorways lead off the pillared hall in all directions. Also, we found some tiny bits of decoration on the walls, and there's a cartouche of Ramesses II in the doorway. . . . " I paused for a moment, my mind racing. "Bruce, we've got to spend more time exploring here. This tomb has possibilities. We could be on to something."

Catharine was scraping mud from her filthy clothes. She looked at me, then at Bruce. "Remember that Elizabeth Thomas"—an American Egyptologist who knew more about the Valley of the

Kings than anyone in this century—"thought this might be a tomb for children of Ramesses II. She had no proof, but her theory should be checked out."

Bruce thought for a moment. "You're right. Okay, I'll get you the money to work here again next season."

Two days later, after hiring an ironmonger to install a door in the tomb entrance, we had to close up after working an eight-week-long field season. I had teaching obligations and the others had jobs or classes to return to. On our last day, while the inspector of antiquities was preparing to seal the tomb, Catharine took a flashlight and tried to peer into the three-centimeter gap between the ceiling and the debris that choked the tomb's first chamber. Her head was twisted and her cheek pushed hard against the ceiling.

"There's a lot of decoration on this wall," she whispered. "I think there's a frieze of cartouches at the top and maybe several columns of hieroglyphs below that."

It was exactly what we were hoping for: such texts would almost certainly tell us for whom KV5 had been carved and when. It was frustrating that we couldn't clear the wall that moment, but we knew that once it was exposed, it would have to be conserved immediately or the texts might crumble to dust. We would have to wait.

Catharine turned to me. "Do you think that the inscriptions here could give us the name of a son of Ramesses II?" We climbed back out of KV 5 and stood in the blazing sun, watching as the inspector padlocked the new iron door for the last time and affixed his official lead seal.

"Wouldn't surprise me in the least. God, I hate to leave for ten months! I have a feeling that KV 5 is going to repay whatever it takes to explore it. Elizabeth Thomas had a feel for such things. But if it is for a son of Ramesses II, it's one of the strangest tombs ever dug for a prince."

IT *was* worth the effort and then some. KV 5 has turned out to be the largest tomb ever found in the Valley of the Kings, perhaps the largest in Egypt, and one of the most unusual and important Egyptian tombs in plan and purpose. Its history spans the reigns of several kings, and it was used as the burial place of not just one son of Ramesses II, but of many. We now know that it contains well over one hundred chambers, and its artifacts and texts already have changed what we know about the reign of one of Egypt's best-known and most powerful rulers. KV 5 has become arguably the best-known archaeological site since the discovery of King Tutankhamun's tomb, and many Egyptologists are calling it one of the most important finds in Egypt in this century.

What follows is the story of the discovery and excavation of KV 5 and an attempt to interpret and explain the meaning of this most enigmatic tomb. It's a personal account, not a technical treatise. I want to share the excitement—and the frustrations—of doing archaeological work in the world's most famous royal cemetery, the Valley of the Kings, and to describe the techniques of archaeological excavation and the ways Egyptologists try to make sense of what they find. I want to show how we Egyptologists, working rather like detectives, have taken minuscule pieces of evidence and constructed much broader pictures of a site (our crime scene), the ancient happenings there (the crime itself), and the people involved in creating, using, and sometimes stealing the materials the site contained (our culprits and victims and innocent bystanders).

In the course of our work, we have been able to reveal exciting new information about the sons of Ramesses II and their role in Egypt's royal court, but the story of KV 5 is a work in progress. We've cleared only a few of its many chambers and corridors, and there are dozens still filled with debris that cover hundreds of square meters each and probably contain many more decorated walls and artifacts. There is decades more work to be done, and we know with certainty that the tomb will reveal even more rooms than the 108 we have already counted.

While our work is frustrating, it is also part of the joy of archaeology—the continuing search for data, the framing of new questions, the revision of theories—it is these that make our current work in KV 5 a prologue to the study of what already has become one of the most interesting and important recent discoveries in the field. It was the kind of discovery I had dreamed of making four decades ago when I first fantasized about becoming an Egyptologist.

CONTENTS

THE LOST TOMB

Chicago House, Luxor

I

THE YEARS B(EFORE) C(HICAGO)

I decided to become an Egyptologist when I was eight years old. I have no idea what first produced in a young boy's mind an interest so strong that an ancient civilization won out over games of cowboys and Indians and dreams of intergalactic travel. I do know that I was fortunate enough to have had several teachers who encouraged my interest by lending me books and talking about the excitement of archaeology. Several of them told me they had wanted to be Egyptologists themselves, and each had a small personal library of books that complemented the small collection on Egypt in our town library. Everett, Washington, where I was born, had a population of about 25,000 then, and most men worked as lumberjacks, pulp-mill employees, farmers, or fishermen. The library definitely didn't have as many Egyptology books as it had Zane Grey novels. My father was a policeman and my mother a medical records supervisor. Neither tried to dissuade me from being an Egyptologist, although several of my more realistic relatives hoped it was a passing fad: one aunt regularly pointed out that an interest in ancient Egypt could not possibly lead to a decent job. My school friends, on the other hand, agreed that cutting open mummies and searching gold-filled tombs were perfectly rational goals and were well worth pursuing.

Whatever the origins of this interest, my fascination with ancient Egypt grew throughout childhood. I cannot remember ever wanting to do anything else with my life than to study Egyptology and—this was my dream!—to go someday to Egypt and dig. When we moved to another small town, Longview, Washington, in 1953, I quickly exhausted its library, too, but again was fortunate to have a teacher who convinced me that the idea of becoming an Egyptologist was not silly but sensible and eminently possible if I seriously worked at it.

The first Egyptologist I ever met was Dr. Ahmed Fakhry, a kind and gentle man who was a professor at Cairo University. We met in Seattle in 1956, when Dr. Fakhry was accompanying the "Treasures of Tutankhamun" exhibition then touring America. We talked for several hours about Egyptology, and Dr. Fakhry generously illustrated his comments with stories of his own projects, at Giza, at Dahshur, in the oases—dropping place names that made me almost dizzy with excitement. He was extremely encouraging when I told him how serious I was about becoming an Egyptologist and offered suggestions about planning a course of study.

I had also received sound letters of advice from Professor John Wilson at the University of Chicago, whom I regularly hounded with requests for information and bibliographical sources. I had by then discovered the wonders of the interlibrary loan system and was ordering Egyptology books from libraries all over western America. Professor Wilson, too, was generous with his time, and his advice was solid: do not specialize too soon; get a good liberal arts education; study foreign languages.

When it was time for university, I chose the University of Washington, in Seattle. It was close by, affordable, and had a good reputation. I majored in anthropology and prehistoric archaeology and minored in ancient history and the history of medicine. I thought these subjects would prepare me for the kind of Egyptology that I hoped to pursue someday. I also took courses in human anatomy and pathology, English literature, Chinese society, plus Greek and French and German. These turned out to be wise choices: I have had many occasions since to use much of what I gained in these areas.

In my senior year at college, Yale University announced its plans for an archaeological expedition in Egyptian Nubia as part of a salvage campaign to save the monuments about to be destroyed by the floodwaters of the Aswan High Dam. I immediately wrote to Yale, and two months later received a letter from the project director, William Kelly Simpson, inviting me to join their project at the site of Arminna West. In November 1963, I flew from Seattle to Cairo (my first time outside the Northwest), and was soon introduced to Ramesses II—first to his mummy in the Egyptian Museum, then to one of his most spectacular monuments, the temples he built for himself and his principal wife at Abu Simbel in Nubia, several hundred kilometers beyond the southern limit of Egypt.

THE TEMPLES OF ABU SIMBEL

I still remember arriving at Abu Simbel for the first time late in the autumn of 1963. I was in ecstasy, sailing on the river I'd dreamed about since I was eight years old. We traveled up the Nile on an aged sailing vessel, a *dahabeyah* that had been built a hundred years earlier for rich European tourists. The boat, although relatively seaworthy (by which I mean it listed only slightly to starboard), badly needed a coat of paint and its decks sagged under one's feet. The masts and sails had disappeared long ago, and we were towed through Nubia by a barge that carried one hundred workmen. As run-down as it was, to me the *dahabeyah* was a floating palace with cabins and lounges that exuded history.

It was a wonderfully romantic trip, sitting on the open deck looking at the narrow strip of plants and palms—never more than a few yards wide—that separated the river from the Nubian desert. We drank tea and watched as huge flocks of geese flew overhead on their winter migration. It was hypnotic. No one dared even open a book for fear of missing any part of Nubia's beautiful desert landscape. I was happy to do nothing: I'd had an emergency appendectomy ten days earlier, almost immediately after my arrival in Cairo, and stupidly, on a dare, had gone swimming in the Nile at Aswan. It was difficult to swim against the river's strong current, and I pulled a stitch. I went to the public clinic in Aswan, where a laboratory aide—the only person on duty—gave me an injection that made me pass out on the examination room floor. I came to a few minutes later and looked up in a daze as he knelt over me. He smiled nervously and said, "*Ma'lish*—no matter—sir, I make the bill very small. And you should be calm for one week."

We arrived at Abu Simbel late on a crisp November afternoon, perhaps two hours before sunset, and moored directly in front of the main temple. No one was there, not even a guard. We were, after all, in the middle of nowhere, 250 kilometers (150 miles)—three days' journey—south of Aswan. Plans had already been drawn up to move the Abu Simbel temples before they were flooded by the waters of the soon-to-be-built Aswan High Dam, but that work wouldn't begin for another year. Building the dam was a controversial project: it would destroy tens of thousands of unexplored archaeological sites between the Nile's First and Second cataracts, but Egypt's need for hydroelectric power and irrigation schemes was deemed more important. Only ten temples, including Abu Simbel, were to be moved to high ground.

We moored not far from the abandoned village of Abu Simbel, itself built on the site of the ancient town of Maha. For thousands of years this area had been home to a fairly large number of people—the very ones who, in the Nineteenth Dynasty, Ramesses II had wanted to impress with this display of monumental architecture. Now, it was dead, empty, awaiting the rising floodwaters of the Nile, which would quickly turn its mud-brick walls to silt. The wooden doors and windows of the houses had been carted away and all that remained were empty shells, surrounded by overturned water pots and fragments of torn woven-reed mats. Mangy dogs wandered the village streets, bewildered, trying to adjust to a new life in which their only food was already becoming nothing but the Nile fish they could catch themselves.

The two temples of Abu Simbel are among Egypt's most impressive monuments, but Egyptologists are still not sure why they were carved here. The larger temple was dedicated to the deified Ramesses and the gods Amun and Re-Harakhty. It was extensively decorated with scenes depicting the king's battle against the Hittites at Qadesh in northern Lebanon. Perhaps Ramesses II carved Abu Simbel and included such scenes to demonstrate for potentially rebellious local tribesmen the invincibility of Egypt's ruler and to assert his claim to Nubia's mineral resources and trade routes. Certainly, the facade of the rock-cut temple is spectacular enough to have inspired awe among the local population: cut directly into the hillside, four gigantic seated statues of Ramesses II, each over twenty-one meters (seventy feet) tall, stare directly toward the rising sun. At smaller scale, beside each of the king's legs, stand figures of Nefertari and the king's mother, Queen Tuy. Between two of the statues of Ramesses, proudly stand figures of the king's eldest principal son, Amun-her-khepeshef; between two others, a daughter.

Perhaps the hill where the temples were carved was a site sacred to some ancient deity. The hill is one of the largest for miles around on the Nile's West Bank, and the only one that impends directly on the river. Its location is so perfectly aligned that twice each year, on the spring and autumn equinoxes, the rising sun sent a shaft of light through its single doorway entrance and down 60 meters (196 feet) where it illuminated statues of gods carved in the tomb's innermost recesses.

We walked around Abu Simbel's temples that day, photographing their huge facades, exploring their decorated rock-cut chambers. That night, we slept in the entrance to the great temple, just as nineteenth-century travelers had done, and awoke before dawn to stare up into the most beautiful, star-filled sky any of us had ever seen. It was a wonderful experience: the desert setting, the

Nile, the four massive statues of Ramesses II, the night sky, the late autumn light at sunrise, the silence—they created a picture that, even after three decades, I remember vividly and with great fondness. In 1873, ninety years before us, Amelia Edwards, one of the nineteenth century's most eloquent Nile travelers, described the night she spent at Abu Simbel, sleeping in this very spot:

> It was wonderful to wake every morning close under the steep bank, and, without lifting one's head from the pillow, to see that row of giant faces [on the statues of Ramesses II] so close against the sky. They showed unearthly enough by moonlight, but not half so unearthly as in the gray of dawn. At that hour . . . they wore a fixed and fatal look that was little less than appalling. As the sky warmed this awful look was succeeded by a flush that mounted and deepened like the rising flush of life. For a moment they seemed to glow—to smile—to be transfigured. Then came a flash, as of thought itself. It was the first instantaneous flash of the risen sun. It lasted less than a second. It was gone almost before one could say it was there. The next moment mountain, river and sky were distinct in the steady light of day; and the colossi—mere colossi now—sat serene and stony in the open sunshine.

To the north of the Great Temple, Ramesses had a smaller sanctuary carved for his wife, Nefertari, and the goddess Hathor: "His and hers" temples, Ramesside scholar Kenneth Kitchen has called them. On the facade of Nefertari's sanctuary six standing statues were carved, four of the king and two of Nefertari who, interestingly, is shown at the same grand scale as her husband. Professor Kitchen believes that Ramesses II and Nefertari may have visited Abu Simbel on either the spring or autumn solstice in the twenty-fourth year of the king's reign to take part in the temple dedication ceremonies. Evidence suggests that this was one of Nefertari's final acts; she died very shortly thereafter, and her mummy was entombed in the Valley of the Queens.

Nefertari was given great prominence at Abu Simbel. Ramesses II had many, many wives by the time of its construction, yet none of the others is even mentioned here, let alone given her own temple. Nefertari obviously was truly deserving of the title "Great Royal Wife." Amelia Edwards attributed the queen's status to her husband's undying love, an explanation that wonderfully illustrates nineteenth-century Europeans' romantic notions of ancient Egypt. It would be more accurate, however, to attribute the queen's position to religious beliefs and political concerns. Nevertheless, Miss Edwards's opinion, written after first seeing Nefertari's Abu Simbel temple, is too elegant to ignore:

> On every pillar, in every act of worship pictured on the walls, even in the sanctuary, we find the names of Rameses and Nefertari coupled and inseparable. In this double dedication and in the unwonted tenderness of the style one seems to detect traces of some event, perhaps of some anniversary, the particulars of which are lost forever. It may have been a meeting; it may have been a parting; it may have been a prayer answered or a vow fulfilled. We see, at all events, that Ramses and Nefertari desired to leave behind them an imperishable record of the affection which united them on earth and which they hoped would reunite them in Amenti. . . . Even in these barren solitudes there is wafted to us a breath from the shores of old romance. We feel that Love once passed this way and that the ground is still hallowed where he trod.

Less than seven years after Ramesses II dedicated Abu Simbel, a massive earthquake struck Nubia. There is an inscription at the temple telling us of the tragedy. One of the four huge figures of the pharaoh on the facade of the Great Temple was damaged. Another cracked at waist level and its entire head and torso—thousands of tons of living sandstone—broke free and crashed to the ground. Inside the temple, pillars snapped free of the ceiling and figures of the king crumbled away. For the next two or three years, the pharaoh's viceroy, Paser, supervised a team of workmen who had been sent to repair the damage. Pillars were rebuilt or shored up with mud brick, some walls were recarved and repainted, but only the simple problems were dealt with: the shattered face of Ramesses II, cracked and broken, was left lying in the sand.

Its damaged state was of no concern to me: Abu Simbel made a deep impression. Over the next three years, I returned to Nubia several times to participate in various archaeological expeditions. Each time, I stopped at Abu Simbel and watched as the dismantling and moving of the temples progressed. On my first return, it was shocking to watch as engineers dismantled the temple. We were digging at a site across the Nile from Abu Simbel, and regularly sailed over to follow the work. I can remember standing in disbelief, watching two men with huge cross-cut saws slice through the head of a sandstone statue of Ramesses II, cutting it into five- or six-ton blocks. I watched as a huge crane lifted the face of the pharaoh high into the air and set it on a truck to be carried to high ground a few hundred meters away where it would be reassembled.

It was an awesome engineering project, but I was almost embarrassed as the figures of one of Egypt's most powerful pharaohs were covered, sliced, wrapped, and carted, like lumps of cheese. Now reassembled, the Great Temple is certainly no less striking than it was before, and certainly we should be grateful that it was not simply left to dissolve beneath the waters of the Nile. But I think Abu Simbel has lost some of the aura it had when I first saw it nearly four decades ago, and I am glad that my memories of the original site have not lost their intensity.

MAPPING ANCIENT THEBES

Three years after my first trip to Egypt, I married Susan Howe, an art major whom I had met at the University of Washington in 1964. Susan had been invited in 1965 to join the staff of another

Nubian archaeological project on which I was also working. The site was Gebel Adda, a Christian city across the Nile from Abu Simbel, and there we fell in love and were married upon our return to Seattle. Susan and I have worked together on every archaeological project we've conducted since our marriage in 1966. When I took my Ph.D. from Yale in 1970, we moved to Manhattan, where I had been hired as assistant curator of Egyptian art at the Metropolitan Museum of Art, and Susan would be working as an artist in the Paleontology Department at the American Museum of Natural History. We both enjoyed our jobs, but we missed Egypt terribly and spent most of our time talking with friends about Egypt, looking through our slides of Egypt, writing about Egypt, thinking about Egypt. So we decided to quit our jobs and return. I accepted a position at the American University in Cairo as assistant professor of anthropology and Egyptology.

Only a year later, in 1973, the University of Chicago's Oriental Institute offered me the directorship of its field headquarters in Luxor. Called Chicago House, for fifty years the institute had been conducting elaborate epigraphic projects, recording and publishing scenes and texts on the walls of ancient Theban temples. It was a four-year appointment, and both Susan and I were ecstatic at the prospect of living in so famous a setting.

We came to Luxor with our two-year-old son, Christopher, and our daughter, Emily, who was only six months old. Luxor was a unique environment in which to raise two young children and the perfect place to work and conduct Egyptological research. Chicago House boasted one of the world's finest Egyptological libraries, and during a very substantial part of its history its staff had been recording and studying monuments of the nineteenth and twentieth dynasties. Chicago House had been built in the 1920s by the Oriental Institute's founder, James Henry Breasted, and its principal benefactor, John D. Rockefeller. The complex of buildings was designed in California Spanish style, and the compound included artists' studios, photographic laboratories, electrical and carpentry shops, garages, tennis courts, gardens, courtyards, and a two-story building with apartments and public rooms. Our staff consisted of ten foreigners employed as Egyptologists, artists, and photographers, and an Egyptian staff of about thirty who ranged from Egyptologists to darkroom supervisors, engineers, and gardeners. We moved to Chicago House in 1973 and remained there until the end of 1976.

Surrounded by so many Ramesside monuments, living in Luxor was a wonderful opportunity to delve deeply into the archaeology of Egypt's Nineteenth and Twentieth dynasties. I'd only spent a week or two in Luxor before we moved there in 1973, and I'd never even seen many of the tombs, temples, shrines, and village sites. During my first year at Chicago House, I was anxious to explore the West Bank at Thebes as thoroughly as possible. Weekends became working holidays, and nearly every Friday (the Muslim sabbath and our day off), I took the local ferry across the Nile, rented a bicycle or hired a taxi, and headed off to the monuments. One week it would be private tombs in Sheikh Abu el-Qurna; the next it would be Malkata, the site of the palace of Amunhotep III; after that, one of the mortuary temples. Nearly every tomb had at least traces of elaborately decorated walls with scenes and texts that offered unique revelations about life in ancient Egypt or were more traditional religious vignettes. Every temple offered variations in architectural details and inscriptions, often some that no one had recorded before.

It was not long before I discovered a problem. It was easy to find the well-known tombs or temples, but when it came to the more obscure, less well-known monuments, the result was often disappointing: they couldn't be found. There are thousands of tombs at Thebes, but fewer than 420 had ever been assigned catalog numbers and been plotted on a map.

"I'd like to see the tomb of so-and-so," I'd say to one of the antiquities inspectors.

"I've heard of it," he would reply. "Do you know where it is?"

"Don't *you* know where it is?"

"No. The old guard, Sheikh Taya, he probably knew, but he died."

I would check one of the few maps of the necropolis that were available, or thumb through a guidebook, but often there was no mention of the tomb or where it was located. It was amazing: tourists had been visiting the Theban Necropolis for two thousand years, archaeologists and adventurers had been probing and digging for nearly two centuries, but there was still no map showing what the necropolis contained or where its monuments were located.

There were two reasons for this. First, Thebes offered tourists an embarrassment of riches. With so many beautiful tombs, so many gigantic temples, travelers ignored all but the finest examples. Poorly preserved monuments were often destroyed in the search for museum-quality pieces. Early visitors hacked scenes from walls and carried them back to Europe, or they converted tombs into residences where they lived for a few weeks while visiting the sites. The smoke from their cooking fires blackened decorated walls; they gouged their names across figures of ancient kings; they crawled through tombs filled with mummies, crushing them, throwing broken or undecorated objects aside in hopes of finding perfect pieces; they burned papyri or wooden coffins for light and fuel.

Second, preparing a map or an inventory of the tombs was a daunting prospect. The Theban Necropolis covers over nine square kilometers (four square miles)—it's a little under six kilometers long north to south, and a little over 1.5 kilometers wide. Along the edge of the cultivation there are nearly two dozen major temples. On the desert hills a few meters west lie the extensive remains of dynastic palaces, town sites, Greek and Roman shrines, Christian churches and monasteries, mingled together with Paleolithic workstations and thousands of ancient graffiti. Cut into these limestone hills are literally thousands of tombs intended for members of ancient Egypt's upper classes and members of its royal families. Some of the tombs are small, poorly dug, undecorated pits choked with debris and fallen stone; others are huge subterranean complexes with well-carved and finely painted walls that extend underground 100 meters (330 feet) or more. In some parts of the crowded necropolis, the tombs were dug so closely together that they often ran into each other. Indeed, in some places, one can crawl from one tomb into another, moving several hundred meters underground before having to return to the surface.

Preparing a map that would show all of this complexity and detail seemed an impossible undertaking. Up to this time, the necropolis maps were usually simple, limited to very small areas, designed for narrow purposes, and often done in haste. They were sketchy, incomplete, and inaccurate. This had serious consequences for our ability to conserve and protect Theban monuments. After all, if you can't accurately locate a monument, how can you protect it?

THE earliest general maps made of the Theban Necropolis were those in the *Description de l'Égypte,* the massive survey of Egypt prepared by scholars who accompanied Napoleon Bonaparte's ill-fated military expedition to Egypt between 1799 to 1802. The maps, which are at very large scale and therefore show very little detail, do little more than point out how few Theban monuments were free of debris in 1800.

Probably the best of the nineteenth-century maps were those of the Englishman John Gardner Wilkinson, who visited Thebes several times between 1821 and 1855, and Robert Hay, who visited intermittently between 1824 and 1838. Wilkinson lived for twelve years in Egypt and received worldwide recognition for his studies, particularly *The Manners and Customs of the Ancient Egyptians* (three volumes), and *Topography of Thebes.* His beautiful maps, and especially his general plan of Thebes, are fine examples of nineteenth-century cartographic technique. The map of Thebes measured 72 by 83 centimeters (57 by 65 inches), and was drawn first in the field in pencil, then revised after Wilkinson returned to

London. The shading technique Wilkinson used gives the topography an almost three-dimensional quality. The map is still useful for its drawings of the visible parts of mortuary temples, and because it covers many outlying areas later surveys ignored. Still, only a few of the necropolis's thousands of tomb entrances were included and none of their subterranean features were shown.

Robert Hay's unpublished manuscripts, now in the British Library, also included maps of the Theban area, but again they contain only minimal topographic detail. The map in Carl Lepsius's *Denkmäler aus Ägypten und Nubien* (1859) is also an attractive piece of work, but it, too, is incomplete. Howard Carter made a few sketch plans of the necropolis, but these were primarily memory aids, not technical productions, and they made no pretense to accuracy.

The best map yet produced of Thebes was that done by an engineer with the Egyptian Antiquities Service, Emile Baraize. He began to prepare a set of 1:500 map sheets in 1904, a combination of sketch plans, measured drawings, and small-area surveys much more accurate than anything that had preceded them. However, the constant encroachment of native buildings into the archaeological areas made the map sheets obsolete almost as soon as they had been prepared. Baraize's map was never completed and never published, but the manuscript served as the basis for several later maps, and for a systematic catalog of Theban private tombs published by the Antiquities Service in 1919.

Before a better survey could begin, tomb robbery, vandalism, the encroachment of modern structures, and deterioration caused by rising groundwater (one of the unwelcome side effects of the original Aswan Dam) were so serious that the need for a map had become urgent. In the 1920s the English Egyptologist Reginald Engelbach consulted with the surveyor general of Egypt on a topographic map of Thebes that would include all monuments visible on the surface, plus the entrances to accessible tombs in the Valley of the Kings and the Valley of the Queens. Unfortunately, the survey limited the number of private tombs to be included to the four hundred that seemed to contain the most significant decoration. Thousands of less well-decorated or unexcavated private tombs were ignored, and large parts of the necropolis were excluded from this survey; some areas were never mapped at all. In the end, much of the map was never published.

From 1959 to 1969, the French Archaeological Institute conducted an extensive aerial survey of the West Bank as part of its study of the thousands of ancient graffiti carved on the Theban hillsides. To locate the graffiti accurately, the French prepared a map of the necropolis based on the aerial photographs. Published in 1969, at a scale of 1:10,000, with five-meter contour intervals, it was the first accurate topographic map of Thebes ever made. Unfortunately, it did not cover the entire necropolis and its scale was simply too large to show tomb entrances precisely or to include detailed temple plans.

Without a detailed map, no regular check could be made on the condition of the Theban monuments. Because existing necropolis surveys were so limited and incomplete, the building of houses, shops, and roads on the West Bank continued largely uncontrolled for another seventy years. This construction damaged archaeological monuments that no one realized were there until it was too late. Roads were laid over tombs; buildings were erected on temple foundations; electrical lines were laid in trenches that cut through ancient floors and mud-brick walls. In recent years the problems of protection have been made even more difficult by the elaborate irrigation schemes in the Nile Valley that have raised the groundwater level and increased local humidity. Also, serious pollution has resulted from the burning of sugarcane fields.

The more time I spent exploring the West Bank, comparing decorated tomb and temple walls with photographs taken of them decades earlier, listening to my colleagues relate horror stories about vandalism, damage, and theft in the necropolis, reading projections of future population growth and tourist development, the more convinced I was that a comprehensive map of Thebes was needed urgently. I was neither an engineer nor a land surveyor and had only a rudimentary knowledge of mapmaking, but it seemed unlikely that anyone else was interested in creating an archaeological database of Thebes, so I decided to do it myself.

Donkeys enroute to the Valley of the Kings. 1995 S.W.

2

THEBES FROM THE AIR

IN 1973, I began exploring the possibility of making a new archaeological map of the Theban Necropolis and, in the process, of creating an archaeological database to help monitor (and, I hoped, prevent) the continuing deterioration of the Theban monuments. Working with David Sims, a friend with a far better knowledge of surveying than I, we made a trial survey to see if mapping the necropolis was even feasible. For the experiment, we chose a small *wadi*—the Arabic word for an arroyo or valley— about three hundred meters south of Howard Carter's house, at the northern end of the necropolis. About one hundred small, generally late New Kingdom tombs had been dug here, most of them partly filled with debris and some of them filled in Graeco-Roman times with cordwood-like stacks of mummies. The quality of bedrock in the *wadi* was extremely poor; but even so, nearly every tomb had traces of painted plaster decoration on its walls, including scenes of daily life and religious ceremonies and hieroglyphic texts. The poor condition of the tombs was a constant reminder of how badly Thebes needed a detailed archaeological map and database if its monuments were to survive.

Every other Friday, David and I would go to the *wadi*, set up our surveying instrument, called a theodolite, and spend four or five hours measuring angles and taping distances. Our goal was first to create an accurate topographical map of the *wadi*, showing precisely each tomb entrance in the hillsides. Then we would crawl into each accessible tomb and prepare as accurate a plan as we could. Crawling was difficult because we had to avoid damaging the mummies that lay half-buried in the debris, as well as the decorated plastered walls, which were in poor condition. We wriggled into pitch-black spaces barely wide enough for our shoulders. Sometimes we frightened a desert fox sleeping in the tomb; sometimes we startled dozens of bats hanging from the ceiling. Flashlights in hand, we used tapes to measure as best we could, and drew up the results in the field. Then we moved on to the next tomb.

The resulting map was not very attractive, but the data it contained showed how useful such a map could be in protecting the tombs. A number of colleagues encouraged me to proceed, though the amount of work the project required certainly raised eyebrows. A frequent comment was, "Weeks, you'll be at this for a hundred years and still not complete the job." In retrospect, I realize that they would still be absolutely correct were it not for rapid developments in computer-aided surveying and for our good luck in enlisting some outstandingly talented people.

SUSAN and I left Chicago House at the end of 1976, when our children came of school age. I accepted a job as associate professor of Egyptology at the University of California, Berkeley. For the next several years, from 7,500 miles away, I continued to worry about the need for a Theban Necropolis map. Finally, in 1979, I managed to raise a small amount of money and established (on paper, at least) what came to be called the Theban Mapping Project.

The TMP was primarily a surveying project, and our first and most critical need was a good surveyor. Just when I was beginning to despair of ever finding someone, I heard about David

Goodman. "He's a character," I was told. "And he's just crazy enough to work on a monster project in Egypt in the heat of summer for no pay."

I first met David Goodman on an abandoned airfield in northern California where he was a principal surveyor for the California Department of Transportation. David is six feet four inches tall, rail-thin, with a goatee. He was wearing a straw hat and size 14 logging boots. He was then fifty years old. It quickly became clear that, no matter what the conversation, David always found a way to boast about his hometown, Paducah, Kentucky, talk about his days on a Mississippi riverboat, and brag about the fantastic vegetables he grows at his home near Sacramento. And somehow he'd always finish by describing the culinary talents of his beloved wife, Mary. I liked David immediately and, much to my surprise, he agreed to join our project, taking time off from his job without pay.

David has been one of the project's most loyal and invaluable members. He has come with us to Luxor almost every year since 1978, and he, more than any other staff member, was responsible for designing the survey procedures that are now standard on the project. In fact, they are now being followed by many other archaeological projects in Egypt.

All the Luxor villagers love David—they call him "Daoud." David speaks no Arabic, but he never seems to have a problem communicating. The mere mention of his name anywhere on the West Bank brings smiles. When Daoud walks through the local villages, hordes of children chant his name and hold his hand and follow behind the tallest and kindest man they've ever met. The adults constantly say, *"Daoud, huwwa ahsen raggil,"* "Daoud, he's the best man!"

We were also joined by two architecture students from my Berkeley class in Egyptian archaeology in 1978—Bruce Lightbody and Richard Smith—and an Egyptology major named Tracey Twarowski. Not only were they bright and hardworking, they were delightful company during the hot and fly-ridden Luxor summers.

We arrived in Luxor on March 28, 1978, and worked without break for the next three months. Our first task was to establish a grid network over the entire necropolis so that we could locate archaeological features with precision. No more of the usual "Well, I think the tomb you want lies down the road, past a broken bread oven, then up the hill a bit." With a grid network, we could locate a feature in terms similar to latitude, longitude, and elevation: "The tomb lies at 9995.211W, 8768.745N, 165.55msl." Prosaic to be sure, but also highly accurate.

Rather than establishing an entirely new grid system, we used one that the Centre Franco-égyptien had laid down a few years earlier over the Karnak Temple complex on the Nile's East Bank and extended it west across the river to the Necropolis. Using their baseline, we created a single, infinitely expandable grid network for the entire Luxor area. The grid's east–west axis ran directly along the axis of the great Temple of Amun at Karnak. Our grid was the same as the one used by the ancient Egyptians when they laid out Luxor's most important temple complex, and it could be extended to cover all the temples and tombs in the Theban area.

Every day during that first season, we slogged back and forth through the West Bank's cultivated fields, running major and minor survey traverses in order to set the grid as accurately as possible. This was no mean feat: we had to contrive ways to avoid vast fields of nine-foot-tall sugarcane and detour around village houses and stands of date palms. We had to hike through flooded fields and ankle-deep mud; walk miles out of our way before we could cross deep irrigation canals; and keep a wary eye out for the vicious and highly territorial village dogs that clearly wanted nothing more than to rip out the throats of strangers. All of this work, from 5:00 A.M. until 1:00 P.M. in temperatures that seldom dropped below 43 degrees Celsius (110 degrees Fahrenheit), had to be done carrying hundreds of pounds of equipment. The battery packs for the electronic distance-measuring machines, for example, weighed forty pounds each; the tripods, targets, theodolite, jugs of water, papers, binoculars, brass markers, and bags of cement added even more weight.

On a typical morning, Bruce and Tracey climbed to the top of a nearby mountain to establish a target site, David hiked into cane fields to set up the theodolite, and I followed him to keep the notes. We called a halt in the afternoon and headed back to the filthy little mud-brick hostel where we were then living, and spent several hours after lunch checking our notes. Twice during the season David had us climb up the mountain above the Valley of the Kings at midnight so we could sight Polaris and align our grid coordinates to true north. Each morning we'd start out again, sometimes switching jobs for variety. Our young helpers, Nubie and Mohammed, however, always insisted on carrying the heaviest loads. "That's why you pay us, Doctor," they said. As the season wore on, we stopped even the pretense of objecting.

The map we wanted to make was to be drawn at 1:500, a scale that would allow us to include archaeological and topographical features in detail. It meant that one centimeter on the map equaled five hundred centimeters (sixteen feet) on the ground. At this scale, any inaccuracies in the early stages of the work would be magnified as work progressed and could quickly grow to disastrous proportions. David therefore insisted on establishing a much more complex set of control points than theoretically was necessary; this doubled our work, but it was certain to save innumerable headaches later. Still, even with the extra work, we had completed the traverses by the end of June and could proudly boast that the grid network was firmly established.

WE knew it would take decades to make a 1:500 topographic map of the Theban Necropolis if we tried to create it entirely from on-the-ground measurements. For a detailed and accurate map we would need stereoscopic aerial photographs—those taken from specially equipped aircraft for use in photogrammetric plotters. But no such stereoscopic photographs of Thebes could be obtained. The French aerial survey taken several years earlier had been flown at too high an altitude to allow making the 1:500 maps we wanted, and the only other aerial photographs I knew about were incomplete surveys made by the British Royal Air Force in 1949. A set was in the Pentagon archives, but I was told that access depended on RAF permission, which would be given only if the Egyptian Air Force first gave *their* permission. My letters to Egyptian Military Intelligence, dozens of them, all went unanswered.

Our only choice then was to take new photographs. At that time, the sole agency in Egypt authorized to fly photo reconnaissance was the Egyptian National Academy of Science's Remote Sensing Center. In December 1979, I flew to Cairo to negotiate with the agency, which I had been told had a reputation for doing poor work at high prices, but it was the only game in town.

To generate topographical maps from aerial photographs, there must be clearly identifiable markers on the ground before the photographs are taken. These "premarks" are large X's, which we made of whitewashed stones, placed at precise positions to allow a photogrammetrist to join individual photographs together with accuracy. Any agency involved in aerial photography knows this, and the Remote Sensing Center promised not to fly the mission until we told them the premarks were in place.

One morning early in April, we heard the sound of a low-flying aircraft, a rare thing in Luxor in the seventies. We ran up to the roof and saw what had to be the center's plane making pass after pass across the necropolis. When I reached the assistant director, he told me they had flown our survey. "Just today, before we talk. We surprise you by doing it early," he said. He sounded pleased.

In spite of their strenuous objections, we made them fly the entire sortie again. All premarks were in place, but this time their flight lines failed to overlap enough to provide the stereoscopic coverage photogrammetry required. We needed about 33 percent overlap; we got less than 15 percent, too little to make an adequate map. Frustrated, we temporarily abandoned photogrammetry. A third run would have cost us a lot more money and we were not convinced that we would get acceptable results.

Not all was lost, however, because the black-and-white aerial photographs provided an outstanding source for the architectural study of Theban mortuary temples and tomb entrances, and they have already provided important data for dozens of studies of Theban monuments.

In our third season, still convinced of the value of aerial photographs, I hired a local charter air service so I could take oblique aerial photographs of Thebes. These would not be stereoscopic photos and could not be used to generate topographic maps, but they would be useful accompaniments to our ground surveys and important sources of information in their own right. To do this, I needed only low-level security clearances, which were relatively easy to obtain. The air charter company apparently had connections with the Egyptian Air Force. The only restriction was that we had to turn over all of our film to Military Security immediately after the flight. They would process it, then deliver the prints (but not the negatives) of the shots that passed military censorship. It wasn't an ideal arrangement, but we had no choice in the matter.

On the appointed day, the air charter company was to have an aircraft at Luxor Airport at 0800. Gaston Chan, another student from Berkeley and an experienced photographer, was working for the TMP that year, and he and I planned to spend three hours photographing the West Bank. We arrived at Luxor Airport at 0730. The plane finally arrived at noon, an aged DC-3, the twin-engine workhorse of World War II. The DC-3 was a legendary plane, well known for its strength and durability, but this one looked tired. Its fuselage had obviously been damaged and mended several times; its engines seemed to sputter; and the pilot was a short, fat man who chain-smoked cigarettes and wore a dirty white shirt and ill-fitting black pants with a broken zipper.

The plane's interior had been configured to carry freight, and there were only two seats forward. Behind the cockpit was a steel-grille floor with tie-down hooks bolted to a bare, aluminum bulkhead, and there were six small windows on each side of the aircraft. I wondered how Gaston and I could possibly take pictures through such scratched and foggy glass. We certainly would have a problem trying to keep the wings and engines out of the shots.

I asked the captain about this. He glanced at his co-pilot, a well-dressed man, about thirty years old, who wore the darkest sunglasses I've ever seen. Both men smiled. The captain pointed to a huge double cargo door at the rear of the aircraft that opened to create a great gaping void about 2.50 meters wide and 2 meters high (8 feet by 6 feet). They would remove the cargo door and leave it at the airport. Gaston and I would sit cross-legged on the floor, in the doorway. For safety— "Very important, safety," the pilot said—they would lash us into position with ropes tied to the bulkhead opposite. "You will have a wonderful view, Doctor," said the pilot. "And, if you want, you can undo the rope and come to cockpit and have coffee. I like to speak English. You welcome."

Gaston had been a Green Beret paratrooper in Vietnam, so he didn't immediately panic, although he did wish aloud for a parachute. For me, however, the plan smacked of sheer lunacy. Trying to calm myself, I rationalized that we had to pay for the plane whether we flew or not; it would be cowardly of me not to do it; I didn't want to embarrass myself in front of Gaston and the pilots; the photographs we'd take would be very useful; Egyptology needed these photos. . . . What the hell! I took a deep breath, faked a smile, turned to Gaston, and said, "Well, let's go!" The pilots tied us down as we sat on the floor in front of the open door, and we tied a bag with extra film and lenses and cameras between us. "Good luck," the pilot shouted, and headed for the cockpit. Moments later, the engines roared and our aged DC-3 headed down the taxi strip.

We turned onto the runway. The plane gained speed and rose quickly, then banked sharply left and headed directly over Karnak Temple, across the Nile, and west to Deir el-Bahari. The wind blew through the cargo doorway and into our faces, and my eyes began to tear. The noise of the engine made conversation impossible, but Gaston and I kept nudging each other and pointing to the sites below. The view was absolutely breathtaking, and I alternated between rapture at the scene four hundred meters (thirteen hundred feet) below and terror as I remembered where I was sitting.

The flight lasted exactly three hours, and in spite of a light cloud cover that gave us less than ideal light, both Gaston and I were sure we'd taken some great pictures. We'd flown back and forth across the necropolis at altitudes ranging from three hundred to three thousand meters. Several times, the plane banked steeply enough that we could feel ourselves on the verge of sliding toward the open door. Gaston and I held our cameras with one hand, and tried to appear calm as we grabbed at the steel-grille flooring with the other. I was convinced that the slightest movement, even the snap of the camera's shutter, could send us sliding out the door and leave us dangling at the end of a rope above the Theban hills. Later in the flight, as we began to relax a bit, Gaston and I had to admit that the angles for taking photographs were perfect.

After we landed, we turned over fifteen rolls of film to the Military Security man. He said that the black-and-white rolls would be processed immediately in the army's own laboratory, while the color-slide film would be shipped to the Egyptian embassy in Germany, because there were then no Kodachrome processing facilities in Egypt. He was almost convincing when he said that we'd have everything in hand in two weeks, "Three at the latest, or four. . . . Three months sure," he said. "Or maybe four months, God willing."

Six months later, we had still heard nothing about the film. We eventually received ten 4 × 5 black-and-white prints—dirty, stained, gray photos, three of them bent and torn. Later, we received twenty color slides, unmounted. They were unusable; all were high-altitude shots and showed little archaeological detail. Fortunately, Gaston had stuck six rolls of color film in his jacket and had it processed in California. We got back 150 excellent pictures of the necropolis, but we never learned what happened to the others.

HOT-AIR BALLOONING

On December 16, 1980, my thirty-ninth birthday, Susan gave me a certificate for a hot-air balloon ride over the vineyards near our home in the Napa Valley. Ballooning is a very popular pastime in California's wine country, and almost every morning we saw balloons over our house. I had often remarked about how much I'd enjoy going up in one. But we were so busy with family matters and with planning for the project and teaching that it was not until August 1981 that I finally booked the flight. Then, on a warm Saturday morning at five o'clock, I stood in a four-man gondola that hung from four cables below a great, multicolored balloon filled with seventy thousand cubic feet of hot air. Not ten inches above my head, a propane-fueled burner sent great bursts of flame into the envelope, heating the air inside to over 180 degrees Fahrenheit.

At first light, as vivid pink rays of sunlight began to pour over the horizon, we rose from our takeoff site, a parking lot in Yountville, California, and floated lazily upward until a gentle breeze nudged us over countless rows of green, leafy vines that covered the valley floor and extended up the sides of the hills that define the Napa Valley. We floated about two hundred feet over the Domaine Chandon winery, then sailed northward, rising to three thousand feet, then sank gradually back down to only fifty. The only sounds were the occasional hiss of the burner or a dog barking as we flew over his territory. The view was spectacular: thousands of acres of vineyards, pine-covered hillsides, and the well-manicured lawns of wineries, their Victorian buildings striped with brilliant morning sunlight and still-dark shadows. The air was crystal clear. For over an hour, we floated above the landscape. It was a truly exhilarating experience, and throughout the flight, I was thinking, "How great this would be in Thebes!"

Hot-air balloons had been used only once before in Egypt, by the archaeologist William Flinders Petrie around the turn of the century, but these were unmanned, tethered balloons that rose

only to a hundred feet or so. No one had ever flown a manned balloon over the Nile and the thought of being the first was irre-
sistible.

I telephoned the pilot who had taken me on the Napa flight,
Andrew "Drew" Brisbane, and asked him if he and his balloon
would come to Luxor for a month of flying. We would pay
expenses but couldn't offer a salary. He accepted, then suggested
that we take two balloons, so that we could photograph one from
the other with the Theban hills in the background. Drew con-
tracted with another pilot, Mark Proteau, to join us.

We had the balloons and the pilots. Now we needed the money.
Bruce Ludwig had already made a generous donation to the project for the year, and I was reluctant to ask for more. Fortunately,
by the purest luck, I was flying to New York a month later to give
a lecture and the airline had bumped me up to first class. I struck
up a conversation with my seat mate, a pleasant fellow I'd never
met before, George Russell, president of a major investment company. I mentioned that we were about to become the first people
ever to fly hot-air balloons over the Nile and suggested that he
might like to come along. Not only was he interested, but he
offered to get a group of people together to do a Nile cruise, take
the balloon ride over Thebes, and contribute to our project. Within
two weeks, George called back and said that the group was assembled.

THE first time we flew, we drove to a level stretch of desert in the
center of the necropolis, then carefully unrolled the balloon and
inflated the envelope, using a hot-air burner and a powerful fan. A
dozen people from the nearby village had awakened early and were
on hand to watch in fascination as the burner ignited and a sheet
of flame and hot air shot into the envelope. Gradually, the brightly
colored balloon took form and rose from the ground. Once it was
inflated, half a dozen of us held tightly to the gondola to keep it
from floating away. The villagers applauded.

There were to be five of us on the first flight: our pilot, Drew; our photographer, Gaston Chan; a donor to the project, Sylvia Frock; our surveyor, David Goodman; and me. At the last minute, Egyptian Military Security decided that we needed someone from their office on the flight to make certain we did not photograph anything militarily sensitive. They never explained what in the Theban Necropolis could possibly have military importance, but we had to bump David for the security man, who it turned out disliked heights and kept asking us to keep the flights as brief and as low as possible. He disliked even more being awakened at 4:00 A.M. After the first few flights, he tired of his job, slept late at the hotel, and never flew again.

"Get ready!" shouted Drew after we were on board. "Let go of the lines!" He turned up the burner, and slowly the balloon began to ascend. Our first takeoff site was directly in front of Queen Hatshepsut's temple at Deir el-Bahari. As we rose above the height of the surrounding hills, a soft breeze from the north began to push us toward the Ramesseum and villages to the east. I had never seen anything more beautiful than the Theban Necropolis at sunrise from a thousand feet in the air. It was breathtaking.

The day was perfect—there was a cloudless sky with bright, early-morning light raking across the landscape and, of course, a perfectly stable platform, the balloon, from which to photograph temples, tomb entrances, hillsides, and houses. We took pictures of Thebes from angles that no one had ever seen before: the roof of the Ramesseum, for example, the laps of the Colossi of Memnon, the hillsides of Qurna, the terraces of Deir el-Bahari. This first-ever balloon flight over Thebes lasted only an hour, but among us we shot over twenty rolls of film, and we were ecstatic.

As we flew, we could hear every sound on the ground, now several hundred feet below us. Dogs barked as our burner disturbed their sleep. Villagers emerged from their homes as we floated overhead, looking up in bleary-eyed amazement, and we heard them saying over and over again, "My God! God is great! My God!" None of them had ever seen a balloon before. Children shouted and waved and ran along below us, laughing in delight.

As our balloon made its descent, landing next to the temple of Medinet Habu, a blue pickup truck sped toward the site. The local village police chief, who obviously had just been awakened and had dressed hastily, walked toward us.

"Why didn't you tell me what you were doing?" he demanded angrily. "My neighbor, Hussein, the schoolteacher, thought you came from the Ayatollah Khomeini to invade Egypt. He wanted to shoot you down. I had to confiscate his gun. This is very bad." I realized that we had told everyone but the local policeman about the balloon flight.

"We are very sorry, sir," I replied. "I can assure you that we did not mean to ignore you. After all, you are the most senior official in this village, and your position is very important. Please excuse us for being so forgetful and not telling you. Tomorrow, would you like to ride in the balloon with us? You would be the first in Luxor to do so."

The policeman smiled. "That would be very nice. Yes, I will meet you at sunrise. And do not worry about the schoolteacher. I told him that you were not the enemies of Egypt."

"Thank you."

The next morning, we waited for the police chief at the takeoff site. He never came. In fact, no one saw him for over a week. Later, we learned that his wife had furiously refused to allow him to do anything so stupid and dangerous as to fly in a balloon. Unwilling to defy her, but unable to think of a face-saving excuse, he avoided us.

I spent the next several days touring with George Russell in Luxor, and we made several balloon ascents with the members of his group. It was a wonderful experience—except for Military Security. The officer assigned to us confiscated everyone's cameras before takeoff. He told us that he was under orders to control all photography. That meant that only Gaston and I could bring cameras aboard, a disappointment to our several guests. I promised that we would send each of them a set of slides after the trip had ended.

Having had such bad experiences in previous years with film

processing, this time we took no chances. Gaston and I told the man from Military Security that the film we shot had to be kept in a box in the refrigerator at our hotel. "You understand," we told him, "it is very important that the film stays cool. Otherwise, the colors will change and we will not get the photographs we need. We will store the film in the refrigerator and give you all the rolls when we finish the work at the end of this month." The man agreed.

Every day, we put the film in the refrigerator. The security man wrote down how many rolls we deposited. In the evening, after he returned to his hotel across the river in Luxor, we replaced the rolls of film in the refrigerator with rolls of unexposed film. The film we had shot that day went into our luggage. At the end of the month, we gave him all the film in the refrigerator and he carried it to Cairo to be developed. "It will be returned to you in one month," he said. "Or two."

We were prepared to act distraught when the film came back blank. Gaston would plead some problem with his cameras. I would whine that we'd been sold expired film. But nothing was ever returned; not a single roll. After the season ended, Gaston and I sat in Cairo, the rolls of film we had spirited away now developed and laid out on a table. The photographs were beautiful. We showed them to several members of the Antiquities Department who were as impressed as we were.

We used the same technique the next season, when we again brought balloons to Luxor to continue the photography. I had organized another fund-raising tour, this one for friends of Bruce Ludwig, and the balloon was one of its principal attractions. This would be our last season of ballooning. The balloons had raised money for our project, but they were expensive to operate and it was time to spend what little money we had for other things. It was sad to abandon ballooning, so we were happy to hear rumors that a commercial firm was going to start hot-air balloon rides in Luxor. We hoped that we could hire their services as needed in future years. Today, I should note, tourists can take commercial balloon flights over Thebes and take photos and videos to their hearts' content. Richard Branson's Virgin Airship Company began operation on the West Bank several years ago, and we've flown with them regularly ever since. In the meantime, however, our balloons went back to California for the last time, and the TMP was grounded.

In fact, it went underground.

S.W. '95

Gurna Murei, West Bank

3

UNDERGROUND:

SURVEYING THE ROYAL TOMBS

I must confess I had assumed that making architectural plans of the tombs in the Valley of the Kings would be simple and straightforward. After all, they were carved by workmen who had only stone axes and copper chisels to dig with and whose surveying instruments consisted of a carpenter's square, a plumb bob, and a piece of string. How complex could the tombs be? We, on the other hand, had state-of-the-art theodolites and electronic distance-measuring units, highly competent surveyors and architects, and, of course, a high degree of naive, can-do cockiness. What problem could an ancient workman possibly pose that we couldn't easily solve? Most of the tombs we were working in were relatively free of debris, or so we thought, and at the outset we were confident that detailed tomb plans could be churned out on an almost daily basis.

I had seriously underestimated the ancient Egyptian workmen. Tombs we thought could be easily planned from, say, five hundred measurements, often required *thousands*; tombs we believed could be mapped in a few days took weeks. The accuracy of the ancient artisans and their attention to detail was remarkable.

For example, in the Egyptian Museum in Turin, Italy, there is a

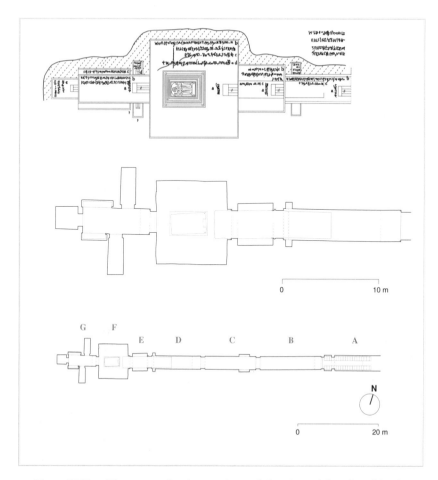

Plan of KV 2. The upper plan is an enhanced drawing of that found in the Turin Papyrus. It is redrawn in modern style (*center*) to facilitate comparison with chambers D–G of the Theban Mapping Project's surveyed plan (*below*).

large papyrus on which an ancient architect had drawn a plan of KV 2, the tomb of pharaoh Ramesses IV. Perhaps it was the very plan used by the men who dug and decorated the tomb. The papyrus was found by the Prussian Egyptologist Carl Lepsius in the mid-nineteenth century, and published by Howard Carter and Sir Alan Gardiner in 1917. The Turin Papyrus gives a plan of the tomb, and its accompanying text gives the name of each chamber and describes its purposes. The papyrus also gives dimensions: usually the length, width, and height of each room.

We wanted to compare the ancient architect's specifications with what our measurements told us the ancient workmen actually achieved. In order to do this, we had to convert the measurements in the papyrus to modern units. The papyrus recorded measurements in cubits, palms, and digits. The size of the Egyptian cubit changed a bit through time: it was the distance from the elbow to the tip of the middle finger and obviously had to be arbitrarily standardized. The value we used—the one in the study by Howard Carter and Alan Gardiner—was the one used by engineers in the Twentieth Dynasty (in about 1150 BCE) when Ramesses IV's tomb was dug:

1 cubit = 0.523 meters
1 palm = $\frac{1}{7}$ of a cubit = 0.0747 meters
1 digit = $\frac{1}{4}$ of a palm = $\frac{1}{28}$ of a cubit = 0.0187 meters

For convenience, we will write the ancient measurements of 2 cubits plus 1 palm plus 3 digits as 2.1.3 cubits. The dimensions given here are in ancient cubits that we have converted to meters, or in modern metric units that we have converted into cubits, palms, and digits. Here, we compare the measurements of three chambers in KV 2, "C" and "D," and "H," and the total tomb length:

PAPYRUS TURIN VALUES *(What They Wanted)*	OUR MEASURED VALUES *(What They Got)*

Chamber C

Length	25.0.0 cubits = 13.078 meters	25.1.1 cubits = 13.189 meters
Width	6.0.0 cubits = 3.139 meters	6.0.0 cubits = 3.140 meters
Height	9.4.0 cubits = 5.006 meters	9.4.3 cubits = 5.070 meters

Chamber D

Length	9.0.0 cubits = 4.708 meters	9.0.0 cubits = 4.710 meters
Width	8.0.0 cubits = 4.185 meters	8.0.1 cubits = 4.200 meters
Height	8.0.0 cubits = 4.185 meters	8.3.0 cubits = 4.405 meters

Chamber H

Length	10.0.0 cubits = 5.231 meters	5.1.3 cubits = 2.750 meters	
Width	3.0.0 cubits = 1.569 meters	4.2.1 cubits = 2.250 meters	
Height	3.3.0 cubits = 1.794 meters	3.3.0 cubits = 1.792 meters	

From Entry Stairs to "E"

Length 136.2.0 cubits = 71.291 meters   134.2.2 cubits = 70.808 meters

From "E" to End of Tomb

Length   24.3.0 cubits = 12.779 meters   19.6.$\frac{1}{2}$ cubits = 10.400 meters

Total Length of Tomb

Length 160.5.0 cubits = 84.05 meters   155.1.2$\frac{1}{2}$ cubits = 81.18 meters

What stands out clearly in these measurements is how remarkably accurate the ancient engineers were in following the specifications for KV 2. In many cases the differences between the measurements given in the papyrus and those from our modern, high-tech methods are only a matter of millimeters. Any significant differences between the two are in the dimensions of chambers at the back of the tomb. This suggests to me that, when the workmen started, they took great pains to ensure accuracy but as the end approached, they became careless. Perhaps Ramesses IV died unexpectedly, and they had to hurry the work.

Work in KV 2 definitely stopped before the tomb was finished. As a result, there is a difference between the total length of the tomb as we measured it and the length given in the Turin Papyrus: in the papyrus it is 84.05 meters (160.5.0 cubits); in our study it is 81.18 meters (155.1.2½ cubits), a difference of 5.3.2 cubits. The last chamber in the tomb, chamber "I," was never finished; the papyrus says it's supposed to be 10.0.0 cubits long; in fact, it's only 5.1.3 cubits. The difference between what it should be and what it actually turned out to be is 4.5.1 cubits. If we add 4.5.1 cubits to our surveyed length (4.5.1 + 155.3.0 = 160.1.1), and compare this with the Turin figure (160.5.0), there is a difference of only 0.3.3 cubits, or 28 centimeters. When completed, the actual length of the tomb was within three tenths of 1 percent (0.3 percent) of the ancient specifications. Not bad for government work.

Such accuracy is remarkable. Certainly, it justified the great care that we took in mapping the tombs and producing detailed plans, sections, and three-dimensional drawings. As we continued mapping KV tombs over the next several years, we were increasingly impressed by the ancient Egyptians' fine workmanship. Carefully examining every accessible part of every accessible tomb, we constantly found small, delicate architectural details, especially fine examples of stone-cutting, and superbly carved and painted walls. Almost daily, one of our crew would wonder aloud, "How on earth did the ancient Egyptians do it?" Fortunately, there are texts and documents that provide an answer.

DIGGING A ROYAL TOMB

When word reached Thebes that a pharaoh had died and his successor had been named, the vizier, priests, and foremen of the workforce not only began to prepare the dead king's tomb for burial, but also began looking around the Valley of the Kings for a place to dig the future king's tomb. This was an important decision, and records indicate that it sometimes took several months. The condition of the bedrock, the structural stability of the hillside, the topography, all had to be considered. Bedrock that was friable, limestone that contained large numbers of hard chert nodules, and hillsides that were badly fractured or showed evidence of a strata of unstable Esna shale would be rejected. In the first half of the Eighteenth Dynasty (from 1524 to about 1420 BCE), preference was given to sites at the base of the sheer cliffs that defined the Valley of the Kings. Ideally, these tombs were situated immediately below a "waterfall," a cliff face over which water from occasional torrential rains poured, carrying tons of debris cascading onto the tomb entrance, burying it under many meters of rubble. The pharaohs of the last half of the Eighteenth Dynasty and the Nineteenth (1293–1185 BCE), were buried at the base of the more gently sloping hills that lay within the valley. These sites were also subject

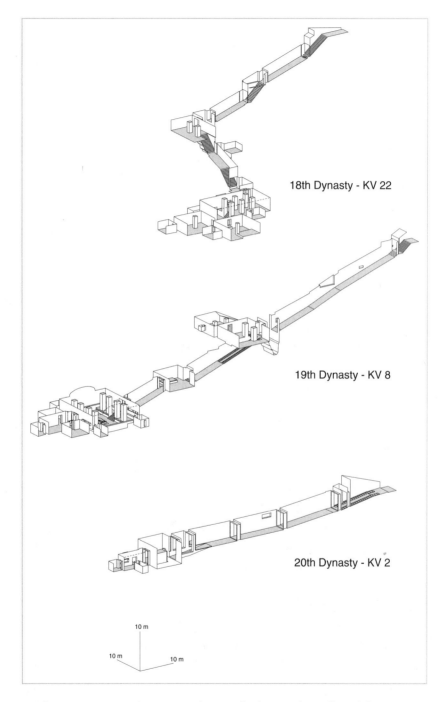

18th Dynasty - KV 22

19th Dynasty - KV 8

20th Dynasty - KV 2

10 m

10 m

10 m

Three common royal New Kingdom tomb plans in the Valley of the Kings.

to flooding. In the Twentieth Dynasty (1185–1070 BCE), the site of choice was changed again, and tomb entrances were dug horizontally into the bases of the valley's small, sloping hills. Such tombs were less likely to flood.

The orientation of a tomb to some geographical or astronomical feature seems not to have been a major concern. For the sake of laying out the decoration, the main axis of a tomb was simply considered to run from east to west, no matter what its actual orientation. Walking down its corridors, one was said to proceed from the horizon of the rising sun to that of the setting, from this life to the next, from the realm of the god Re to the realm of Osiris.

As the Valley of the Kings became increasingly crowded, the choice of sites became increasingly limited. Apparently, there was no master plan of the Kings' Valley, and on several occasions workmen digging a new tomb unwittingly cut into an earlier one. In such cases, they either abandoned the work, made a sharp turn in another direction, or they incorporated the earlier tomb into the new one. Each of these options was used at one time or another.

Once a site was chosen, a plan was prepared. Tombs could vary enormously in size. The pharaohs seem to have deliberately tried to make their tombs larger than their predecessors'. However, this did not always happen, and neither is there is a correlation between the length of a king's reign and the size of his tomb. The plan of a royal tomb followed one of three or four basic layouts, although here, too, there was room for variation. The different plans followed the same chronological scheme as the changes in the choice of site.

Tombs of the Eighteenth Dynasty were usually L-shaped, with alternating corridors and staircases that sloped steeply downward toward two pillared halls, the second of which served as the burial chamber. The burial chambers were either rectangular or oval (cartouchelike), and around them were four small chambers for the storage of funerary equipment. To a degree, the plan of the tomb was seen by Egyptian priests as a reflection of the Netherworld, providing a schematic map of the Beyond.

At the end of the Eighteenth Dynasty, and in the Nineteenth Dynasty, too, the L-shaped plan was abandoned in favor of a straight line of corridors, stairs, and chambers that descended deep into the hillside. The purpose of any royal tomb was basically to protect the body of the pharaoh and provide for his needs in the Afterlife. Enlarging the plan of a tomb, as happened in the reigns of Horemheb, Seti I, and Ramesses II, was simply a way of ensuring that those needs could be more fully met; it did not necessarily imply any major changes in religious beliefs, nor did it reflect the inflated ego of its owner. Chambers and corridors in larger tombs were separated from each other by gates with double-leaf wooden doors, and there was a much more elaborate system of decoration than had been common in Eighteenth Dynasty tombs. Whereas Eighteenth Dynasty tombs were clearly sealed and inaccessible after the pharaoh's mummy was interred, Nineteenth Dynasty tombs may have been partly accessible to priests on ceremonial occasions after the pharaoh's death. Wooden doors, sealed with sliding bolts and stamped-wax impressions, could be reopened; perhaps the only part of the tomb that was intended to be permanently walled off was the burial chamber and its surrounding storerooms.

Tombs of the Twentieth Dynasty, which were smaller in total volume than those of Dynasty 19, had wider corridors and higher ceilings. (It is possible roughly to date royal tombs on the basis of their relative internal dimensions.) Also, instead of making a steep descent, Twentieth Dynasty tombs were cut almost horizontally into the hillside.

No matter how the plans of the New Kingdom (Dynasties 18, 19, and 20) royal tombs changed, there were some basic elements of design and decoration that remained constant. The main entrance, called "The Passage of the Way of Shu," meaning that it was a corridor open to the air (Shu was the god of air), was followed by "The Passage of Re," because it was the farthest corridor into which the sun's rays could penetrate. This was followed by other corridors, including "The Hall Wherein They Rest," "they" being a reference to the statues of various gods that were kept there. Beyond that lay a deep shaft or well, sometimes called "The Hall of Hindering." This well once was thought to be a catchment to prevent floodwater from penetrating the tomb or, alternatively, an obstacle to keep robbers from entering farther into the tomb. But some of these wells have decorated chambers at their base, and some Egyptologists now believe that they also served as a symbolic burial place of the god Osiris. Beyond the well lay the first pillared hall followed by a corridor called "The Ramp." The burial chamber, "The House of Gold," came next, and off it, four storerooms, two of them intended for food and drink, two for wooden statuettes and other ritual equipment.

Before work on a new tomb was begun, priests consecrated the building site by performing what Egyptologists call a "foundation ritual." This involved digging a small pit near the proposed entrance to the royal tomb in which offerings were placed, including model tools and amulets. Shortly thereafter, work on the actual tomb would begin.

The organization of the labor force digging a royal tomb was fairly simple. The men formed two "gangs," referred to as the "left gang" and the "right gang," each consisting of anywhere from twenty to fifty workers. In the narrow confines of a tomb, only two or three men at a time could actually dig. Using wooden mallets, copper chisels, and chert hand axes, taking advantage of natural fractures and cracks in the hillside, they cut into the bedrock, breaking and levering away large chunks of limestone. Other men broke these into manageable pieces, and still others carried them away in leather or reed baskets, dumping them on nearby hillsides. Great piles of this ancient debris still lie in the valley (and I do not doubt that some of them cover the entrances to other lost or undiscovered tombs).

Digging in the valley was not especially difficult—limestone is a soft, easily carved material—but it was dangerous, because of the risk of falling stones and because broken limestone has extremely sharp edges. There are no records of injuries or deaths during the work, but we can assume that they occurred. Yet it was not the fear of injury that made the work unpleasant; much worse was the intense discomfort. As the men cut deeper and deeper into the hillside, the work space became increasingly claustrophobic, dusty, hot, humid, and dark. I can sympathize with those ancient workmen: the conditions in which we work in KV 5 are also unpleasant, even though we, happily, have much better tools—as well as hard hats, face masks, safety devices, and electric lights.

The amount of work accomplished each day by the ancient workers was measured by the number of baskets of broken stone they carried out of the tomb. The length of their workday was measured by oil lamps and wicks. Each morning, workmen were given clay bowls in which they placed twisted lengths of linen soaked in wax and sesame oil. A pinch of salt was added to the oil to prevent it from smoking. Two of these wicks were given to each of the gangs, one for the morning work, the other for the afternoon. Both pieces were of equal length and each burned for about four hours. Thus, the workday consisted of two four-hour-long sessions with a lunch break between them, and when a wick was gone the workmen knew that it was time to stop. We know, too, that in the Nineteenth Dynasty the workweek was eight days long, followed by two days off, and that there were many holidays scattered throughout the year.

Two men, digging forward, starting at the top of a corridor and working down to the floor, roughly cut each corridor or chamber or stairway, passing the chunks of stone to basket carriers who carted the pieces out of the tomb. Following behind them, other men worked more carefully, straightening and smoothing the walls, using a simple carpenter's square, plumb bobs, and string to ensure that walls were vertical, corners close to 90 degrees, and floors parallel to ceilings. The foreman made frequent checks to make sure that the design specifications were correctly followed. A third group of men followed still farther behind, applying a layer of gypsum to the walls in preparation for the decoration.

Decorating the tomb also was an assembly-line operation. First, a scribe drew in red pigment an outline of the figures and hieroglyphic texts to be carved. Then, a second scribe checked the outline, using black pigment to correct spelling errors or alter the proportions of figures. Artisans cut away the background to create raised relief, and still others smoothed the raised outlines and modeled details of the figures and hieroglyphs. Finally, the walls were painted using the usual New Kingdom palette of colors—red, yellow, white, black— made from naturally occurring minerals or vegetal materials, as well as blue, which was made from ground faience.

The subject matter of tomb decoration changed along with the tomb's location and plan during the course of the New Kingdom. In the Eighteenth Dynasty, there was an emphasis on describing the nighttime journey of the sun through the Netherworld. In the Nineteenth Dynasty, this story was given less emphasis, and instead walls were given over to elaborate descriptions of Osiris and his role in the Afterlife. In the Twentieth Dynasty, both the journey of the sun and the stories of Osiris were given more or less equal billing.

The texts of these theological discussions have been generically labeled "The Book of the Dead." In fact, there were several differ- ent texts, each dealing with different theological subjects. For example, "The Book of Gates" discussed the divisions of the night into twelve hours. It was carved on the walls of Nineteenth- and Twentieth-Dynasty burial chambers. The *Amduat,* called "The Book of That Which Is in the Underworld" or "The Book of the Hidden Chamber," recounted the sun's nighttime journey and was found in royal burial chambers throughout the New Kingdom. "The Litany of Re," a text of praise for the sun god, was found just inside the entrances of many Nineteenth- and Twentieth-Dynasty tombs. "The Book of Coming Forth by Day," a collection of much earlier prayers and spells for the deceased, can be found in several Nineteenth- and Twentieth-Dynasty royal tombs.

The quality of the decoration in the royal tombs varied from good to outstanding, and many tombs fully deserve the praise given by Arthur Stanley, an English traveler who visited Thebes in 1853. Of his first visit to a KV tomb, he wrote:

Nothing that has ever been said about them had prepared me for their extraordinary grandeur. You enter a sculpted portal in the face of these wild cliffs, and find yourself in a long and lofty gallery, opening or narrowing as the case may be, into successive halls and chambers, all of which are covered with white stucco, and this white stucco brilliant with colors, fresh as they were thousands of years ago, but on a scale, and with a splendor, that I can only compare to the frescoes of the Vatican Library.

THE WORKMEN'S VILLAGE

The men who dug the royal tombs lived in a village about two kilometers south of the Valley of the Kings. Called Deir el-Medineh (meaning "the village monastery," an Arabic reference to a fifth-century Coptic (early Christian) monastery that lay nearby), this workmen's village is one of Egypt's most fascinating and important sites. Few tourists ever visit it, and those who do often walk quickly past it on their way to the tombs. That's a pity because even today the village offers the clearest view of what it might have been like to be an ancient Egyptian.

What makes the site so remarkable is that when it was abandoned at the end of the New Kingdom, five hundred years after its founding, when the royal court moved permanently north and kings were no longer buried in the Valley of the Kings, memory of Deir el-Medineh faded and it was buried by blowing sand. Thousands of ostraca—limestone chips used as memo pads—statuettes, and other artifacts were left behind, and the site lay utterly ignored for three thousand years. But when eighteenth-century explorers and local villagers began to scratch about in Deir el-Medineh's blowing sand, the artifacts they found rapidly led to more extensive digging.

The excavations of the Italian scholar Ernesto Schiaparelli from 1905 to 1909 and, even more dramatically, the extensive work undertaken by the French Institute in Cairo between 1917 and 1947 and again after World War II, proved Deir el-Medineh's importance. So much material was recovered that, even today, only a small part of it has been fully published. What has appeared provides us with a remarkable picture of life in Deir el-Medineh. We know, for example, the names of the workmen who lived there and the names of their parents, children, and wives; we know which village houses the families lived in; we know how long they lived there and where they were buried. We even know when they took ill or went on holiday, what they ate and what they bought and sold.

Deir el-Medineh lay about half a kilometer west of the nearest cultivable land. Food and water had to be delivered to the villagers several times a week. The narrow *wadi* offered privacy but precious little else. The village was hemmed in by hot, dusty, sand-covered hills and there are no beautiful views. It was not a large village: perhaps 130 meters long, 50 meters wide, covering about 6,500 square meters (70,000 square feet). Yet three thousand years ago, this was home to several hundred people. They lived in seventy houses, with fifty or so public buildings and workshops laid out along a single north–south lane hardly wide enough for two donkeys to pass. For nearly five hundred years, twenty-five generations of workmen and artisans lived and died here, digging and decorating the royal tombs and passing their craft on to their children.

Today, Deir el-Medineh is a maze of stone and mud brick walls that rise not more than a meter above the windblown sand. From a distance, there seems to be little of interest here until, suddenly, over an ancient enclosure wall, there appears a maze of walls. These are the remains of scores of houses, their doors opening onto a narrow central street. With proper signing and explanatory displays, the village could be made as exciting and informative as Pompeii or Herculanaeum.

The people of Deir el-Medineh must have been as full of life as the inhabitants of the modern villages nearby. Of course, these ancients were linguistically, religiously, and politically a world apart from us. But these are superficial matters. Deeper down, theirs was a life very much like our own, and at Deir el-Medineh—more there, I think, than at any other site in Egypt—you can feel the presence of a people who share the same basic emotions and concerns as we do.

Among the professionals living in the Deir el-Medineh community were sculptors, woodworkers, quarrymen, painters, and plasterers. The scribes Ramose and Huy lived here. Both may have worked on the tomb of Ramesses II and perhaps KV 5 as well.

The homes in Deir el-Medineh varied slightly in size and plan, but their basic layouts were similar. Each house had a ground floor with a reception room with a central column, private rooms, a kitchen, and a shaded roof terrace. Small niches were cut into the walls to serve as shelves for clothing and the statuettes of household deities such as Bes, Isis, or Hathor. We have an ostracon ordering such a statuette: "Please manufacture for me a *Weret*-demon because the one which you manufactured for me has been stolen. . . . " The homes were furnished simply; wood was expensive, so mud brick, woven reeds, basketry, and pottery were the principal materials. The craftsmen of Deir el-Medineh were paid in kind, and small cellars were cut into the floors of each house to store food they received. What were they paid? Another ostracon gives the answer:

[The mayor] of the West of Ne (Thebes) Ramose communicates to the foremen of the crew, namely, [to] the foreman Nebnefer and to the foreman Kaha and the entire crew as well. To wit:

Now the city prefect and vizier Pazer has written me saying, "Please have the wages delivered to the necropolis crew comprising vegetables, fish, firewood, pottery, small cattle, and milk. Don't let anything thereof remain outstanding. [Don't] make me treat any part of their wages as balance due. Be to it and pay heed!"

In other words, they were paid in food and other goods, but not in money.

Deir el-Medineh lay in a relatively isolated and inconspicuous valley, hidden from the cultivated Nile floodplain behind a barren hill. Each day, workmen left the village early in the morning and spent an hour climbing over the hill to reach the Valley of the Kings. They returned along the same path, although there was also a small collection of stone huts—a rest house of sorts—at the top of the hill if they chose to spend the night in the cool evening breezes that bless what Egyptologists have termed the "village de repos."

It is not a long or particularly difficult hike from Deir el-Medineh to the narrow, high plateau where the "village de repos" was built. But the climb is hot because the surrounding hills block most of the winds and even in winter months it is possible to work up a good sweat. The climb is worth this minor annoyance. Once one is on the plateau, a light breeze nearly always blows and there is one of the most stunningly beautiful views anywhere in Egypt. It is the best place to understand Egypt's natural environment, the topography of Thebes, and the reasons why the Valley of the Kings was the obvious choice as the place to bury the New Kingdom pharaohs.

The plateau is narrow and covers no more than a few hundred square meters. Its four sides are defined by two hills and two cliffs that rise up to it. To the south is a mountain that resembles a great wall whose face extends nearly two kilometers to the southernmost limit of the Theban Necropolis. To the north is a series of low hills and plateaus that extend for several kilometers before dropping down to a large desert plain, a part of Thebes called Ta'arif, the ancient necropolis's northern limit. The western cliff drops 150 meters into the Valley of the Kings. The eastern cliff drops two hundred meters into the narrow strip of desert separating the Theban hills from the Nile floodplain.

In this narrow strip of desert below to the east lie the entrances to hundreds, more probably thousands, of Eighteenth and Nineteenth dynasty tombs, most of them still not explored except by thieves. Beside them stand the temples of New Kingdom pharaohs, great stone columns and pylons and thick brick walls jutting from the desert sand. Two kilometers north stands the mortuary temple of Seti I; a kilometer south stands Medinet Habu, the mortuary temple of Ramesses III. Midway between them lies the Ramesseum, the mortuary temple of Ramesses II. These three temples are fairly well documented. But there are dozens of others that even today have been only cursorily explored. From this vantage point it is easy to see why: between cliffs and cultivation, an area only a few hundred meters wide and six kilometers long, there lie more tombs, temples, shrines and villages than in almost any other area in Egypt—more, perhaps, than anywhere else in the world. It is hard to imagine where one should begin to clear or record them.

This monument-rich area is not only beautiful, it is daunting.

THE Valley of the Kings, where the Deir el-Medineh artisans worked, is a small *wadi* that, at first glance, seems little different from any of the hundreds of others here on the edge of the Western Desert. Shaped like a human hand with fingers splayed, KV is defined by vertical cliffs of limestone that rise fifty meters above the valley floor. This valley is small compared to others in the area: its floor covers only about four hectares (9.88 acres).

There is only one entrance into KV, originally "a narrow steep passage about ten feet high . . . broke down thro' the rock." But early in the twentieth century, that passage was cut away, leveled and widened so that donkeys could be ridden into the valley, then widened again in the 1950s to accommodate a paved road leading directly into the heart of the valley. From there, an intricate web of footpaths extend across the valley floor and onto the hillsides beyond. These paths are not ancient. Most were laid down in the last century using thick layers of white gravel taken from the debris dumped by tomb excavators. But ancient paths still meander across the upper slopes of KV leading from the valley to temples and ancient workmen's homes. Their dusty-white surfaces contrast with the dark brown fields of chert that cover many hill slopes.

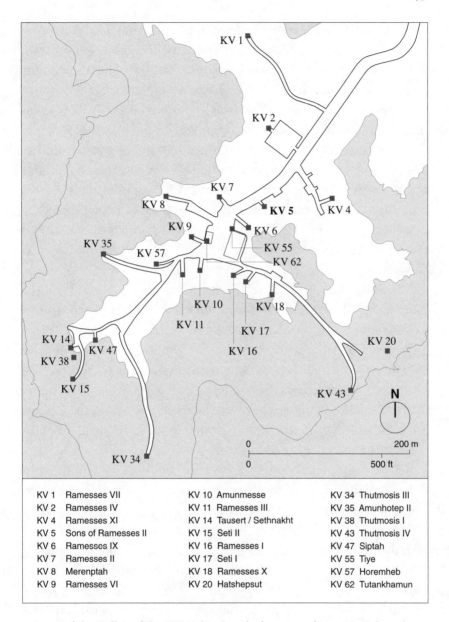

KV 1	Ramesses VII	KV 10	Amunmesse	KV 34	Thutmosis III
KV 2	Ramesses IV	KV 11	Ramesses III	KV 35	Amunhotep II
KV 4	Ramesses XI	KV 14	Tausert / Sethnakht	KV 38	Thutmosis I
KV 5	Sons of Ramesses II	KV 15	Seti II	KV 43	Thutmosis IV
KV 6	Ramesses IX	KV 16	Ramesses I	KV 47	Siptah
KV 7	Ramesses II	KV 17	Seti I	KV 55	Tiye
KV 8	Merenptah	KV 18	Ramesses X	KV 57	Horemheb
KV 9	Ramesses VI	KV 20	Hatshepsut	KV 62	Tutankhamun

Map of the Valley of the Kings showing the location of its principal tombs.

Actually, there are two "Valleys of the Kings" at Thebes; appropriately, they are collectively referred to in Arabic as *Wadayn*, "The Two Valleys." We have been describing just one of them, the East Valley, referred to as KV. Immediately adjacent is a much larger valley, the West Valley, usually referred to as WV. WV has only two major tombs in it (that we know of), those of the pharaohs Amunhotep III and Ay, and a handful of smaller, undecorated tombs belonging to lesser nobility. But although it contains fewer tombs than KV, the West Valley is topographically the most impressive. It is a long, narrow, meandering *wadi* surrounded by dramatically rugged cliffs and mountains. Tourists rarely visit it (only the tomb of Ay is open to the public), and it is a special treat to walk here alone, wrapped in its silence and beauty.

Towering over KV is the Qurn, meaning the "Horn" or the "Forehead." From KV—and from no other place in Thebes—this 455-meter (1,500-foot-high) peak looks like a pyramid. Some Egyptologists believe that this natural symbol of the sun god Re explains why the valley was chosen as the site of royal tombs. The Qurn also was sacred to the goddess Meret-seger, "She Who Loves Silence," and to Hathor. They were believed to dwell in these western hills, waiting to meet and assist the deceased on their way into the Afterlife.

KV was selected also because it had good-quality limestone in which structurally solid tombs could be dug; its well-defined shape and the sheer cliffs surrounding it made it easy to guard; it was close to the Nile Valley; and it lay directly west of Deir el-Bahari and the royal mortuary temples, a symbolically important geographical relationship. It was also convenient: although today the road from the cultivated floodplain to KV follows a nine-kilometer-long arc, giving the impression that the valley is isolated and distant, one actually can walk over the hill from Deir el-Bahari to KV in about half an hour and from the workmen's village at Deir el-Medineh in under an hour.

What today in English we label the Valley of the Kings, modern Egyptians call the *Wadi Biban el-Melouk*, the "Valley of the Gates

of the Kings." The ancient Egyptians called it "The Great and
Noble Necropolis of Millions of Years of Pharaoh (May He Live,
Be Prosperous and Healthy!) on the West of Thebes" or, less formally, "The Hidden Place" or "The Great Place." During most of
the New Kingdom, from about 1524 to 1070 BCE, a period of over
four centuries, it was here that the pharaohs of Egypt were buried,
in what arguably are the most famous tombs in the world.

Sheikh Ali Abdel Ressaul, Qurnah, Luxor. ("Mersam Hotel")

4

MAPPING IN THE VALLEY

OF THE KINGS

BEFORE we could begin mapping the Valley of the Kings and making plans of the tombs it contains, we had to review the work that had already been done there, most of it within the last two centuries, but some two thousand years ago. Diodorus Siculus, a Greek historian who visited Thebes about 65–40 BCE, said that priests gave him a list of forty-seven tombs in the valley. His figure agrees with that of Strabo (64 BCE–CE 21), a Roman geographer, who claimed that there were about forty tombs. (Today, we count sixty-two tombs, plus about two dozen unfinished pits.) The only tombs accessible to Greek and Roman visitors who came between 332 BCE and CE 251, however, were nine Ramesside tombs—those of Ramesses II, III, IV, VI, VII, IX, XI, Merenptah, Amunmesse, and Seti II. At least, they are the only tombs with Greek or Latin graffiti on their walls, and these graffiti are the only sure proof we have that Greeks and Romans visited them. In the early Christian period, Copts used several tombs as hermitages or churches and also left graffiti in them and in the tomb of Ramesses VI. These graffiti are the first evidence we have of "modern" interest in the Valley of the Kings. In fact, they are the only evidence of visitors to the valley before the seventeenth century. In 1668, two French priests, Protais and François, alluded in their journals to "the place of mummies called biban el melouc," but they left no description of what they saw. These early records were brief and uninformative, and most visitors didn't know for whom the tombs had been dug or what their painted scenes and texts might mean.

In 1708, for example, a Jesuit priest, Claude Sicard, visited the valley. Remarking on the "admirable" decoration he saw, he reported that the scenes and texts told "the story of the lives, virtues, acts, combats and victories of the princes who are buried there." His description was inaccurate because *those* kinds of stories are told (exaggeratedly) on temple walls, not in royal tombs where, invariably, the scenes have purely religious content. But Sicard's view was widely held for over a century.

One of the earliest travelers to leave a fairly detailed record of his visit was the Englishman Richard Pococke, who visited the Valley of the Kings on September 16, 1739:

> . . . There are signs of about eighteen [tombs] . . . now there are only nine that can be enter'd into. The hills on each side are high steep rocks, and the whole place is cover'd with rough stones that seem to have rolled from them; the grottoes are cut into the rock in a most beautiful manner in long rooms or galleries under the mountains, which are of a close white freestone that cuts like chalk, and is as smooth as the finest stucco work . . . some of them [are] painted, being as fresh as if they were but just finish'd.

Pococke's chief claim to fame, however, is the map that he drew of the valley. His is the oldest KV map we know of and, in spite of its rather quaint style, it shows the valley's topography with some degree of accuracy, although the positions of the tomb entrances have caused much confusion. Some can be identified, but others are puzzling. Pococke reported eighteen tomb entrances, apparently nine of them at least partly accessible, but KV 5 was not among them.

In 1768, an English traveler, James Bruce, visited the valley and devoted an afternoon to copying some of the beautifully preserved scenes in the tomb of Ramesses III (KV 11). Inaccurate and highly stylized, Bruce's drawing of a harpist in the tomb nevertheless struck a chord in European imagination and generated considerable interest in ancient Egypt and its art. KV 11 inevitably came to be known as "Bruce's Tomb." However, European knowledge of the valley and its contents remained vague and uninformed until early in the nineteenth century, when *Description de l'Égypte,* the massive record of Egypt's culture and environment left by scholars who accompanied Napoleon's expedition up the Nile, included an impressive map of KV, surveyed and drawn by Edmé Jomard and the baron Louis Costaz. The map included simple plans of eleven tombs in the valley and references to five others said to be inaccessible, their entrances indicated by black dots. One of those dots marked the entrance to KV 5.

Giovanni Belzoni's 1818 map of KV included sketchy topography of both the East and West valleys and the simple, unscaled plans of the tombs he had excavated there. Robert Hay, who visited the valley in the 1820s, and James Burton, who came in 1825, also made sketch maps. The quality of each map's cartographic work was a great improvement on its predecessors, although none of the nineteenth-century maps were based upon anything more than casual observations and paced-off distances.

John Gardner Wilkinson, whose elegant map of the Theban Necropolis we mentioned earlier, was responsible for establishing the system of KV tomb numbering that is still used today. In 1827, armed with a brush and a bucket of red paint, he walked through the valley writing large numbers on the bedrock above the entrance of every tomb he could find. Wilkinson's numbering system was ordered geographically: he began at the entrance to the valley, proceeded southward to its end, then moved on to the eastern spur, where the tombs of Ramesses I (KV 16), Seti I (KV 17), and Thutmosis I/Hatshepsut (KV 20) were located. Wilkinson numbered twenty-one tombs, but there are seven more entrances shown on the sketch map he made of the valley, meaning that twenty-eight tomb entrances were visible at the time. Wilkinson's system has been added to since 1827, with tombs KV 22 through KV 62 assigned numbers in the order of their discovery. The most recent number, KV 62, was assigned to the tomb of Tutankhamun.

Wilkinson was aware of the entrance to KV 5 during his original numbering project, but just barely: apparently, so little of the doorway was exposed that he could not find a place to write the tomb number. KV 5's doorway was also partly visible in 1849: a peculiar book called *Journal of a Voyage Up the Nile,* by "An American" refers to it, stating that "No. 5 is the tomb of Chamed." I do not know who Hamid (the more nearly correct spelling) might be, however.

Carl Lepsius, whose monumental book, *Denkmäler aus Ägypten und Nubien,* offered Europeans twelve volumes of plates devoted entirely to the ancient monuments, also surveyed the Valley of the Kings (in 1844–1845), recording scenes in several of the accessible tombs. His map showed twenty-five tomb entrances in the Valley of the Kings, KV 5 among them.

MAPPING THE VALLEY OF THE KINGS

Sometime around 100 BCE, a Greek traveler in the valley scratched a graffito in the tomb of Ramesses VI: "I, Dioskorammon, looked upon this nonsense and found it bewildering!" They may be bewildering, but to most people the tombs are among Egypt's most fascinating monuments. When we announced that our second season of work at Thebes would be devoted to mapping KV and planning its tombs, the number of Berkeley students who volunteered nearly doubled.

Our goals were to prepare plans, sections, and three-dimensional renderings of each of the KV tombs; to explore the valley's surface meticulously for traces of ancient building or digging; and to prepare a precise topographic map of KV and its surrounding hillsides. Back at Berkeley, we spent the winter collecting all the historical data on KV we could find. In the field, our team of surveyors from the previous year returned, and we added another Egyptologist, Catharine Roehrig, then my graduate student at Berkeley but who has since become a senior curator at the Metropolitan Museum of Art. Catharine immediately displayed a flair for surveying. Under David Goodman's guidance, she learned to use the theodolite in only a few weeks, and by the end of the first month, I put her in charge of surveying inside the KV tombs.

There were several reasons why we began our Theban survey in the Valley of the Kings and not elsewhere in the necropolis. The rapid increase in mass tourism that had begun in the late 1970s seemed likely to continue. It was especially heavy in KV, and careful planning would be required to keep the tourist threat to a minimum. Nonetheless, tourism and archaeological preservation are not necessarily antagonistic, so long as tourism is properly controlled. Mapping KV and preparing architectural studies of its tombs—in effect creating an archaeological database—were required to protect these ancient treasures.

We began in KV 1 and 2, and we discovered early on that the survey techniques we were initially using needed to be changed if we wanted to achieve a level of accuracy and still work efficiently. At first, we had simply placed the theodolite on a tripod at the entrance to a chamber, leveled the telescope, and then taped measurements left, right, up, and down from the optical line thus created. However, this process was hard to control and introduced errors into the work. After a few days, David had us measure angles with the theodolite, working in turn from several stations that we would establish in each tomb, sighting from them to such architectural features as walls, ceiling, floor, corners, and edges.

The distance from the theodolite to the feature was then taped. This was much more accurate and much faster. Once our crew had become accustomed to it, they grew a bit cocky and talked about how anxious they were to work in what one of them called "a tomb that will really challenge our skills." As we went on, we found that no tomb seemed more likely to pose a challenge to us than KV 20, one of the strangest tombs in the Valley of the Kings. In our second season, we decided to work there.

SURVEYING HATSHEPSUT'S TOMBS

The work undertaken by the Deir el-Medineh quarrymen and artisans varied greatly over five centuries both in quantity and quality: some of the tombs were large, carefully dug, and elegantly decorated; others were small, hastily finished, and hardly decorated at all. Some of the tombs followed standard plans, but a few were unique—wildly divergent from the norms.

One of the oddest was the intriguing and challenging tomb ordered by Queen Hatshepsut (1498–1483 BCE), the daughter of Thutmosis I, wife of Thutmosis II, and stepmother of Thutmosis III. Hatshepsut was reviled after her death, treated as an interloper, and ignored in later king lists. But her memory lived on in one of the most spectacular monuments of dynastic times, her mortuary temple at Deir el-Bahari. It was a remarkable building whose setting in a dramatic amphitheater of rugged limestone cliffs made it one of the most beautiful monuments of ancient times. The temple lies immediately east of the Valley of the Kings, and its axis is the same as the first few corridors of KV 20, one of two tombs that have been ascribed to Hatshepsut.

It now seems likely that KV 20 was originally dug for Thutmosis I. His architect, Ineni, boasted that he undertook the work, "no one seeing, no one hearing," a claim that probably meant only that he was the senior project supervisor. At the time, the tomb extended about fifty meters into the hillside. Later, Hatshepsut usurped the tomb, increased its length, and arranged that both she and Thutmosis I be buried in it.

KV 20 is also one of the most unpleasant tombs. Its entrance was cut high in a cliff at the easternmost edge of the valley, well concealed in a deep cleft about 280 meters (900 feet) west of Hatshepsut's temple. Its doorway was cut in fair-quality limestone; had the tomb been dug more or less horizontally, it would have been a solid piece of work. Instead, the corridor was cut steeply downward, and within a few meters of the entrance workmen had dug below the stratum of limestone and into a layer of shale, called *tafla* in Arabic. *Tafla* is an extremely weak stone that has the appearance—and the strength—of dark gray oatmeal.

At one time it was thought that Hatshepsut had her tomb dug here so that its burial chamber would lie immediately behind or beneath her mortuary temple. It is true that the first part of KV 20—the part dug for Thutmosis I—lies roughly on same east–west axis as Hatshepsut's mortuary temple. But about fifty meters into the tomb, beyond the first chamber where Hatshepsut had begun her work, the corridor began a huge clockwise turn, moving sinuously downward and curving back on itself. The tomb extends over 213 meters into the hill and descends 97 meters in the process, from 197.5 meters above sea level at the entrance to 101.2 meters at the burial chamber. (The mortuary temple at Deir el-Bahari lies at about 114 meters above sea level.)

John Gardner Wilkinson cleared the first part of KV 20 in the 1820s. The work was extremely difficult because "in parts the rubbish was so hard that pickaxes were necessary, and one could hardly tell whether the men were cutting the rock or the rubbish." James Burton also experienced difficulties when he worked here: ". . . he was obliged to abandon his researches owing to the danger of the mephitic air, which extinguished the lights." Howard Carter finally cleared the lower reaches of the tomb, and revealed a series of decorated limestone blocks apparently intended to line the rough-cut walls of the descending corridors.

We mapped KV 20 in 1980. Four of us arrived early one morning at the entrance, loaded down with tripods, theodolite, bags of tape measures, plumb bobs, and note forms. The tomb had a wire-mesh door at its entrance, but the lock had been broken and the door obviously had stood open for years. From inside the tomb wafted the unmistakable urinelike stench of bat guano. Bats love Theban tombs.

The corridors of KV 20 slope downward at a 30-degree angle and are covered with a fine dust, a combination of powdered limestone and bat guano that makes walking almost impossible. Nubie, one of our workmen, hadn't gone ten meters into the tomb when he slipped and fell, sliding another several meters down the slippery slope. I shone the flashlight down the corridor to where he lay. The clatter of his falling equipment bag and the light from the flashlight startled the bats in the tomb, and suddenly the air was thick with flapping wings and high-pitched screeches as the creatures flew in panic toward the doorway. At first, there were only a few dozen of them. Then their cries startled others and within seconds thousands of bats were flying past us, their wings stirring up dust and flapping against our faces.

"*Watazveet!*" Nubie shouted the Arabic word for bats. "They will get stuck in your hair! I hate them!" He rolled over and lay facedown on the ground, covering his head with his hands. The rest of us sat down against the wall. It took several minutes before things began to quiet down. Not all the bats had left the tomb by any means, but several thousands of them had, and the air was thick with the stench of the fine dust they had stirred up. None of us wore a face mask, and we spent the rest of the morning coughing and sneezing, anxious to get back to the hotel and wash the bat guano out of our hair and clothes.

After that first experience, work in KV 20 over the next week followed a regular routine. We entered the tomb, trying to make as little noise as possible, shining deliberately dimmed lamps only at the floor or at survey targets. We found that it was easier and quieter to sit and slide down the corridors than to try to walk. Climbing out of the tomb was dirtier and even more difficult than sliding in. In places, we had to crawl on hands and knees. In spite of our silence, at least a dozen times a day we had to sit in corners while great clouds of bats flew by.

During our third field season, we discovered that the second tomb attributed to Hatshepsut posed other problems for us. We had been mapping the numerous minor tombs in the West Bank's outlying *wadis* for over six weeks. Most of them were fairly straightforward: they were pits cut vertically into the *wadi* floor, small, undecorated, poorly carved, and poorly preserved. Hatshepsut's tomb, however, was another matter. It lay in the remote Wadi Sikket wu Tagga ez-Zeid, several kilometers southwest of the Valley of the Kings, and its entrance was halfway up a sheer cliff over 110 meters (360 feet) high. The only way into the tomb was to rappel down from the top of the hill, forty-two meters above its door.

The tomb, designated WA-D, was first cleared by Howard Carter in 1916. Its plan was simple: a long corridor makes a right turn and leads to a small burial chamber. Inside the chamber, Carter found a large, yellow quartzite sarcophagus inscribed for the "King's Daughter, King's Sister, Wife of the God, Great Royal Wife and Lady of the Two Lands, Hatshepsut," evidence that the tomb had been dug for her before she assumed the throne. It must have been a major feat of engineering to have maneuvered a huge sarcophagus into such an awkwardly located tomb. No less impressive must have been getting it out. That job was undertaken seventy years ago by the engineer Emile Baraize, who had it removed to the Egyptian Museum in Cairo. His description of the problems he faced when building a mud-brick ramp, using block and tackle and rollers to move the monolith, is another reminder of the ancient Egyptians' remarkable patience and skill.

One member of our project that field season, Berkeley

Egyptology student Joel Paulson, had rock-climbing experience. Anticipating that our work would include WA-D, I had asked Joel to bring his climbing paraphernalia to Thebes. After two days of careful planning, checking where one could tie a rope at the top of the cliff, studying the cliff face through binoculars, and constructing a harness that would permit Joel to carry the needed survey gear with him and still keep his hands free, we hiked the five-kilometer-long trail into the *wadi*, then made our way along another three-kilometer-long path that led to the hilltop. Making everything ready took a good three hours, and it was not until late morning that Joel was finally ready to descend into the tomb. As he slowly backed over the edge of the cliff, I stood on the *wadi* floor, watching with the binoculars and taking photographs. Joel's descent was slow, steady, and uneventful. We all applauded as he stopped in front of the tomb entrance and maneuvered himself and his heavy equipment inside.

Not thirty seconds later, Joel literally jumped out the tomb doorway into thin air and made a rapid descent to the *wadi* floor. I rushed over to where he had made a rough landing.

"What happened?" I asked.

"As soon as I got inside, I thought I saw something move. I turned on my flashlight and there was a cobra, maybe three feet long, ten paces down the corridor. I'm not going back in!" How a cobra got into such an inaccessible tomb is a mystery. It may have followed a small animal down one of the many crevices connecting the tomb with the surface above. We abandoned work in WA-D that season, promising ourselves that we'd return. We've not yet found time to do so.

JOEL got another chance to use his climbing equipment later that season. During one of our balloon reconnaissance flights, we were blown off course by an unexpected gust of wind that sent us into a remote area north of the Valley of the Kings. As the pilot maneuvered to land, one of our crew spotted a rectangular doorway cut into the cliff face of a small *wadi*. We suspected that it might be a tomb similar to those we'd mapped in other outlying areas, so we marked its location at the top of the cliff and, with Joel and his climbing equipment, hiked back to explore it.

The entrance was all but invisible from the ground below. It lay halfway up a forty-meter-high cliff, and Joel outfitted himself as he had at WA-D, muttering the hope that there would be no unwelcome creatures lurking inside this tomb. He rappelled quickly down the cliff to the doorway and hung outside for a minute or two, shining his flashlight into the dark interior. Nothing seemed to be moving, so he proceeded inside.

After about ten minutes, Joel reappeared and shouted a description of what he'd found. Nothing inside suggested that this was a dynastic tomb. Instead, there were four small rooms; floors littered with early Christian pottery; and walls brilliantly painted with figures of Christ, animals symbolizing the four evangelists, Coptic texts, elaborate crosses, and geometric designs. Almost certainly this was a Christian hermitage, probably of the seventh century CE, when Thebes was home to a large number of monasteries. Many of the monks considered even a monastic life too worldly for their taste, and they opted to live as hermits in isolated caves in the Theban hills, depending upon their brothers to bring them food and water. Perhaps once or twice a week, a monk came from a nearby monastery and lowered a basket of bread, vegetables, and water to the hermit. The hermit then spent his solitary days in prayer, meditation, and wall painting. We have published a plan and several photographs of the hermitage, but I hope that one day we will be able to return and thoroughly document what may very well be the best-preserved, most elegantly decorated hermitage in all of Upper Egypt.

KV 17: THE DEEPEST TOMB OF ALL

The tomb of Seti I, father of Ramesses II, known as KV 17, is fascinating not only because it is one of the largest and best-decorated tombs, but also because it boasts a peculiar corridor that bores more than 150 meters (500 feet) beyond the already deeply dug burial chamber. The news of its discovery by Giovanni Belzoni in 1817 caused as much furor in the European press as Tutankhamun's tomb would 105 years later.

Belzoni, born in Padua in 1778, was an enormous man, six feet seven inches tall, who had worked for years in England and Europe as a weightlifter in a vaudeville show. (His performance consisted of lifting an iron bar with a dozen men hanging on to it.) Belzoni had originally trained as a hydraulic engineer and in 1815, acting on a rumor, sailed to Egypt in the hopes of selling the Egyptian government his design for a hydraulic device for lifting water. The government wasn't interested. In need of a job, Belzoni found work with the British consul in Egypt, Henry Salt, who was impressed with his engineering credentials and hired him to move a huge statue of Ramesses II from Thebes to Alexandria, where it would be shipped to the British Museum. Belzoni accomplished the feat in only a few weeks; the statue is now one of the largest pieces of Egyptian sculpture outside Egypt.

Over the next several years, Belzoni explored numerous archaeological sites, including the Pyramids at Giza, but his most important work was in the Valley of the Kings, where he uncovered six royal tombs. Seti I's, of course, was the most famous. Belzoni wrote that its discovery

has paid me for all the trouble I took in my researches. I may call this a fortunate day, one of the best perhaps in my life. . . . [I had] the pleasure of discovering what has been long sought in vain, and of presenting the world with a new and perfect monument of Egyptian antiquity . . . appearing as if just finished on the day we entered it. Not fifteen yards from the last tomb I described [KV 16, tomb of Seti's father, Ramesses I], I caused the earth to be opened at the foot of a steep hill, and under a torrent, which, when it rains in the desert, pours a great quantity of water over the very spot I caused to be dug. No one could imagine, that the ancient Egyptians would make the entrance into such immense and superb excavation just under a torrent of water; but I had strong reasons to suppose, that there was a tomb in that place, from indications I had observed in my pursuit. The Fellahs who were accustomed to dig were all of the opinion that there was nothing in that spot as the situation of this tomb differed from that of any other . . .

He instructed his workmen to dig out the entrance of the tomb as rapidly as possible, and two days later, on October 18,

about noon, the workmen reached the entrance, which was eighteen feet below the surface of the ground. The appearance indicated, that the tomb was of the first rate: but still I did not expect to find such a one as it really proved to be. The Fellahs advanced till they saw that it was probably a large tomb, when they protested they could go no further, the tomb was so much choked up with large stones, which they could not get out of the passage. I descended, examined the place, pointed out to them where they might dig, and in an hour there was room enough for me to enter the tomb through a passage that the earth had left under the ceiling of the first corridor, which is thirty-six feet two inches long, and eight feet eight inches wide, and, when cleared of the ruins, eight feet nine inches high. I perceived immediately by the painting on the ceiling and by the hieroglyphs in basso relievo, which were to be seen where the earth did not reach, that this was the entrance into a large and magnificent tomb.

Crawling through a small channel cut by his workmen into the debris, Belzoni found that a rainstorm two days earlier had sent water cascading into the tomb and had damaged parts of the first few corridors. The cause was his own excavations of the

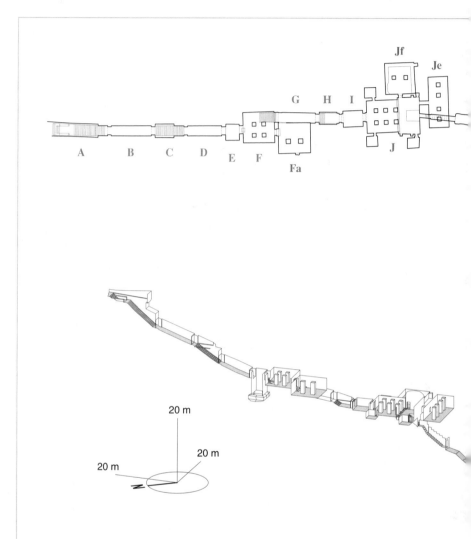

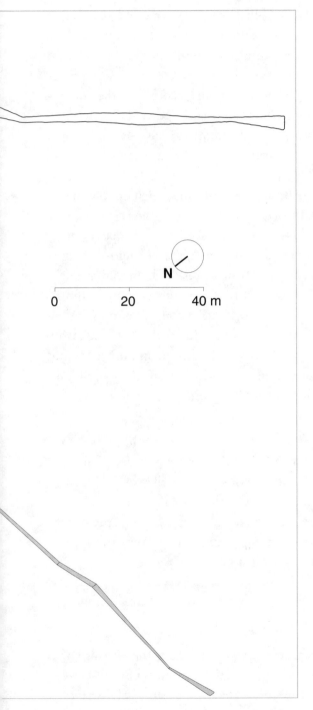

N

0   20   40 m

Plan and isometric
drawing of KV 17, the
tomb of Seti I.

entrance, which removed the blocking that formerly had acted as a dam. Belzoni's offhand reference to water in KV 17 is one of the earliest records of flood damage to tombs in the Valley of the Kings. But it was by no means the last. Since his time, damage from rainfall, as well as from unthinking visitors to the tomb—and from Belzoni himself, whose squeezes and casts badly damaged the painted walls—has brought about dramatic and unwelcome changes to the brightness and character of the wall paintings.

In 1829, a decade after Belzoni, Jean-François Champollion, the man who is credited with deciphering Egyptian hieroglyphs, also described the awful condition of the tomb: ". . . it decays every day. The pillars are cracking and splitting. The ceiling is falling in pieces and the paint is coming off in flakes." Champollion had a remarkable solution to preserve the tomb: cut it up and ship its best scenes off to France. This "solution" soon came to the attention of Joseph Bonomi, an artist who had worked at Thebes on archaeological projects with Burton, Wilkinson, and other famous nineteenth-century recorders of tomb decoration. Champollion's proposal so agitated Bonomi that he wrote him a letter:

> Sir, I have been informed that certain people have arrived here at Gourneh by your orders to cut certain pictures from the tomb in the Valley of Biban el Molook [the Valley of the Kings] opened by Belzoni at the expense of the late English counsul Mr Salt. If it be true that such is your intention I feel it is my duty as an Englishman and a lover of antiquity to use every argument to dissuade you from so Gothic a purpose. . . .

Champollion wrote in reply:

> Rest assured, Sir, that one day you will have the pleasure of seeing some of the beautiful bas-reliefs of the tomb of Osirei [Seti I] in the French Museum. That will be the only way of

saving them from imminent destruction and in carrying out this project I shall be acting as a real lover of antiquity, since I shall be taking them away only to preserve and not to sell.

In fact, a section of Seti's tomb wall was sent to the Louvre. It was a superbly carved and painted scene of Seti I receiving a necklace from the goddess Hathor. Both figures are as elegantly modeled as any in KV 17, and the subtlety of the painting is remarkable.

In 1905, Howard Carter, who was an inspector of antiquities in the Valley of the Kings, observed that the damage was still serious:

> The limestone rock in which it [KV 17] is hewn and sculptured is, though of a fine nature, very shaley and full of natural cracks which in many cases have become disintegrated from age; these parts of the surface have scaled and fallen away. This condition has not been improved by former explorers and antiquity hunters. The painted sculptures have been defaced by making wet squeezes. The sculptured walls have been hacked indiscriminately, to gouge out cartouches as well as pretty pieces of reliefs. Parts of columns and doorjambs, which acted as supports, have been removed. The ceiling is totally blackened by smoke from torches and candles.

Seti's decoration is still in trouble. At least three different attempts have failed to consolidate and protect it during the past fifty years. The most recent, in late 1996, was being undertaken by a team from the Egyptian Antiquities Organization who, because of budget cuts, arrived with no equipment, supplies, or plan. Our conservator interrupted his work in KV 5 for a day to offer advice and donate some of our chemicals and supplies. Another project, under American auspices, seems unlikely to succeed because of bureaucratic delays.

Belzoni saw no evidence that the tomb's entrance had been sealed in ancient times, but about fifty meters inside, immediately beyond a ten-meter-deep pit, he wrote that the corridor had been closed up, "plastered over, and painted." Ancient thieves had used a rope to descend into the pit on one side, then a second rope to climb back up the other side. At that point, they had cut a small "aperture" through the plastered wall and continued farther into the tomb.

Belzoni thought that the pit (labeled "E" by American Egyptologist Elizabeth Thomas, whose KV chamber designations are now standard) was a way of preventing water from traveling farther inside the tomb should there be a rainstorm in the valley. He also thought that perhaps it was a means of preventing thieves from reaching the burial chamber. Recent studies of royal tomb architecture, however, indicate that such pits—and they are found in several royal tombs—were actually intended to serve as symbolic burial places of the god Osiris. Some of the tomb-pits have small chambers at their bottoms; the top of the pit in KV 17 has scenes of Seti and various deities painted on its walls. This is another example of how, in the Nineteenth Dynasty, the relationship between Osiris and the pharaoh was increasingly emphasized, bringing the two of them closer and closer together in death and in life.

Belzoni, his wife, and the artist Alessandro Ricci made a fifty-foot-long model of the tomb and a set of full-sized painted plaster casts of two of its chambers—the casts that did such serious damage to the original walls. These were exhibited in London in the "Egyptian Hall" at Piccadilly in the summer of 1821, a triumphant show that became the talk of the town. Audiences were in awe of the size of the tomb, the brightness of its decoration, and the beautiful composition of the scenes. And despite the deterioration these scenes have suffered, KV 17 is still one of the most impressive tombs in all Egypt. It was the first royal tomb to exhibit what Egyptologist and Valley of the Kings specialist Erik Hornung calls "a complete program of decoration," meaning that virtually every wall and pillar was carved and painted, and nearly complete copies of religious texts were painted in well-organized fashion throughout the tomb.

Immediately inside the tomb entrance, in corridor "B," two scenes were painted that henceforth appeared in nearly all New Kingdom royal tombs: one showed the pharaoh offering to the god Re-Harakhty; the other was a scene of the sun god—represented in two forms, as a ram and as a beetle—placed inside a solar disk flanked by two of the sun god's enemies, a snake and a crocodile. Ra is, of course, the most common name of the sun god; Harakhty means "Horus of the Horizon," the daytime manifestation of Re. The accompanying text is called the "Litany of Re," a hymn of praise for the sun god, here described in seventy-five different forms. These scenes, elegantly painted and filling every available bit of wall space, continued in the succeeding stairway and corridor. To them are added texts from the *Amduat*, the "Book of the Hidden Chamber," which describes the Afterlife from the point of view of the sun god as he journeys through it each night.

Beyond the pit (Miss Thomas's pit "E"), lie two pillared halls, labeled "F" and "Fa," the former decorated with scenes from "The Book of Gates." This is a description of the gates that divide the night into twelve hours. One especially fascinating scene here is on the east wall of chamber "F." It is perhaps indicative of how international Egypt's view of the world had become during Seti I's reign. It shows four groups of elaborately dressed and coifed male figures, each representing one of the four races of humankind recognized by the Egyptians: an Egyptian, an Asiatic, a Nubian, and a Libyan. These foreigners are usually depicted as Egypt's mortal enemies; yet here, in Seti's tomb, they, too, are protected by Egyptian gods.

The decoration in chamber "Fa" is unusual: only simple but elegant black and red outlines define figures of pharaoh and gods. There are none of the vivid colors that characterize the rest of the tomb. Belzoni was impressed: "I gave it the name of the drawing-room, for it is covered with figures, which, though only outlined, are so fine and perfect, that you would think they had been drawn only the day before." Some Egyptologists believe that the two rooms, "F" and "Fa," were intended to deceive tomb robbers: not only does the decoration appear to be unfinished, but the tomb seems to end abruptly, as if it had not been finished. In fact, it continues along a new axis, shifted to the left and cut through the floor, presumably where thieves would never have thought to look for it. However, if the intention was to thwart thieves, the ancient architects failed because when Belzoni found it it was nearly empty of artifacts.

Beyond these final corridors lies a pillared hall, then a vaulted burial chamber. The vaulted ceiling in the burial chamber is spectacular. It offers one of the best-preserved and most complete astronomical ceilings ever found in an Egyptian tomb. Instead of simply showing the sky goddess, Nut, swallowing the sun at evening and giving birth to it each morning or, even more simply, showing a geometric pattern of five-pointed stars, the ceiling gives us a complex map of the northern hemisphere's night sky. Against a dark blue background, red stars are overlaid on figures that represent the constellations as the ancient Egyptians saw them. The figure of an ox represents Ursa Major; a man with arms outstretched is Cygnus; a crocodile crawling atop a hippopotamus is Boötes; a running man is Orion. Especially prominent are the "Imperishable Ones," the circumpolar stars that fascinated the Egyptians because their position in the heavens never changed. Aesthetically, the ceiling is a delight. It is also a scientific document and a statement of religious belief, an attempt to explain how the universe operates.

But Seti's burial chamber offers more surprises. Without doubt the tomb's most unusual feature lies beneath the floor of the burial chamber. Unlike in any other tomb in the Valley of the Kings, the ancient artisans had cut a long, steeply sloping passageway that extends beyond the burial chamber and continues at least another 150 meters (500 feet) into the mountain. Belzoni must have had considerable difficulty crawling with his huge frame down this corridor:

The sarcophagus [lying in the burial chamber] was over a staircase in the centre of the saloon, which communicated with a subterraneous passage, leading downwards, three hundred feet in length. At the end of this passage we found a great quantity of bats' dung, which choked it up, so that we could go no farther without digging. It was nearly filled up too by the falling in of the upper part. One hundred feet from the entrance is a staircase in good preservation; but the rock below changes its substance, from a beautiful solid calcareous stone, becoming a kind of black rotten slate, which crumbles into dust only by touching. The subterranean passage proceeds in a southwestern direction through the mountain. I measured the distance from the entrance, and also the rocks above, and found, that the passage reaches nearly half way through the mountain to the upper part of the valley. I have reason to suppose, that this passage was used to come into the tomb by another entrance; but this could not be after the death of the person who was buried there, for at the bottom of the stairs just under the sarcophagus [sic] a wall was built, which entirely closed the communication between the tomb and the subterranean passage. Some large blocks of stone were placed under the sarcophagus horizontally, level with the pavement of the saloon, that no one might perceive any stairs or subterranean passage was there.

Since Belzoni's day, other explorers and archaeologists, too, have been prevented from making their way more than 45 meters (150 feet) down this passage by the many stones that have fallen from the passageway's ceiling and by debris that completely chokes its lower levels. Gardner Wilkinson, for example, described the passage in 1843 as "an inclined plane, which, with a staircase on either side, descends into the heart of the agrillaceous rock for a distance of 150 feet." He was certain that it continued farther, but exploration was impossible. In 1903, Howard Carter explored the accessible part of the passageway, but also failed to make further progress. Carter labeled the passage "Q," but Elizabeth Thomas refers to it as "chamber K," and we'll follow her system here.

For many years, the Qurnawis, the people who live in Qurna, the desert edge of the West Bank at Thebes, have maintained that a tunnel joined the Valley of the Kings with some monument to its east, perhaps the Temple of Karnak across the river, and that within this tunnel lay great, unplundered treasure. The passageway in KV 17 was believed by many to be this tunnel. Others have argued that chamber "J," the room we call the burial chamber, was another false room intended to deceive thieves. The *real* burial chamber, they claimed, lay at the end of chamber "K" and is still filled with gold and jewels. Tunnel or burial chamber, either way one wins: since Belzoni's day, the Qurnawis have wishfully talked about digging farther in Seti's tomb. Whoever clears the tunnel, they say, will become very, very rich.

Early in the 1950s, in what must rank as the oddest excavation permit ever issued by the Egyptian Antiquities Organization, the Qurnawi sheikh Ali Abd el-Rassoul, whose family has been intimately connected with tomb robbing and the smuggling of antiquities for over a century, somehow managed to obtain government permission to clear chamber "K."

Sheikh Ali was a tall, very distinguished-looking man with a great mustache and an imposing presence. When I knew him, in the early 1970s, he was already over seventy years old. He delighted in showing off his strength and virility by lifting me off the ground whenever we met at his family-run hotel behind the Colossi of Memnon. He would carry me across the courtyard to meet the newest addition to his ever-growing family. He was a descendant of the nineteenth-century men responsible for finding—and plundering—the cache of royal mummies discovered in a tomb (DB 320) near Deir el-Bahari. I know of several people, myself included, who were offered genuine papyri, statuettes, amulets, and jewelry by various of his relatives while drinking tea at the family's "Ramsum Cafeteria" adjacent to the Ramesseum.

It is ironic that Sheikh Ali was given permission to supervise about forty of his relatives in the clearing of "K," a part of the tomb of Seti I whose mummy was one of those that the Abdel-Rassouls had found and plundered. It also is strange that permission was given even after several EAO employees protested that such clearing in KV 17 would stir up dust, damage the reliefs, interfere with tourism, and threaten the structural integrity of the tomb. Yet, in spite of the complaints—and all were valid and proved absolutely correct—a large-scale project was undertaken, and substantial amounts of debris were removed from chamber "K" until lack of funds finally forced a halt to the project. Before stopping work, however, Sheikh Ali had managed to dig a tunnel more than 136 meters (450 feet) through the debris-filled passageway "K."

During the second season of our Theban Mapping Project, we made a plan of "K" as part of our work to prepare a detailed plan of KV 17. It was the most dangerous operation we had ever attempted. The bedrock was fragile, the air poor, and the occasional wooden braces in the passageway were rotten. The silts covering the sloping floor made it impossible to keep solid footing, and we would grasp a rope and literally slide down the passageway to continue our work each morning. Coming out was even more difficult: we slid back two feet for every three feet we moved forward. On one occasion, while we were blithely taking measurements deep inside chamber "K," a block of stone weighing several hundred pounds fell from the ceiling, halfway between us and the door. We did not hear it fall, but we found it on our way up the passageway; it blocked our exit for nearly half an hour until we could maneuver it aside and crawl past. It was then that we finally realized how foolhardy it was to work in "K." Still, in retrospect, it was worth doing, because the plan we made of "K" offers the best clue yet as to the passageway's purpose.

Sheikh Ali's work in chamber "K" was shoddy at best. His men had dug with no supervision, and he kept no records of the work. But he did show that the floor consisted of a staircase with a ramp down its middle third and that there were gates at intervals along the passageway. We were able to include one of them on our plan. All of these features clearly indicate that "K" was a well-planned, carefully executed, and integral part of Seti I's tomb, a passageway that had been cut and sealed before the alabaster sarcophagus was dragged into place in chamber "J." This careful planning is further emphasized by the care taken to ensure that the axial line of "K" was close to that of the preceding passageways (which we label "G" through "J," following Elizabeth Thomas's system).

The dimensions of "K" in relation to the first parts of KV 17 are interesting. Chambers "A" through "J" slope downward at an average angle of 16 degrees. Chamber "K," however, slopes at an average of 32 degrees, and in some places reaches 47 degrees, angles steep enough that we had to use ropes in order to move up or down it.

The distance from the entrance of KV 17 to the burial chamber is 94 meters (310 feet). The length of "K" from its entrance in the floor of the burial chamber to the limits of Sheikh Ali's excavation is 136.21 meters. Thus, the total length of KV 17 is at least 230.21 meters (760 feet), longer than any other tomb in the Valley of the Kings; at a minimum, "K" represents 60 percent of that length.

KV 17's entrance lies 178 meters (580 feet) above mean sea level. The burial chamber, "J," and the entrance to "K" lie at 152.53 meters. The farthest accessible point in "K" lies at 79.1 meters, almost 100 meters (330 feet) below the tomb entrance. This point is only 2 meters (7 feet) above the average level of the Nile Valley floodplain at Thebes, and only 4 meters (13 feet) above the mean level of the river itself. In dynastic times, this would have been below the level of the Nile floodwaters. And this is perhaps the crucial fact in explaining chamber "K."

If "K" is not the path to untold wealth, then what was it? One view was expressed by Egyptologist Elizabeth Thomas. She noted that most royal tombs have small chambers off the burial chamber.

She believed that "K" was merely a more elaborate form of such side chambers. I doubt this: the chambers around the burial chambers in KV tombs are usually rooms for storage of offerings and funerary equipment. Chamber "K" seemed utterly unsuited to such a purpose.

Chamber "K" cannot have been intended to join some area east of KV, because it is dug far below the level of any such feature and, in any case, it heads south. For the same reason, it cannot have led to any known structure elsewhere in the Valley of the Kings. Dr. Gerhard Haeny, the former director of the Swiss Institute in Cairo, suggested to me that perhaps "K" was simply heading for water. He observes that physically joining the burial chamber to groundwater may have been a goal similar to that achieved in the cenotaph (a symbolic tomb) of Seti I, the Osireion, at Abydos. There, too, a burial chamber (or, rather, cenotaph) was connected to a chamber that allowed the Nile floodwaters to seep in. The late University of Chicago Egyptologist Henri Frankfort thought that this was an "attempt to imitate the actual burial of the god." And this may also have been the purpose of "K." The passage makes as direct a plunge toward groundwater as geology and engineering would permit. Therefore, there is a good chance that "K" leads to a chamber where groundwater was intended to seep, not to a chamber filled with the gold and jewels of Sheikh Ali's dreams. Its purpose was not to hide treasure, but physically to unite the burial chamber of Seti I with the primeval waters of Nun. It was a union that symbolized the site of the world's creation and the pharaoh's rebirth.

Seti's sarcophagus, which Belzoni found lying over the entrance to "K," is a magnificent monolith of inscribed Egyptian alabaster. Belzoni shipped the piece to London, hoping to sell it to the British Museum. The trustees found the price too high, so it went instead to Sir John Soane, whose home in Lincoln's Inn Fields is now a museum. The sarcophagus sits in a cramped basement room, poorly lit and difficult to appreciate, surrounded by an eclectic assortment of ancient objects from the many different cultures that Sir John had found of interest. Still, the piece is impressive, a beautiful block of stone elegantly carved and painted with scenes from "The Book of Gates," the same texts found in the tomb of Ramesses I and in Seti I's burial chamber, but more complete than either of them. Belzoni described it as:

> not having its equal in the world, and being such as we had no idea could exist. It is a sarcophagus of the finest oriental alabaster nine feet five inches long, and three feet seven inches wide. Its thickness is only two inches; and it is transparent, when a light is placed in the inside of it. It is minutely sculptured within and without with seven hundred figures. . . .

The mummy of Seti I that once rested in this sarcophagus was moved in antiquity by priests to a royal cache nearby in Deir el-Bahari in hopes of protecting it and other royal mummies from tomb robbers who, by the end of the New Kingdom, had become extremely active in the Valley of the Kings. The cache was discovered in 1871 by members of the Abd el-Rassoul family. The mummies are now in the Egyptian Museum in Cairo.

The mummification techniques used on Seti's body were of the highest quality, the wrappings well executed of fine linen. The mummy of Seti, in fact, is one of the best-preserved royal mummies we have (only Ramesses II's mummy comes close), and it has served as the model for a score of Hollywood horror films. I was co-director of an expedition (with James Harris) in the early 1970s to X-ray the royal mummies in the Egyptian Museum, and Seti I's was one of those we were most anxious to examine. It is a truly wonderful example of the embalmer's art. The X rays showed that small amulets, including an Eye of Horus, had been inserted into the wrappings, perhaps during one of at least three rewrappings the body received from later priests. Seti's arms were crossed, Osiris-like, across his chest. The X rays showed that during middle age, the pharaoh had lost a tooth. But his well-mummified remains had suffered greatly after death: the head and neck were broken from the body and the abdomen was crushed, perhaps by careless priests who moved the body several times after its original burial.

workers at entrance to KV5, 1995

5

LOST TOMBS

BY the end of our 1988 season, we had finished mapping the Valley of the Kings, the Valley of the Queens, and all of Thebes's outlying *wadis*. We had walked, crawled, slipped, slithered, rappelled, and climbed into every accessible tomb and the accessible parts of every partially blocked tomb we could find. We had worked in some of the most fascinating places we'd ever seen, and also in some of the most unpleasant and dangerous. We had fought off bats, foxes, snakes, and scorpions; taken measurements through gaggles of inquisitive tourists; developed skin rashes that fascinated our dermatologists back home; suffered sinus infections and bouts of coughing; worked for hours in temperatures as high as 50 degrees Celsius (120 degrees Fahrenheit); and over the years probably suffered a collective weight loss of a quarter of a ton. But the data we acquired were worth these inconveniences. Never had such detailed notes been taken on the Theban monuments.

Unfortunately, we did not have enough money to publish the maps and plans in the comprehensive and proper format. Field notes had to be transformed into drawings, then elaborate computer programs had to be used to create three-dimensional tomb models. The cost alone for salaries to pay the data analysts, engineers, and architects was way beyond our budget. In fact, we finished the 1988 season with $2,000 in the bank and a promise of $10,000 the next year from our benefactor Bruce Ludwig and his friends. I decided to gamble, take that $12,000, spend one more season in the field, and *then* worry about future publication money. God willing, some other sources of funds would appear. In the meantime, I felt certain that we had just scratched the surface of the Valley of the Kings. There was still a lot to learn, and I was anxious to get back.

BY 1989, the Theban Mapping Project had been surveying in the Valley of the Kings for over a decade, and our data were about as complete as we could make them. But there was one more thing that could be done in KV, and I wanted to devote one additional season to finding out about tombs that were "lost" or had gone missing. It seemed impossible that so intensively studied an archaeological zone could have lost tombs. After all, how does one lose a tomb?

We know that a few nineteenth- and early twentieth-century visitors to KV referred to tomb entrances that are missing today. Some tombs are thought to exist because nineteenth-century sketch maps of the valley have question marks or "Xs" in places that seem geologically and topographically appropriate for a tomb. These marks are found on the map in the *Description de l'Égypte*, the maps of Burton and Belzoni, and several working drawings of Howard Carter. These maps give us a general idea where a "lost" tomb might lie, but their unscaled simplicity usually leaves us to guess the part of a hillside where the tomb might have been dug; we cannot determine its exact location. We had already made extensive studies of every early map of KV and had pored over dozens of early explorers' journals. We found references to nearly a dozen tombs or unfinished shafts that had been seen a century ago but were "lost" today.

KV tombs disappeared for two reasons. First, torrential rain-storms have hit Thebes once every two or three centuries and have washed vast quantities of silt and debris down from the hills and into low-lying areas of the valley. That was where most tomb entrances were dug, and most of them were affected to some degree by flooding. Over the past three millennia, many tomb entrances have been filled and deeply buried beneath the flood debris. The second reason is that many early excavators ordered their workmen to dump the debris from their excavation atop another tomb nearby. Once a tomb was buried, it was quickly forgotten. It took only a generation or so before the memories of guards and thieves faded and knowledge of its location disappeared.

Thirteen tombs had gone missing since the eighteenth century: KV 5, 21, 27, 28, 31, 33, 41, and 48 through 54. Some had been cursorily explored both in the nineteenth and early twentieth centuries, but usually very little published information was available and knowledge of their location had simply disappeared. Still, the nineteenth-century maps gave us a general idea of where the tomb had been dug.

The simplest way to relocate these "lost" tombs would have been to dig along each KV hillside until a tomb entrance turned up. But since our search areas were relatively small and we were virtually certain that there were "lost" tombs in KV, this seemed an excellent time also to test various geophysical instruments being used in other parts of the world to locate archaeological sites. If we could test geophysical devices here, we might later be able to use them for other searches—in the West Valley, for example, where huge areas had never been archaeologically explored. In such areas, geophysical equipment might be an efficient and cost-effective method of exploration. A few geophysical surveys had already been made in Egypt, at one or two sites in the Delta and in the eastern part of the Karnak Temple complex, but these were areas of waterlogged silts in which archaeologists were searching for stone walls, an environment very different from KV or almost any other Egyptian mortuary site, for that matter.

In 1984, I contacted the Southwest Research Institute of San Antonio, Texas, which had a long and solid reputation in geophysical testing, and they proposed using electrical resistivity surveys and VHF electromagnetic tests. We tried these methods at several different sites, dragging the heavy and cumbersome equipment across the hillsides, trying to spot "anomalies" in readings that might indicate that a tomb lay below the surface. Unfortunately, the nature of KV's geology made the test results ambiguous and difficult to interpret. The equipment simply didn't work.

In 1986, we tried other geophysical techniques, working in association with Vincent Murphy of Weston Geophysical Company in Boston. These included ground-penetrating radar, seismic refraction, and magnetometry. The first two techniques were not helpful. But the magnetometer (a device that measures tiny, local variations in the earth's magnetic field) did give useful results—at least for tombs that were nothing more than single, empty chambers at the bottom of vertical shafts. In such cases, magnetometer readings over the tombs differed from those in the immediate surroundings, and relocating the tomb entrance was straightforward: dig where the magnetometer showed an anomaly and there would be a shaft.

Magnetometers are not tomb locaters, however. They simply identify anomalies, which might be air pockets in debris, old tin cans buried in sand, or a stone that differs from its surroundings. Criss-crossing the hillsides with the equipment (which looked like a shoebox taped to a walking stick), we watched a needle move across a small dial as we took readings at one-meter intervals: 5 . . . 5 . . . 1 . . . 5 . . . 4. The "1" obviously was the anomalous reading in this series. We marked the location, then dug below it. Twice we relocated small, vertical-shaft tombs in this manner: KV 48 was the tomb of Amunemopet, the mayor of Thebes under Amunhotep II, and had been dug in 1906 by Edward Ayrton. KV 49, also dug by Ayrton, was intended for an unknown Eighteenth Dynasty official and was reused at the end of the New Kingdom as a storeroom for linen used in rewrapping of royal mummies. Both tombs had been covered with debris from later excavations nearby.

OF the several "lost" tombs, I was particularly interested in relocating KV 5, which according to early maps was said to lie near the valley's entrance. I was curious about the tomb's unusual plan, which was suggested by the sketch in the 1825 notebook of James Burton, and about Elizabeth Thomas's belief that KV 5 might date to the reign of Ramesses II. There was also a much more prosaic reason. In 1989, the Egyptian Antiquities Organization announced its plans to widen the roadway at the entrance to the valley. The roadway was only about ten meters wide and its shoulders were crammed with dozens of kiosks where local villagers sold postcards and fake antiquities. Scores of tourist buses pulled up there, then had to maneuver backward down the road through throngs of tourists and other buses in order to exit. It was an awkward and potentially dangerous situation. Widening the roadway seemed logical and necessary. But if the nineteenth-century maps were correct and a tomb was located somewhere in the hillside next to this roadway, any roadwork would almost certainly cause it damage. This gave us an immediate reason to relocate KV 5, and in 1989 the EAO agreed. That summer we began work.

THE REDISCOVERY OF KV 5

KV 5 was apparently not known to early visitors in the valley or, if it was known to Greek, Roman, Christian, and other travelers, they had ignored it. But from the nineteenth century onward, its existence was referred to fairly frequently in the journals of travelers and on Egyptological maps. Richard Pococke, for example, may have seen the entrance in 1738, if we correctly interpret his rather fanciful map. It was marked on the *Description* map, on Lepsius's *Denkmäler* map, and on several others. The pit where

KV 5's door was cut is clearly visible in a sketch made by Robert Hay or one of his artists in 1825. None of these early sources revealed anything about what lay beyond the doorway or precisely where that doorway was, but they did generally agree about the hillside where the entrance had been dug.

We began by using several geophysical techniques to survey that hillside, but again only the magnetometer produced even remotely promising results. It gave us readings that indicated scores of "anomalies" at random intervals all across the hillside. The anomalies were so numerous and scattered that they seemed to represent nothing more than either air pockets under loose stones, variations in bedrock density, or perhaps the ramblings of a faulty magnetometer. In hindsight, we were probably picking up the presence of a tomb, but as we later learned, KV 5's chambers were of different sizes and were filled with materials of different densities. They also often contained pillars that registered as solid bedrock on the magnetometer. All of this conspired to create a nearly meaningless hodgepodge of readings. And KV 5's octopuslike plan complicated things even more.

Even if we had been certain that a tomb lay beneath our feet, we could not simply have blasted through the bedrock. We had to locate the tomb's one and only entrance—and there was no geophysical device that could tell us where that was. So, somewhat frustrated, we abandoned our geophysical devices and returned to old-fashioned archaeological excavation: digging with a pick and shovel.

The maps showed KV 5's entrance in the southern half of a long slope not far from KV 6, the tomb of Ramesses IX. There was a wide, shallow gully about five meters up the hillside that seemed a logical spot for a tomb entrance. But after three days of digging, it was obvious that the ancient Egyptians had not shared our assessment. The only things we found were broken fake antiquities, thrown out by the vendors in the nearby kiosks.

"Another likely spot for a tomb entrance would be at the very base of the hill," I suggested to our foreman, Ahmed, early on a hot Sunday morning. "Let's dig a trench adjacent to the paved road, from the gully south to the ticket kiosk." That was a strip of about 40 meters (130 feet), lined with bright yellow kiosks filled with hawkers' postcards, plaster statuettes, and cotton hats. We put our workmen at intervals along this stretch, digging close behind the kiosks. The workmen made good progress the first day, but we learned nothing except that the hillside was covered with a much deeper layer of sand and stone chips than we had expected. Some of the debris clearly had been laid down in the 1960s as a foundation for the paved road, but much of it had been dumped earlier. A photograph of this hillside taken in about 1910 shows a shelter standing where the kiosks were. The shelter was erected to provide a shady resting place for the donkeys ridden by tourists. The photograph shows the hillside clean and largely free of debris, though photographs taken several years later show at least three meters of debris covering the slope. That debris probably resulted from the excavations of Howard Carter and Theodore Davies. It's certainly ironic that Carter and Davies inadvertently buried one of the valley's most spectacular tombs.

ON a hot Tuesday morning in July, I set our workmen to digging a trench along the base of the hill at the valley entrance, just east of the roadway. This, I believed, was the hillside where Burton claimed to have seen KV 5. Our men worked in a long row, carting away stone chips and sand as they dug a trench down to bedrock, several meters below the surface.

For over a week, our workmen dug a narrow trench along the base of the hillside. They worked slowly and carefully, even though the hillside was littered with tourist curios, fake plaster statuettes, and scarabs dumped from the adjacent tourist kiosks. They dug from north to south adjacent to the asphalt road, cutting a trench a meter wide, digging down twenty centimeters, and forward two meters a day. The debris was loose and dry—clearly it was detritus from earlier excavations in the valley—and the workmen methodically loaded it into baskets, then dumped it into sieves a few meters away. Tourists gave us a wide berth as they walked into the valley, covering their faces, cursing the clouds of dust we created.

By the end of the week, the trench was over fifteen meters long, and I began to wonder if Burton really had seen a tomb entrance here. But on Wednesday, traces appeared of vertical faces cut into the bedrock and, after several hours' work, the faces defined a pit, about two meters wide and four meters long, lying beneath and beside the asphalt roadway at the base of the hill.

For the remainder of the week, we continued to clear the entrance pit. We were well below the level of the paved roadway now, and the debris we were removing had come, not from Carter's dig, but from ancient rainstorms that had washed down from the valley's high hills. The debris was a mixture of limestone chips and sand, and our baskets were filled with potsherds from Dynastic, Roman, and Christian periods.

Friday was our day off, so I spent the morning reviewing my notes on Burton's work in the valley in anticipation of Bruce Ludwig's arrival later in the afternoon. I wanted Bruce to appreciate how potentially important KV 5 might be, and I knew, too, that he would enjoy learning more about one of nineteenth-century Egyptology's more eccentric characters.

JAMES BURTON

Burton may have been the first person since ancient times to venture beyond the door of KV 5, and he was perhaps one of only two or three Europeans ever to do so prior to our rediscovery of the tomb in 1989. Certainly, he was the first to leave a record of what he saw.

James Burton was born in London in 1788. He graduated from Cambridge University in 1810, then worked briefly for Sir John Soane, a prominent English architect. Soane was an avid collector of art and antiquities with rather eclectic tastes that included a minor interest in ancient Egypt. Soane most likely inspired Burton's initial interest in Egypt and its monuments.

In 1819, Burton traveled to Italy, where he met John Gardner Wilkinson and several other Egyptophiles, who urged him to extend his trip to Cairo and seek work there. Burton was not especially anxious to return to England, so he booked passage to Alexandria and soon took a job with a geological survey in the Red Sea hills. He was ill-suited to the task, because he knew nothing about geology (the project he joined was searching for coal deposits), and he didn't stay on the survey long. He then joined Wilkinson and Edward Lane on a trek across the Eastern Desert and later cruised with them up the Nile.

In 1825, Burton visited Luxor and remained there for several months. On June 12, he moved into the valley of the Kings and set up camp in the entrance of KV 9, the tomb of Ramesses VI. His goal was to sketch a map of the Valley and to compile notes, plans, and drawings of its accessible tombs. The doorway to KV 5 was barely visible then, its entrance apparently completely blocked with rubble. Burton's curiosity led him to hire a few local men to clear away enough of the debris so that he could squeeze through KV 5's doorway and crawl inside. His men cut a trench about fifty centimeters (twenty inches) high, fifty centimeters wide, and twenty meters long through the top of the debris. Burton was able to crawl into what we now label "chambers 1–3," and he could peer through doorways into five of the side chambers. Limestone chips, silt, and sand filled the chambers almost to the ceiling, so he couldn't see their walls and had no idea that they were decorated. Burton couldn't have spent more than a few hours in the tomb; the notes he made cover less than a third of a page in his journal. He never returned to KV 5, but he did make a sketch plan of the rooms he visited, roughly measuring distances from the channel where he lay to the chamber walls by probing them with a stick. The plan was not to scale, and it left out some important features, but, given the awful working conditions, it was a credible job.

For the next several years, Burton remained in Egypt and

worked with several Egyptological missions along the Nile. At some point between 1825 and 1834, he bought a Greek woman, Andreana Garafaliki, at a Cairo slave market, and when he returned to London in 1835, he took her with him, along with several slaves, a veritable circus of animals, and a sizable collection of antiquities. Not surprisingly, Burton's parents were scandalized. Burton was always a thorn in his family's side, and within three years, his father had disowned him. Disinherited and worried about money, Burton sold his collection of Egyptian antiquities at auction in 1836, and the proceeds kept him solvent until his death, on February 22, 1862, at the age of seventy-three. His wife, Andreana, lived on, provided for by his savings, until her death a few years later.

Burton's brother, the very successful architect Decimus, donated James's notes and journals to the British Museum. None has been published. They fill over sixty-three folio volumes, a strange collection of scraps of paper written in pencil and ink and pasted onto the pages of bound blank folios. The writing is difficult to read, and the text sometimes runs diagonally across the page. The entries are in no discernible order. On one page there will be a penciled note like this:

> In the brain and belly of the mummies of the richer sort are found 2 substances, a yellow one rubbing into powder and burning with the odour of labban looking the colour of Gumbase—and a white harder substance wrapped in linen. . . . The yellow is used by the Fellaheen for wounds and venereal complaints.

Then might follow the measurements of a tomb, or drawings of a tomb relief, or notes on the condition of the monuments:

> My friend Mr Hay says "The tombs . . . have been sadly destroyed, since the days when you can remember them—and I fear that the work of destruction goes on daily—whenever

the fellaheen fly to the mountains, I think, they employ themselves to kill time in chipping the painting and sculpture with
their spears—and in these cases, tombs have been cut up for
sale."

Burton was not a scholar and his journal entries are sometimes
inaccurate, but his sketch maps and plans are greatly valued today,
because they locate and describe many monuments that have since
been damaged or lost.

THE day that Bruce Ludwig arrived in Luxor for his annual visit,
we went to the Pharaohs Hotel to have a beer in the hotel garden
and talk about future plans. I went over Burton's notes with him
and told him what we were doing with KV 5.

"This is great," he said, looking through the folder of information I had put together over the previous several months. "But
what do we really know about this tomb? Whose is it, anyway? Do
you plan to dig inside it?"

"We know almost nothing about KV 5, Bruce. Originally, I'd
just wanted to relocate the entrance and make sure that any EAO
roadwork would avoid damaging the tomb. But the more I look at
Burton's plan, the more the tomb fascinates me. Either Burton's
plan is a complete fiction or KV 5 is unique in Egypt."

I took the KV 5 folder and pulled out a photocopy of Burton's
journal entry.

"Here. Look at this. Burton labeled the tomb 'M,'" I said, pointing to his nineteenth-century map of KV. "And he located it fairly
accurately, at the valley entrance. Now, here's his plan of the tomb."
I showed him Burton's unscaled drawing and pointed out the
entrance and the first two small chambers. "But look at what he
shows just beyond these two chambers: there is a huge sixteen-pillared hall with chambers leading off it in all directions. I can't find a
reference to a tomb anywhere in Egypt with a plan like that. And his
journal entry: it's very brief, but he makes some interesting com-

ments." I read aloud Burton's description of tomb "M," stammering occasionally as I tried to make out Burton's crabbed handwriting:

> This tomb is all in a state of ruin. On the ceiling alone which has in general fallen in vast masses are to be seen some small remains here and there of coloring. The substance of the rock between the small chambers and the large ones above cannot be more than 18 inches. Being full of mud and earth the descent from the pillared room to those underneath is not perceptible. The Catacomb must have been excavated very low in the valley or the valley much raised by the accumulation of earth stones and rubbish brought down by the rains. I found a large piece of breccia verdántico, evidence of those quarries having been used in this king's time and of some sarcophagus having been in the tomb of this material. It is possible there is some passage leading from below the center of the pillared chamber into that where the sarcophagus stood.

"Obviously," I said, "Burton thought there was more to the tomb than he was able to explore. Another explorer, Edward Lane, visited the tomb about ten years after Burton." I flipped the page and began reading from Lane's unpublished journals. In them, he describes the "8th tomb" in the valley, but it was KV 5 that he was referring to:

> Situated quite at the base of the hill and entrance concealed by rubbish taken out. Entrance narrow. Passage has been quite filled up by rubbish washed in by rains and by frag. of stone which [have] fallen in consequence of the damp on such occasions; but a way has been cut thro this mass, leaving part all along to support the loosened masses of rock above. Impossible to trace any plan or order.

I explained to Bruce that the "way" Lane refers to almost certainly is a channel dug by Burton to gain access to the tomb. I told him I wanted to continue clearing the doorway to see if Burton's channel was still there. Then I'd crawl inside. I also wanted to check the accuracy of Burton's sketch plan and to see if there's anything he might have missed.

BY the end of work on Thursday, we had exposed what clearly was a step at the western end of the pit, and by early the following week, we had exposed most of a badly worn staircase cut into the limestone bedrock that led steeply down toward the east. There was no doubt that this was the entrance to a tomb: there are many examples of such pit-and-staircase tomb entrances in the Valley of the Kings. We were all excited by the discovery, and the men insisted on working overtime for the next several days as they carefully cleared the pit and exposed ancient steps that had been cut into the limestone bedrock, each one taking us closer to the entrance to the tomb.

A few days later, we found a doorway in the eastern wall of the pit, about four meters below the surface of the hillside. It took several days to expose the upper part of the door, because it was filled with debris much denser than that on the hillside. Digging slowed considerably. Debris completely choked the doorway and the chamber beyond, but the channel that had been cut through the dirt and limestone chips by James Burton in 1825 was still there, still well defined after 164 years. Catharine and I immediately decided to crawl inside.

"LET'S see where Burton's channel leads," I said to Catharine. I asked the workmen to remove several large stones that had been washed into the tomb entrance by a rain-fed flood early in this century, then I climbed down into the pit and peered into the doorway. I was met by a great rush of hot, foul-smelling air. In the 1950s, a sewer line had been inadvertently built over the entrance to KV 5 from a nearby tourist cafeteria to a septic tank lying down the hill. It had broken several decades ago, and it was appallingly obvious that raw sewage had been flowing into the tomb ever since. The smell was awful.

"Can you see anything?" Bruce asked teasingly, quoting the line Lord Carnarvon is said to have uttered when Howard Carter first peered through the door of Tutankhamun's tomb, a hundred meters away. Carter's answer had been, "Yes, wonderful things!"

Mine was, "Yes. Shit." I climbed out of the pit and took a deep breath of fresh air.

"There's some serious cleaning to be done, Bruce. The entrance is a mess, so full of debris that I can't see more than a few centimeters inside." Fanning myself with my hat, I backed away from the doorway and turned to the workmen.

"Mohammed, I want you and Saleh to clean up this area. Be careful, wear gloves, and put the debris in the large plastic bags up topside. We'll dispose of it later."

"*Haddir*," Mohammed replied. "It will be done."

While Mohammed and Saleh cleared Burton's channel, Catharine and I took brushes and flashlights and began examining the exposed upper parts of the doorjambs. In the 1850s, the Prussian Egyptologist Carl Lepsius, who also had seen the doorway of KV 5, wrote in his journal that there was a cartouche of Ramesses II and the figure of a deity on the jambs. (A cartouche is the oval outline surrounding the hieroglyphic name of an Egyptian pharaoh.)

"There's the cartouche," Catharine said, her flashlight bringing out the faint, worn hieroglyphs of a royal name. "It's badly weathered, but it's Ramesses II: I can see parts of User-Ma'at-Re Setepen-Re." Those were two names borne by Ramesses II.

I brushed dirt from the left jamb. "And there's a goddess carved here," I said. "It looks like a kneeling figure of Ma'at." You'd expect to find her in the entrance to a Nineteenth Dynasty tomb. We climbed out of the pit, and I began making notes on the entrance while Mohammed and Saleh continued to clear Burton's channel.

*   *   *

A few days later, when Catharine, Mohammed, and I crawled along the trench, we found that Burton's sketch plan of KV 5 was essentially correct—as far as it went. However, we found traces of decoration on every wall visible to us, something that no earlier traveler had noticed. More than that, KV 5 was clearly not just an unimportant, undecorated, unused hole in the ground, as early explorers in the Valley of the Kings had thought. To us, the tomb looked promising, and we all were disappointed we had to leave at the end of the season. Ten months is a long time to wait when one has found a "lost" tomb in the Valley of the Kings.

INTO KV 5

When we returned to Thebes the following season, our first objective was to reopen KV 5 and clear its first chamber. Once again, what we thought would be a fast and easy task turned out to be a slow and meticulous process that kept us occupied for the next four years. During our ten-month-long absence, the tomb entrance had become filled with empty plastic water bottles, candy wrappers, newspapers—all from thoughtless tourists and sloppy caretakers. On our first day back, Ahmed and Mohammed removed the debris, then we impatiently waited for our inspector to climb down to the steel door, break the lead seal, and remove the padlock.

The next morning, with about ten workmen, we began again to dig. Almost immediately, we encountered serious engineering problems. Since 1950, when the roadway was laid into the valley, thousands of huge tour buses had driven past KV 5, stopping not five meters away from its entrance with their motors running. The vibrations had seriously weakened the stone of KV 5's first chamber, and several huge blocks of limestone had broken free of the ceiling. Some of them weighed several tons. These blocks had to be broken up with hammer and chisel, then carried away. (We know that virtually all of the ceiling damage in chamber 1 had occurred quite recently: the large stones lay in the upper layers of debris, whereas farther inside the tomb, there is no evidence of modern ceiling damage but plenty of ancient collapse.) As we dug, we installed steel screw jacks to ensure that no other pieces would break free from the cracked and damaged ceiling. The last thing I wanted was for a workman to be injured on the job. It took only a few moments of contemplating this possibility before I telephoned the American University in Cairo to arrange for liability insurance for our project as soon as possible.

Our goal during the next several weeks was to dig forward into the center of chamber 1 and in the process carefully study the layering—the stratigraphy—of the tomb debris. This was necessary for two reasons. First, using what we already knew about flooding and flood debris in other tombs, the stratigraphy in KV 5 could let us trace the history of flooding here. It might not reveal specific dates, but at least we could gain some idea how many floods had hit the tomb.

There was also a question of who had been in KV 5. Our first examination of the debris in chamber 1 and the distribution of artifacts within its strata suggested that nobody had entered KV 5 from the late New Kingdom until James Burton three thousand years later. There were many potsherds from the Roman and Christian periods, but many were waterworn and abraded, and had almost certainly been washed into the tomb with the flashfloods. There was none of the other evidence—graffiti on the walls, for example, or traces of smoke on the ceiling from the lamps and torches carried by early visitors—to suggest otherwise.

We actually know the name of one of the last men to enter KV 5 in ancient times: he was the thief who robbed the tomb and he was called Kenena. His name is found in a papyrus written in the reign of Ramesses III (1194–1163 BCE), perhaps fifty years after the death of Ramesses II. Several workmen from Thebes had been arrested for robbing the tombs. They were brought to trial, tortured, and forced to confess their crimes, and those confessions were written down by a scribe—an ancient court reporter—on a piece of papyrus. That papyrus is now in the Turin Museum. In it, one of the thieves testified as follows:

> Now, Usihe and Patwere have stripped stones from above the tomb of Osiris King (Ramesses II), the great god. . . . The chief artisan Peneb, my father, caused men to take off stones therefrom. [He has done] exactly the same. And Kenena the son of Ruta did it in this same manner above the tomb of the royal children of Osiris King (Ramesses II), the great god. Let me see what you will do to them, or I will make complaint to pharaoh my lord and likewise to the vizier my superior.

We began to wonder if anyone had been in KV 5 between Kenena's entry and Burton's 1825 exploration. That was definitely worth checking out, even though it meant that we would have to work slowly and meticulously to gather evidence, keeping track of the stratigraphy and noting precisely where each piece of pottery and every object came from.

Flood debris filled chamber 1 to the ceiling. Over the last three millennia, it had hardened to an almost concretelike density and our only choice was to use pickaxes to dig it out. Only two men dug at a time. Mohammed broke up the debris, Hussein loaded it into baskets, and ten men then formed a bucket brigade to carry it out of the tomb. Next to the row of bright yellow kiosks, it was sifted to make sure that no sherd or bone or bead, however small, escaped notice. At the end of each day, a truck hauled the debris off to the desert. We kept careful records of where each object had been found, the stratigraphic context of the potsherds, and the context and associations of every trace of human activity. We produced notes, drawings, sketches, and plans almost as rapidly as we generated basketsful of debris.

After two weeks of work, Mohammed and our crew had dug about a meter through the doorway and had reached floor level. The damage that floods and tomb robbers had done was obvious the moment we reached that floor. Hundreds of broken objects—

potsherds, bits of jewelry, fragments of wooden furniture, pieces of alabaster, chunks of stone sarcophagi—lay scattered around the room. But although the objects were broken, they were informative. For example, in one corner of the room we found a cluster of small alabaster and faience statuettes called *ushabtis*, figures intended to work magically as servants for the deceased in the Afterlife. Several had black-ink inscriptions on their bodies. In another corner, fragments of alabaster canopic jars lay side by side with the wooden drawer pull from a small box that once perhaps held unguent jars or jewelry. Canopic jars, which come in sets of four, were containers intended to hold the internal organs of a mummy (one each for liver, lungs, stomach, and intestines). Scattered around the room were "wiglets," cone-shaped twists of faience that had once been attached to the head of a wooden statue or a wooden coffin to suggest an elaborate braided hairdo.

In chamber 1, there were other artifacts as well. For example, in 1993, we found the broken base of an imported Canaanite amphora that had been reused by an ancient artist as a paintpot. It still contained the blue paint he was applying to scenes of a god's kiosk and lay on the floor against the wall where the scene had been painted. The pot had been knocked over in antiquity and the paint had spilled, leaving a large blue stain on the floor. Perhaps the artist had suddenly stopped work and accidentally kicked over his paintpot as he left the tomb and never returned.

About a month into the first full season in chamber 1, I took a powerful lamp and began to examine the wall where Catharine had seen hieroglyphs the year before. Mohammed knows never to dig too close to decorated walls with his heavy pickax, so with trowel and paint brush, I slowly began to pull away the uppermost part of the thick face of debris that he had left lying against the plaster. Removing the debris required patience and a gentle touch. The limestone bedrock in this part of the chamber was cracked and of relatively poor quality. Instead of carving the relief decoration directly into this crumbling stone, the ancient artisans had applied a thick coat of plaster to the wall and cut the relief into that. Once the carved plaster had dried, it was painted. Originally, the wall must have been beautiful, but now it was in poor condition. Many floods had taken their toll, as had the vibrating tour buses, and the leaking septic line. In some areas, the water damage was so great that the plaster had simply turned to mush and had slipped off the wall to form thick puddles on the floor. Our work was slow and tedious, but by the end of the day, we had turned up part of an inscription. I called Catharine over.

"Do you remember what you said last season? About this being a tomb for sons of Ramesses II? Well, take a look at this." I turned on the flashlight and shone a raking light across the exposed part of the wall. There were traces of several columns of hieroglyphs on the wall immediately adjacent to the doorway. I pointed to the signs.

"*Sa nesu tepy,* 'The Eldest Son of the King,' " I read in one column. I moved the light past a layer of debris and illuminated part of another column of text. "*Imun her-* . . . *Amun-her-* . . . the rest is broken off. But the text has to be the name and titles of Amun-herkhepeshef, the eldest son of Ramesses II. You and Elizabeth are correct: at least one of his sons is buried here."

"That's wonderful!" She smiled. "How many more sons do you think are in here? Want to pick a number?"

"Not yet. But I'll bet there's more than one."

The late Egyptologist Elizabeth Thomas argued that KV 5 was "the tomb of the royal children" mentioned in the Turin Papyrus, and that KV 5 belonged to royal sons. We now know that she was correct.

OVER the next several seasons, as our work in chamber 1 continued, I grew increasingly concerned about the heavy salt incrustations that covered large parts of its walls. The salt crystals would continue to grow and their presence threatened the condition of the wall and its inscriptions. Limestone normally contains a high percentage of salt, and when it comes in contact with moisture—

as had happened in KV 5, with floodwaters and sewage—the salt dissolves and migrates to the wall's surface. There, in contact with air, it crystallizes. As the salt crystals grow, they push ancient plaster away from the bedrock until it falls to the floor of its own weight. Many wall areas had already lost their decorated plaster surfaces, depriving us of important ancient texts. But many of those fragments lay buried in the debris that filled the chamber. One of the reasons it took so long to clear chamber 1 was because we tried to recover those fragments so that we could reconstruct (on paper) the scenes they came from. We have already dug carefully near the walls and have recovered hundreds of plaster fragments. From such fragments, often no bigger than a postcard, Susan can reconstruct on paper tens of square meters of wall decoration. She has an amazing eye, but she also had help from our conservators.

During the 1993 field season, we hired a talented Egyptian conservator, Lamia el-Hadidi, to clean and protect the damaged walls of chamber 1. Gently brushing, blowing, and cleaning with various solvents, Lamia removed much of the salt that covered the walls, reattached precariously hanging bits of plaster, and cleaned their painted surfaces. Hovering over us as we cleared debris away from the wall, Lamia quickly stepped in to stabilize wall sections as we exposed them. It was all done slowly, a square centimeter at a time, but by the end of the month, we had uncovered and cleaned the southwestern corner of the chamber. We already knew that the name of the firstborn son was there. Now we could see the figure of the son himself, Amun-her-khepeshef, being presented by Ramesses II to the gods Hathor and Sokar and, above the figure, we could read nine short columns of text: "Ramesses Mery-Amon, Revered before Osiris, The Great God, Lord of the West, First King's Son, Heir, Prince, Royal Scribe, Effective Confidant, Beloved of Him, Amun-her-khepeshef, Justified before Osiris." Four weeks later, on the south wall, we uncovered another scene. Here, before a figure of the god Nefertum, was a figure of the king's second son, Ramesses. We immediately dubbed him

Ramesses Junior to avoid confusion with his father. Above Junior's head were four lines of text: "The King's Principal Son of His Body, the Generalissimo, Ramesses . . . Justified." Just as Elizabeth Thomas had suggested, KV 5 was indeed the burial place of *sons,* plural.

By now, KV 5 had become a tomb of more than passing interest. The burial place of sons of so powerful and important a pharaoh was of potentially great historical importance. The fact that we were already finding extensive decoration on the walls of chamber 1 and a great number of potsherds and artifacts lying on its floor meant that it was no longer enough simply to add Burton's sketch plan to the TMP's survey of the Valley of the Kings. The tomb needed to be accurately planned, its chambers cleared of debris, its walls conserved and stabilized, and its objects and decoration recorded and studied. This was a parenthetical addition to the primary goals of the Theban Mapping Project, but it clearly was worth doing. Anyway, looking at Burton's plan of the tomb—apparently a small number of small chambers that led nowhere—we thought that work here wouldn't occupy us for more than another short season or two. Today, nine years later, we've cleared and conserved parts of only ten chambers.

limestone offering table

canopic jar fragments

clay figs - an offering to osiris

wooden head - sarcophagus

a trio of alabaster shawabtis

6

KV 5: MORE CLUES

BY 1994, five seasons after we began work in KV 5, we had managed to clear about three quarters of chamber 1 and two thirds of
chamber 2. We were still digging slowly, moving less than two
cubic meters of debris a day, working as much with trowels,
brushes, and sieves as with picks and shovels. These are expensive
procedures, but this meticulous approach taught us enough to
make it worth the extra time and money. Gradually, we developed
an outline of KV 5's history, drawing on the stratigraphy in chambers 1 and 2, and on what we could glean crawling along Burton's
channel into the undug and still barely accessible parts of chambers 3 and 4.

Visitors to KV 5, as well as several colleagues and antiquities
inspectors, have often been astonished by how slowly our work in
the tomb goes. For example, when we explained that we were
recording the stratigraphy of the floodborne debris, they shook
their heads in amazement. "Why do you waste time and money
studying the garbage," one visitor asked me incredulously, "when
there is a banquet awaiting you in texts and objects?"

In the past, many archaeologists chose to work at a particular
site simply because they might find museum-quality objects. They

were not interested in broken objects, certainly not in pottery unless it was decorated, and sometimes they even hacked through mud-brick walls, searching for ones that were of carved and painted stone. Unfortunately, some excavators in Egypt continue to use this approach, and stratigraphy still remains a foreign concept to some of them. Although archaeologists elsewhere in the world have been concerned about this problem for over a century, only recently has stratigraphy become an important tool in Egyptian archaeology. Stratigraphy—the study of how soil and debris are laid down—is one of our most potent and valuable tools. By modern standards, an archaeology project that ignores stratigraphical analyses is more an exercise in moving dirt than an archaeological excavation. The damage such projects do and the information they destroy is appalling.

All else being equal, the layers of debris in an archaeological site were deposited from bottom to top, the earliest layers laid down first, successively more recent layers on top of them. This obvious fact—called the "Law of Superposition"—means that even if a site has no datable artifacts, archaeologists can still develop a relative chronological sequence for its objects, features, and architecture.

Also important are the sands, silts, and other debris that constitute the fabric of a site; they often contain information that would have astounded archaeologists even two generations ago. It is possible to recover from microscopic seeds, grains, pollen, and other floral material evidence of what the climate might have been like at a site thousands of years ago. Fragmentary bits of animal bones—the sort of garbage no self-respecting archaeologist of the past would even have glanced at—can reveal a people's diet and, in the case of KV 5, the kinds of food offerings brought to the tomb. Knowing, for example, that a certain kind of pottery was found in a KV 5 chamber associated with a certain kind of animal bone might reveal the purpose of the room where the finds were made. Knowing that bits of plaster in the debris lay nearer one wall of a chamber than another can allow us to reconstruct from the fragments the entire scene that was carved and painted on the wall.

Comparing the strata in KV 5 with those in other KV tombs may one day allow us to develop a 3,000-year-long history of climate and flooding. These are exciting and important possibilities, in their own way as valuable as a lovely statuette or an inscribed tomb wall. But the evidence must be collected slowly, which makes archaeology an expensive undertaking.

In the case of KV 5, the power of the floods that washed debris into the tomb and tossed things about has complicated the stratigraphy, making its evidence more equivocal and its study especially costly. However, the general rules of stratigraphic analysis still hold. By carefully identifying and studying the different layers of debris and noting the kinds of artifacts they contain, we have been able to construct a history of KV 5 from its ancient beginnings until today. This includes not only a history of flooding in the tomb, but also a history of human activity in chambers 1 and 2 that is divided into seven major phases. The evidence for some of these phases is admittedly rather tenuous, and the lines we have drawn among them are sometimes rather arbitrary, but the general outline provides a useful framework for the study of KV 5. It has been key to convincing us to give KV 5 continued and meticulous attention.

ARCHAEOLOGISTS invariably dig a site from the top down, exposing recent strata before the earlier levels that lie below. That's why I start with the tomb's most recent history and move downward, moving backward through time. I'm not going to describe the two earliest phases of KV 5's history until later, after we've more closely examined the reign of Ramesses II.

The most recent period in KV 5's history is called "Phase Seven." It began at the end of World War I and continues today. During those eight decades, KV 5 suffered serious damage. In the early 1920s, when Howard Carter used the hillside above KV 5's entrance as a dumping ground for debris from his excavations, the tomb was buried under several meters of limestone chips and dust.

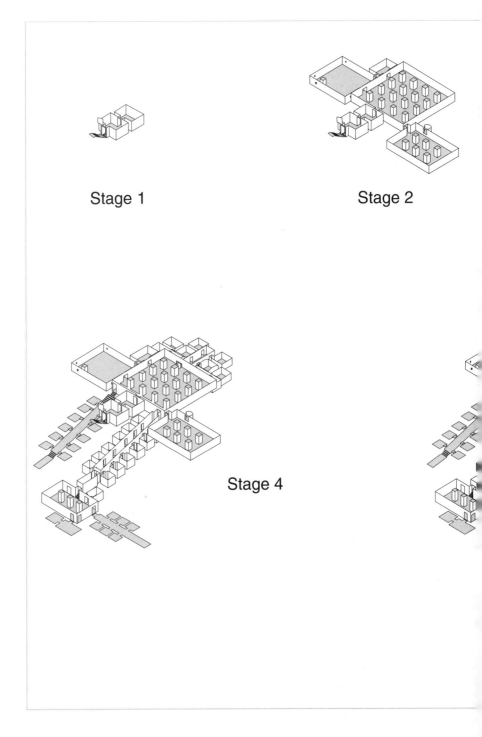

Stage 1

Stage 2

Stage 4

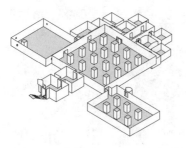

Stage 3

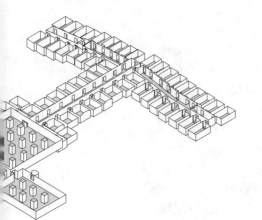

Stage 5

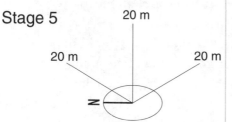

Stages of growth of KV 5.

Also, since the 1950s, a leaking sewer pipe and countless vibrating tourist buses have damaged the tomb entrance. Damage to the tomb stopped only in 1988, when our Theban Mapping Project began clearing and conservation work. Except for a washed-in broken champagne glass that may have belonged to Howard Carter, we have yet to find any objects in KV 5 that date to this phase.

Phase Six lasted from late in the nineteenth century until the beginning of Phase Seven. During this phase, in 1902, Howard Carter's workmen cleared the entrance to KV 5. The stratigraphy of debris in the tomb entrance suggests that his men had started to dig along the midline of the tomb entrance but, for some reason, stopped working after digging less than a meter. Carter didn't see any of the chamber's decorated walls or its artifact-strewn floors, and apparently believed that the tomb was an unimportant and undecorated pit. He was almost certainly unaware of Burton's unpublished notes in the British Museum Library and had not seen the plan Burton had made. A covered rest area for tourist donkeys was built directly above the buried entrance to KV 5 sometime at the end of the nineteenth century.

During Phase Five, which lasted through nearly all of the nineteenth century, the entrance to KV 5 was visible—but just barely. It was completely choked with debris, and the tomb itself was not accessible. But several early travelers made note of it, and Wilkinson gave it the designation "KV 5," although so little of the entrance could be seen that he could not find a place to paint the number above its door. In 1825, James Burton entered the tomb and made a sketch plan of its first few chambers. Robert Hay, Edward Lane, and Eugene Lefebure commented on how unexciting it appeared to be. None of these visitors saw any decorated walls. The only evidence these visitors left inside the tomb was a graffito giving Burton's name, written in lampblack on the ceiling of chamber 3, and the trench that Burton's workmen dug through the first three chambers. A few nineteenth-century travelers after Burton—Edward Lane was one—also crawled along

Burton's trench, but none attempted to explore the tomb further.

There is no evidence that KV 5 was accessible at any time during the 1,500 years from late Christian times to the nineteenth century in Phase Four. I doubt that more than a handful of people entered the tomb during this time, and certainly none of them seem to have stayed for more than a few minutes. The only thing that left a mark, in fact, was flooding; several torrential rains during this phase account for the debris lying 90 to 200 centimeters (36 to 78 inches) above the floor. We have identified at least six major floods during this time, but we cannot determine how many years separated them from one another. The layers of debris contain a mix of limestone flakes, stones, and silts, usually deposited in that order as a flood's force declines. These layers are separated from each other by other layers of fallen ceiling blocks and plaster from chamber walls.

In Phase Three, from the end of the reign of Ramesses II in the New Kingdom (1080 BCE) to the end of the seventh century CE, a period of about 1,600 years, KV 5 may have been occasionally accessible, but there is little evidence that anyone bothered to go inside. The few who did were probably tomb robbers whose activities we can pick up from a series of papyri and, less obviously, from the condition of several KV 5 chambers and their contents. We have found pottery from Phase Three lying in the debris that lies ten to ninety centimeters above the floor in chambers 1 and 2. Nearly all of it is broken, and most of it either was washed into the tomb during flashfloods or was dumped into the tomb entrance by early tourists, then churned about by floodwaters. A few Late Period pottery bases may have been used as lamps for visitors near the end of dynastic history, but there aren't many of these bits of pottery, and they could easily have washed into the tomb during floods. However, if KV 5 had been visited during this period (as several other tombs were) and perhaps used as a storeroom, resting place, hermitage, or church, we would most likely have found graffiti on the walls, lampblack on the ceiling, and caches of whole vessels in the corners of the first two rooms. But we didn't find anything like this. KV 5 was probably ignored because its entrance was awkwardly located: the doorway lies in a pit several meters below the footpath at the valley entrance. It was inconvenient; there were several other tombs nearby—those of Ramesses IV, VI, IX, and XI, for example—that were easier to get to, were more comfortable, better ventilated, and better lit. Also during Phase Three, the tomb of Ramesses IX, KV 6, was hewn about thirty meters south of KV 5, into the same hillside. The workmen were apparently unaware of KV 5's existence and dug KV 6 directly over much of it, coming within two meters of breaking into KV 5's southern transverse corridor (corridor 10).

For the last three thousand years then, in Phases Three through Seven, KV 5 was thought to be an unimpressive, undecorated, unfurnished, unused, unimportant hole in the ground of no possible interest to thieves or archaeologists. Also, the tomb lay in such an exposed position, right at the entrance to the valley, that anyone walking by probably assumed that it must already have been examined and found empty. It wasn't until 1989, when our Theban Mapping Project found inscriptions and artifacts in chambers 1 and 2 and not until 1995, when we discovered the enormous size of KV 5, that the real significance of the tomb became clear. No one was more surprised by the importance of KV 5 than those of us who were digging it.

THE SIXTEEN-PILLARED HALL

In 1995, a European television reporter visited us at the KV 5 site. As her camera rolled, I began answering her first question—"What are you doing here?"—by briefly describing our work in the first two small chambers of the tomb. When she asked what we were digging at the moment, I described our work in chamber 3, the tomb's huge pillared hall.

"This is one of the largest pillared halls ever found in an Egyptian tomb," I said.

"Did you also find colored balls?"

I did a double take. "I'm sorry?"

"I mean, were billiard halls common in ancient Egypt?"

I had trouble keeping a straight face as the camera rolled. When the interview was over, I suggested that we film it again.

"Billiard hall? Pillared hall? What difference does it make? Who cares?" she replied. "Besides, it makes a better story."

From the beginning, I was convinced that clearing the pillared hall would almost certainly help us understand the purpose for KV 5's unusual plan. However, there was a problem. During the 1994 season, as we anticipated work in chamber 3, I asked several friends who are engineers in Cairo to come to Luxor and check out the tomb's geological stability. Don Richards, an American mining engineer working on the construction of a new Cairo subway line, was an expert in tunneling and mining safety. He and several colleagues volunteered to serve as consultants to our project. They flew to Luxor one spring weekend and spent two days exploring every accessible part of KV 5—chambers 1 through 6—studying the overlying bedrock and making comparative studies of other KV tombs. Saturday afternoon, when their surveys were finished, Don and I crossed the river to Luxor for a hamburger.

"All things considered," he began, "KV 5 is in good condition. The damage at the entrance is recent, as you said, caused by the sewer line and tour buses. The ceilings in chambers one and two can easily be patched and stabilized. Chamber four is sound, chambers five and six are in need of more extensive study. What worries me is chamber three." He took out a pen and paper and drew a quick sketch of the sixteen-pillared hall.

"First, there are a couple of major cracks in the ceiling." He drew two lines diagonally across the room plan. "In themselves, they're nothing serious, but there's another problem, too. Put simply, the ceiling is being held up by the pillars. Many of the pillars are either badly cracked or have completely broken away because of the enormous weight of the mountain above them. The only thing holding up the pillars is the debris packed around them. Remove the debris, the pillars collapse, and the ceiling falls in on your head. There are several ways we can solve this problem, but

I'd like to make some more tests next season. I think you should put off doing any clearing in chamber three for a few months."

I thought for a moment. "Could we dig along the front wall of the chamber? The ceiling in that area is solid and that would leave plenty of debris packed around the pillars. At least we could see the chamber walls."

"Yeah, that would work," he said. "But don't dig more than a meter away from the wall itself." He put the pen back in his pocket. "I'm going to contact some guys I know in Cairo and maybe a fellow in Colorado who's one of the world's experts on this kind of thing. We want to get it right the first time, especially since it's expensive work."

"How much is expensive?" I asked nervously.

"Can't say yet. Maybe fifty thousand dollars, probably more."

My face fell. That was more than double our budget for an entire season. "Well, I guess it's got to be done." We shook hands and I walked him to the taxi stand. He was flying back to Cairo in an hour. "Thanks, Don. I'll let you know in a month or so how much money I've been able to raise."

Several months later, after hitting every source I could think of, I called Don at his home in Cairo.

"Bruce Ludwig, as usual, has been able to come up with some money, but I couldn't raise everything we need. We're going to have to put off doing any engineering work in chamber three for at least another year. I'm going to start clearing the debris along the room's front wall, but there's no way we can make a start on fixing the pillars."

There were two ways we could do this in the next season. We could clear the debris along the front wall of chamber 3, which Susan was anxious to get started on because she had been looking at only the top 3 centimeters of the wall that was exposed above the debris and she was sure that extensive decoration was there.

Or we could leapfrog over chamber 3 and find out what lay beyond the four doorways cut into its north, south, and east walls. To me, it seemed best to do this first. Once we dug along the front

wall, movement of men and baskets through the chamber would
be more difficult. If we removed debris from whatever rooms lay
beyond chamber 3, the workmen could lie atop the chamber 3
debris and form a bucket brigade to pass the dirt out of the tomb.
It would be a tight fit, but the fill formed a fairly level surface
where the baskets could be safely slid. After much discussion, we
decided that digging beyond chamber 3 was our best option, and
we also agreed first to check out the door in the rear wall of the
chamber.

The fill in chamber 3 completely choked the front and center of
the room, but it stopped about forty centimeters short of the ceiling along the east and south walls, and once past the middle of the
room, we could crawl around relatively easily.

Now that we'd decided on our plan, Catharine, Mohammed, and
I set off to check the uppermost parts of the pillars and walls for
traces of decoration. Burton had done some digging along the rear
wall of the pillared hall when he was apparently trying to locate a
door along the main axis of chambers 1, 2, and 3. There was no door
in the center of the wall, and he quickly gave up. But his 1825 sketch
showed there was a doorway several meters north of that main axis,
a door whose top lay more than two meters below the ceiling. Burton
had dug a pit in front of the door to gain access and had crawled a
meter or so into it. His plan showed that it led into a small room,
which had several side chambers off it. We decided to clear away
more of this doorway so that we could see what lay beyond. In this
way, we would determine if Burton's plan was accurate. It would
then allow us to make plans to clear enough debris from the area so
that we could make a rough, but complete, plan of KV 5.

WE had already tied kneepads to knees and elbows to protect
against the sharp limestone chips in the tomb, donned hard hats,
and strapped extra flashlights to our belts. Now we moved to the
back wall of chamber 3 and stared apprehensively at the narrow
crawl space that exposed the doorway.

"It's a tight fit, Mudir," Catharine said, kneeling in a pit dug into the debris at the back of chamber 3 and peering into the doorway leading into what we were calling chamber 7. "I'm a lot thinner than you. I'll go see what's there. Besides, I want to be the first inside." She took a second flashlight from our equipment bag, then proceeded to crawl head first down into the pit, through the door, and up onto the fill in the chamber beyond. "It's not so bad once you get past the door," she called back to me. "Come on in!"

"I'll try," I said. "Mohammed, you wait here in case something happens."

I slid down into the pit and moved into the doorway. At this point, my feet were atop the debris in chamber 3, my stomach fifty centimeters lower, beneath the top of the door. My head was twisted painfully into the tiny space between the fill and the ceiling of the next chamber, sharp stone chips cut at my cheek, and fine silts turned to mud on my sweat-covered face. I was bent backward nearly in a U-shape. My back scraped the lintel, my elbows the sides of the door. My hair caught in the many fine cracks in the ceiling. As I tried to move through farther, I got stuck. My feet and hands could find no purchase, and I couldn't crawl either forward or back. My flashlight was fading, the air was hot and humid, the silence total. Catharine had vanished into a side chamber, and Mohammed was somewhere behind me. For the first time in my life, I was hit with an attack of claustrophobia.

"Pull me out, Mohammed! Pull me out! For God's sake, get me out of here!"

At first, Mohammed could not hear me. But when I began to thrash about in the tight confines of the door, he knew something was wrong. He grabbed my feet and, with a great burst of energy, pulled me in a single movement backward through the doorway. My mouth and nose were filled with dirt, and I was bleeding slightly from being dragged across sharp stones. But I was out! I coughed and spat and took a welcome drink from our water bottle. I sat, waiting for my pulse rate to drop. Mohammed looked concerned. I gave him a sickly smile.

"*Il hamdulillah!*" I said, "Thanks be to God!"

After a few minutes, I had recovered enough to crawl back down into the pit—not through the doorway, but far enough inside that I could talk to Catharine.

"What's in there?"

"Come in and look around," she said teasingly.

"Not today, thanks."

"Well, there is a room with a slightly vaulted ceiling off to the left, and I can see the tops of two doorways inside it that lead below the pillared hall. Otherwise, everything is blocked by debris. It's a very strange plan, but it's just like Burton drew it."

"We can't do anything more in the next few days," I said, more to myself than to Catharine. "But next season, let's see what's in there." I tried brushing away the silt that had caked on my soaking-wet shirt. It was futile. "Let's go outside and get some cold water. We've had enough fun for one day."

TWO weeks later, after spending several days on a Nile lecture-cruise, Susan and I returned to Luxor and were immediately told that a woman from El-Gezira, whom we had once met, was waiting to take the car ferry across the river and had gotten her foot caught in a twist of steel cable on the pier. She was literally cut in half by the boat's steel boarding ramp as it came into dock. The whole village was in mourning, and it seemed appropriate that, at about 6:00 P.M., the sky turned coal-black, lightning flashed, great claps of thunder drowned out conversation, and we were suddenly hit with a torrential rainstorm. In only ten minutes, at least 4 centimeters (1.5 inches) of water were dumped on parts of the West Bank. At our hotel, we all grabbed brooms and worked frantically to sweep the water off the hotel balcony before it flooded the adjacent rooms.

The morning after the storm, I drove to the valley to inspect the damage. There were huge puddles of water by the road along the way, and I drove slowly through them to avoid drowning the engine. The valley had also been hit by the heavy rain—numerous piles of sand and debris had washed down mountainsides—but KV 5 and the other tombs that I examined were all untouched by the flood. Thank God! After four years of meetings in the Antiquities Organization, the plans to develop a flood-protection plan for the valley are still "in discussion," and nothing has yet been done.

Supposedly, heavy rainstorms and resulting flashfloods hit the West Bank only every few centuries. But several years ago, I had checked the official meteorological data available for the last sixty years in Luxor, and had searched out scattered references in journals and diaries from the past 150 years, and found that such storms actually come much more frequently and in three- or four-year clusters. Every two to three decades, there are periods of heavy rain and flooding. Howard Carter witnessed several; so did Wilkinson and other travelers.

In November 1994, for example, a torrential downpour hit at the north end of the Theban Necropolis, destroying KV 13, the tomb of Bay, and doing serious damage to the temple of Seti I. The mortuary temple built for Seti I lies at the north end of the West Bank, not far from the small hillock on which Howard Carter built his home. The temple is rarely visited by tourists—"Too small, too far away," one tour guide told me—but it has two special things going for it, one good, the other bad. Thanks to a dedicated guardian, the temple is probably the cleanest, most frequently swept monument on the West Bank. Second, in 1994 the temple lay directly in the path of a torrent of floodwater, so it offers a depressing but dramatic lesson on the disastrous effects of rain on Egyptian monuments.

Late on the afternoon of November 4, heavy rains fell suddenly on the hillsides surrounding the valley. Within minutes, many centimeters of water had fallen and hundreds of tons of stone, silt, and sand washed down the mountainsides and into the low-lying parts of the valley. The water that poured out of the valley watershed met even heavier runoff from other *wadis* farther north. Near the house of Howard Carter, half a kilometer north of the Seti temple, these several streams met and created a wall of water that residents in northern Thebes said was two or even three meters deep. Boulders the size of buses were tossed about like toys. Moving at great speed, this deluge raced down the paved roadway, crossed a narrow stretch of barren land, and poured directly into the enclosure of the Seti temple. The result was devastating. Two days later, the German Archaeological Institute, which had been excavating there, found their storerooms were filled with three meters of water, and thousands of archaeological objects on the shelves were utterly destroyed. Limestone stelae and sphinxes that had stood before the temple simply turned to mush; mud-brick walls had vanished; stone architectural elements, some weighing hundreds of kilograms, were washed away. Within five minutes, the raging waters had poured through the temple and into the neighboring village, destroying scores of buildings, leaving a thousand people homeless, and killing several villagers and scores of animals. The cost was enormous, and the damage has still not been completely repaired.

What particularly interests me about this sad event is that it was not unique—and that it was preventable. There are records of many other storms in the Luxor area during the past two centuries, scattered references to storms even earlier than that, and some references to rains that fell over three thousand years ago. In the recent storms—and doubtless in earlier ones as well—the same pattern can be seen: in the northern part of the necropolis, the water that poured from the Valley of the Kings watershed joined runoff from the *wadis* farther north; together they raged east toward the Nile Valley, their path leading directly through the low-lying area where the temple of Seti I was built. The question is why the ancient Egyptians, who seem to have been keen observers of nature, who were very much aware of the problems of desert flooding, built the Seti temple in such an exposed location. Had so little rain fallen in the century preceding Seti's reign that memory of such storms was lost? Were storms less severe than those of today? Had the Egyptians been farsighted enough to dig diversionary channels or other protective measures that have since disappeared? I don't know, but the more we excavate around the temple, the greater the chances are of finding evidence of such construction. In the meantime, the flood-protection measures being discussed for the valley should be accompanied by measures to prevent these problems from recurring throughout all of Thebes and in the villages beyond.

After inspecting KV 5, I crossed the Nile in midmorning on business. Immediately, I noticed that the character of the river had changed completely. The heavy rains had turned the water so reddish brown that the ferrymen were calling it the Red Sea. I was reminded of the first plague on Egypt described in the Bible, when God turned the waters of the Nile to blood. The young boatman, Yassir, said he had never seen the Nile like this before.

"It makes me afraid," he said. "My neighbor says if we drink this water we die. Since yesterday, I drink only wellwater and Fanta."

The nineteenth-century Egyptologist Gaston Maspero said that the floodwaters "turned from grayish blue to dark red, occasionally of so intense a color as to look like newly shed blood." Such color changes were typical of the annual Nile flood, and one ancient text said that the river looked like red carnelian. Today, with the flood no longer an annual event, such color changes occur only after heavy local rainstorms. Young people like Yassir don't think of them as part of an annual river cycle but as a bad omen caused by an angry God.

When I got to the site, I put three men to work outside the entrance to KV 5, constructing a low stone and concrete wall adjacent to the stairs. I figured that if the Antiquities Organization wouldn't implement their master plan for flood control in the valley, we would have to protect KV 5 ourselves. I put Nubie, Abdallah, and Taya Hassan to work building the wall.

Taya Hassan is a good workman. He's about forty years old, strong, good-natured, and bright, but his eyesight is poor, so we usually have him work on projects that don't require careful observation. He is especially good at wall building, having worked for the EAO on a couple of projects several years ago.

They were all working for an hour or so, and Taya and Abdallah were talking about last night's soccer match. Without thinking, Taya slid his hand under a large stone and was almost instantly bitten by a scorpion. Immediately, everyone started shouting, and several of the workmen ran over. One of the men crushed the scorpion with a trowel; the others led Taya to our work tent.

The way Sa'idis treat a scorpion bite is based on a long tradition of local folk medicine. My offers of the first aid kit or a ride to the local clinic were politely refused. Instead, Ahmed tied a tourniquet around Taya's finger and made a small incision over the bite. Taya sucked on the finger to extract any part of the scorpion's stinger that remained in the wound. Then, the wound was washed with water and lemon juice and wrapped in a piece of cloth. Ten minutes later, Taya returned to work. For the next two days, he drank a mixture of olive oil, lemon juice, and crushed garlic, and a local sheikh recited the Koran at his side each evening.

These procedures aren't so different from those prescribed in ancient Egyptian medical papyri—mixtures of religion, magic, and home remedies. The pain from a scorpion bite can be terrible, but the bite is rarely fatal unless the victim is very old, very young, or in poor health.

The sheikh who recited the Koran over Taya, by the way, is a fellow highly regarded in a nearby village for his ability to rid homes of scorpions and snakes. He used to come to the Valley of the Kings almost daily, with three or four scorpions in his pocket (he had removed their dangerous tails). He would show them off in front of tourists, taking them out and letting them crawl over his face.

Last season I failed to give this charmer any baksheesh on our final day of work, not realizing that he apparently considered himself a part of our workforce. He took me aside and warned me that, next year, if God willed it, our tomb might be plagued by more snakes and scorpions than we could possibly imagine. Then he took two scorpions from his pocket, placed one on each shoulder, stared me in the eye, and slowly backed away. The next year, I tipped him generously.

Statue of Osiris, God of the Dead, K.V.5; Valley of the Kings

7

THE DISCOVERY

WE began our 1995 season earlier than we had previous ones: I was given a sabbatical from the American University in Cairo and looked forward to spending January through April in the valley, continuing where we had left off in KV 5. Shortly after New Year's, we resumed work clearing the doorway in the back wall of chamber 3.

Several times this season and last, the workmen began joking that whenever I leave work to go to the National Bank in Luxor, one of them finds something interesting in KV 5. Last season, it had been Sethy's canopic jar and an ostracon. On the morning of February 2, 1995, I had to go to the bank so I could meet our payroll, and again Ahmed said, "I think we will find something nice while you are gone."

An hour later, I returned, empty-handed. The bank had said apologetically that an authorization we had arranged from Cairo ten days ago had still not arrived. They suspected it was being sent by regular mail instead of by fax. The local mail service is a disaster, and it might take another two weeks for the letter to arrive. Worse, this was the second day of Ramadan, the Muslim holy month of fasting, and already the pace—and the efficiency—of life in Egypt had slowed dramatically. I walked up to the site and could see the men's faces fall as I approached. There was nothing in my hands, no bag of money, no wad of bills; the men knew they would not be paid today. Several of them were counting on the money to pay bills. I shrugged my shoulders and muttered the customary line: *"Ma'lish."* It's an untranslatable word, but it means something like, "Don't worry, things will all turn out well in the end."

"Ma'lish," they replied.

Hussein, at fifty-four years of age our oldest workman, added, "Money is not important, Doctor. God will provide."

"Il hamdulillah! " the men chimed in. "Thanks be to God."

Mohammed was standing at the top of the stairs into KV 5. "We need you inside," he said. I put on a hard hat, and we went inside the tomb.

For the past two days, we had been working to clear the doorway in the rear wall of chamber 3. Burton had gone through it in 1825; this was the same door I'd gotten stuck in last season, when I almost became a permanent inhabitant of KV 5.

We had widened the space through the doorway and had begun digging into the chamber beyond. We assumed that the chamber would be small—perhaps similar to chambers 1 and 2—and that a door in its north wall would lead to three more tiny rooms. That's what Burton's plan showed, and what Catharine had confirmed the year before. Other than that, we didn't expect anything of particular interest; the purpose of our clearing was simply to correct and complete Burton's plan of the tomb. At the time, I wasn't even sure that we would have to excavate down to floor level. All we needed to know was where the walls lay, and we could determine that by probing and measuring the walls at ceiling height.

This time I was able to struggle through the narrow crawl space and into the chamber beyond. Mohammed was already there with Marjorie Aronow, an Egyptology student who was with us for the season, doing research for her Ph.D. thesis on the sons of Ramesses II. Marjorie had already crawled into the newly enlarged channel cut beyond the doorway.

"Look," Mohammed said, pointing to the wall of debris that lay ahead.

Here, as elsewhere, flood debris filled the chamber to within a few centimeters of the ceiling. Mohammed dug away a bit of the limestone rubble and asked me to shine the flashlight into the gap. About 50 centimeters ahead of us, the debris began to slope downward. The doorway had been blocked by pieces of stone fallen from the ceiling, which had apparently reduced the amount of flood debris that could pour farther into the tomb. I shone the light into the gap, but there was nothing to see but blackness. It was strange that the light did not reflect off a rear wall, and that I couldn't see any abrupt change in the ceiling level. There was no densely packed fill—nothing but a black void. The chamber obviously continued deeper into the hillside, and was clearly not the small room we had thought it would be.

I left Mohammed and went topside to get some fresh flashlight batteries. In the tomb's high heat and humidity, even the best batteries begin to dim in a matter of minutes. When I came back not five minutes later, I could hear Marjorie, her shouts faintly echoing in the tomb.

"Kent! Kent! It's fantastic! Oh, it's so wonderful! Come back here! Please!"

During my five-minute absence, she and Mohammed had removed enough debris that they could crawl farther into the chamber through space not more than forty centimeters high and wide that curved around a huge block of fallen ceiling. When I shone the newly revived flashlight into the space, I saw that this was not just another small chamber but a long corridor. I clambered up and slithered through the narrow gap to join them. It was a tight fit, but Mohammed grabbed my hand, pulled, and I was through.

Once I was beyond the fallen block of ceiling, I saw that the debris dropped downward and there was nearly a meter-high void between the debris and the ceiling. Considering what we'd crawled through, it seemed spacious; there was actually enough room to crouch. I shone the light around me.

The corridor was about two meters wide. As far as the flashlight beam could reach, the side walls of the corridor continued forward into blackness. The walls were punctuated by doorways. There was one door on the left, another on the right, then two more, then four—we counted as we crawled slowly forward along the corridor: ten, twelve, sixteen, eighteen. . . . Most KV tomb corridors have only one or two doorways cut into their walls. I had never seen a corridor like this in *any* Egyptian tomb.

"This is incredible," I muttered.

The doorways were in poor condition. There were deep cracks through many of them, and some had been almost completely destroyed, crushed by the weight of the hillside above or, perhaps, forced downward into a void below. Fallen blocks of ceiling and debris lay strewn on the floor, and some of the doorways were so badly broken they looked as if they had exploded. Others, however, were well preserved and even decorated. We paused a moment to collect our thoughts and wipe our brows. The heat in the corridor was stifling and the humidity fogged my glasses.

Mohammed turned his flashlight down the corridor. "What's that?" he asked, suddenly. He pointed toward the end of the corridor. I wiped my glasses on my soaking shirt.

"Oh, my God!" said Marjorie. In our flashlight beams, we could make out a vaguely human form in the darkness. "It's a statue!"

Mohammed began whispering a prayer from the Koran.

Cut into the back wall at the end of the corridor was a niche, about two meters (six feet) high, two feet wide and one foot deep. Inside it, was a shadowy figure. As we crawled closer, the form became clearer: it was a beautifully modeled standing figure of the god Osiris, ancient Egypt's quintessential god of the Afterlife, the god with whom the good and pure—and the upper class—ancient Egyptians were united at death. The figure, itself about five feet high, was elegantly proportioned, plastered, and painted with dark gray-green pigment. A deep crack ran across the statue's head and through the wall behind it. The face was missing; it had probably fallen off in antiquity. We could see traces of mortar in the break—

an ancient artisan's attempt to glue the piece back in place. There's a chance, I thought, that we might find that face lying underneath our feet.

We sat for several minutes at the foot of Osiris, slowly moving the flashlight's beam over the statue, from head to toe, head to toe, again and again. Finally, I turned the beam to the doorways to the left and right of the statue. More surprises. These doors did not lead into small side chambers, as the other doorways in the corridor had done, but into even more corridors that extended even deeper into the bedrock. And more doorways were cut into *their* walls.

"I can't believe it!" Marjorie kept repeating. "I just can't believe it!"

All I could think to say was, "It's incredible, absolutely incredible!" The distance from the entrance of KV 5 to the Osiris statue was at least sixty meters (two hundred feet), and the transverse corridors—the arms of this T-shaped plan—extended at least another twenty meters (sixty-five feet) to the left and right. Suddenly, KV 5 was much more important than a small tomb with seven or eight chambers. We quickly crawled down the corridor again, recounting the doorways. There were twenty of them between the corridor's entrance and the Osiris statue, ten in each wall. And there appeared to be another sixteen doorways down the transverse corridor to the left of Osiris, and sixteen more to the right of the statue.

"How many rooms are there then?" Marjorie asked.

I counted aloud. "Sixteen plus sixteen plus twenty . . . that's fifty-two. Plus the corridors themselves, fifty-five. Plus the rooms at the front of the tomb, six more, that's sixty-one. And from what we've seen, some of the doorways in this corridor lead into suites of rooms, not single rooms. Burton's plan showed one such suite, just inside corridor seven." I stopped and thought for a moment. "My God! There have to be over sixty-five chambers in the tomb." No tomb in the Valley of the Kings has more than thirty chambers—most have only six or eight—and I can think of few tombs anywhere in Egypt that have anywhere near sixty-five chambers, and those are more like storage cells than rooms.

There was something else: we knew from inscriptions in chambers 1 and 2 that KV 5 was the burial place of several sons of Ramesses II: we'd already found the names of two sons carved on the walls of chamber 1. It is known that Ramesses II had nearly thirty principal sons, but we knew where only two of them—Khaemwese and Merenptah—were buried.

"Could all the other sons be here?"

"There's certainly room for them," Marjorie replied.

All at once I was overcome by a strange feeling, as we sat sixty meters underground, in utter silence, our light focused on a statue of *the* god of the Afterlife. Here, in the tomb of the great royal sons, in my imagination I could see the ancient funerals that took place three thousand years ago. I could hear ancient priests chanting prayers and shaking tambourines; I could feel the floor shake as great sarcophagi were dragged down the corridor; I could smell incense and feel priestly robes brush my arm as the funeral procession moved slowly past. For an instant, I felt transported back in time: it was 1275 BCE, and this *was* ancient Thebes.

I sat in the dust and debris and looked at the scene around me. Walls and corridors extended in several directions, doorway after doorway leading into chambers and suites of rooms, all of them filled with the silt and detritus of at least a dozen flashfloods during the last three millennia. There were traces of decoration on these walls and artifacts lying on the floor. Marjorie, Mohammed, and I were the first people in over three thousand years to see these corridors, to touch these carvings, to breathe this stale air. Three thousand years. One hundred and twenty generations! What a privilege, what a humbling experience to sit here where Ramesses II had once come on sad occasions to bury his sons. None of us said a word.

Twenty minutes later, we crawled out of the tomb, sweating and filthy and smiling. As the magnitude of our discovery began to sink in, I thought to myself, "I think I know how we're going to be spending the next twenty years." I turned to shake hands and receive congratulatory hugs from our ecstatic workmen. Everyone smiled and laughed and kept repeating, "This is the biggest tomb in the valley! The biggest tomb in the valley!"

THE ANNOUNCEMENT

Later, I sat and pondered the protocol of informing the Egyptian Antiquities Organization, our sponsors, and others about what we had found. Clearly, it was an important find and a very exciting one. I did not want an inadvertent error on my part to result in hurt feelings or worse. Several of my colleagues have suffered embarrassing recriminations for failing to follow the unwritten (and often capriciously changing) rules the Antiquities Department expects foreign Egyptologists to follow. First, I had to inform our on-site inspector of what we had found; he and I would then together inform the chief inspector of the Valley of the Kings; the three of us would then inform the chief West Bank inspector. He alone would inform the inspector of Upper Egypt, who would send a fax to inform the Antiquities Department in Cairo. Cairo would then decide when—or if—to inform the press. I went off to find our inspector, who was having tea in the rest-house office and brought him back to visit the tomb. He declined to crawl into the new chambers until we had cleaned them further, but he did realize the importance of what we had found and agreed to come with us to the inspectorate. I left instructions to the staff to widen the crawl space so that the inspectors could visit the new corridor tomorrow.

While we were starting our slow climb up the EAO's chain of command, the local West Bank grapevine had already been at work. By the time we arrived at the inspectorate, two or three dozen people were milling about excitedly. Gossip in Thebes travels faster than any Land Cruiser, and everyone rushed up to shake hands and offer congratulations.

"Congratulations, Mudir! We are very happy!"

"I am very glad it was your discovery, Doctor. My son, who works for you, told me he was sure the tomb would be important."

"Now you will be needing more workers, Mudir. Please remember me and my large family."

I talked to the West Bank chief inspector, Sabry Abu-Sallam, an extremely kind and helpful man who is truly committed to protecting Egypt's monuments. His eyes grew wide as we described what we had found, and he kept shaking his head in amazement.

"This is wonderful, Doctor. I am very anxious to see the work. Let me phone Doctor el-Sughayyer, then we can go to the site."

Dr. Mohammed el-Sughayyer is the director of all Upper Egyptian archaeological sites. He has played a major role in the development of plans to protect Thebes. As he and Sabry spoke over the telephone, his voice grew louder and louder. It was obvious that he, too, was excited.

By coincidence, the chairman of AUC's board of trustees, Frank Vandiver, former president of Texas A&M University, was in Luxor on February 2 with his wife and daughter. I met them for drinks early that evening in the lobby of the Jolieville Hotel. As I described to them the discovery, trying unsuccessfully to keep the excitement in my voice at a reasonable volume, I drew on a napkin a crude sketch plan of the tomb, building slowly to the climax.

"We've got sixty-five chambers or more here, Frank. Nothing anywhere near as large has been found in the Valley of the Kings before."

Frank's Texas accent grew even heavier as his excitement mounted. "Wow! By God, that's a tomb! Damn, that's excitin'!"

His daughter asked about the possibility of finding objects or inscriptions in the tomb.

"I'm sure we'll find things," I said. "In fact, we already have: pottery, alabaster jar fragments, pieces of jewelry, inscriptions. But we know that the tomb was robbed in antiquity. How much we'll find of high-quality pieces and how good their condition will be, I can't say."

As we talked she, too, grew increasingly excited. Suddenly, she jumped up and rushed out of the lobby.

"Now, where's she goin'?" Frank muttered.

In less than five minutes she was back, clutching a wad of hundred-dollar bills. "Here," she said, "take these for the project. It's all I've got with me. I was going to go shopping, but this is much more exciting and fun." I protested, but only mildly. With no money available at the bank, I'd had to borrow from Big Ahmed at our hotel to put fuel in the Land Cruiser. I had just enough money on me to pay for a taxi back to the ferry landing.

"Take the money! Take it all! It's only seven hundred, but won't that help pay for another week's work in the tomb? This is so wonderful!" She looked down at the sketch I'd been making. "Will you autograph that and let me have it to hang at home? I'd love to have the first plan ever made of the tomb." I signed my name and gave her the drawing.

"Seven hundred's a lot of money for a doodle by an unknown Egyptologist," I said.

"You won't be unknown for long, my man," Frank replied. "I think AUC's got itself another Howard Carter. Next drawing you do, you hold out for two thousand bucks!"

I left the Vandivers gushing about the tomb and went to fax the president of the American University in Cairo, Donald McDonald, telling him about the discovery. Then I sent another fax to Bruce Ludwig in Los Angeles. Paraphrasing the telegram that Howard Carter had sent to Lord Carnarvon when he discovered the tomb of Tutankhamun in 1922, I wrote, "Bruce: Have made wonderful discovery in Valley of the Kings. Awaiting your arrival. Kent." Bruce would get the joke.

The next day was Friday, and I spent the morning at Chicago House, poring over excavation reports and tomb publications, trying to find evidence of something at some Egyptian site—anything at all—that was even remotely like KV 5. There was nothing. I did not mention what we'd found to colleagues in the library; it seemed best to wait until the EAO decided how to handle matters before announcing the news, but Susan and I did telephone our son and daughter in America. They both know the Valley of the Kings well, having spent a good part of their childhood roaming around

Thebes, and they asked perceptive questions about the tomb, most of which I could not answer.

Donald, Bruce, and I talked by telephone the next evening. In what turned out to be a wise move, we asked Dr. Abdel Halim Nur ed-Din, head of the EAO, for permission to delay any announcement of the new chambers in KV 5 until after the end of the current field season, which would be early in April. We knew that considerable press attention was likely, and it would become nearly impossible to continue working to figure out what KV 5 was all about if we were deluged with reporters, cameramen, and more tourists.

"Just as important," said Bruce, "don't forget that AUC's celebrating its seventy-fifth anniversary early in May. That's just three months from now. Wouldn't it be great if we could make the announcement at the anniversary ceremony in New York? It'll be at the Explorers Club—that's appropriate—and it'll be great for everybody: AUC, the project, the EAO." We all agreed that it would be a great publicity coup for the university, and an auspicious way for AUC to begin its fourth quarter-century in Egypt.

I had one serious qualification. "Before deciding on anything, we've got to clear whatever we do with the Antiquities Organization."

It's not an official rule, just a tradition that is very politic to observe, but the first announcement of any archaeological discovery must be made by the Egyptians in Cairo to the Egyptian press. I asked Donald McDonald to contact Nur ed-Din and sound him out. Two days later, Donald phoned me back in Luxor.

"We had a good meeting," he said. "Nur ed-Din is a very easy fellow to talk to and he saw the benefits of delay. He's agreed to hold off until the AUC anniversary in May. He says he likes to have as much information as possible before going public with announcements anyway, and another month of work in KV 5 may offer some more clues about what we've got there."

Later, Donald discussed with Dr. Nur ed-Din the procedures to be followed. I remained in Luxor, but kept in daily contact to see how things were progressing. Nur ed-Din, Donald said, was convinced that the announcement would generate considerable publicity.

"He told me, 'This is a very exciting discovery, Doctor McDonald, and it will be very good for Egypt. Especially now.'" He was referring to a recent decline in tourism following several terrorist bombings in the Middle East. "This is important.'"

Over the next week, we laid out a plan. We would invite Dr. Nur ed-Din to the AUC ceremony in New York, where he would join us in making the announcement. Several hours earlier, in Cairo, his office would issue a formal press release in Arabic announcing the discovery to the Egyptian press. This would give the local journalists the opportunity to break the news first. Actually, because of the seven-hour difference between Cairo and New York, the two events would be separated by only a few hours, a small enough delay that we were not likely to anger foreign reporters, who dislike being scooped by the local press.

For the next twelve weeks, we were all sworn to secrecy. Our group continued to work in KV 5, trying not to give any hint of the discovery as colleagues and tourists came by and asked questions about our work. We were all on an emotional high, which was heightened due to the fact that we could talk about the new corridors only among ourselves.

The excavation was also going very well. Every day produced new material—more pottery, of course, along with faience beads and inlays, broken glass vials and alabaster vases, hieratic ostraca, pieces of a beard once worn by a statue, and small glazed "wiglets." At the end of each day, we returned to our hotel and talked for hours, proposing theories to explain KV 5's size and shape, wondering which sons were buried there. Everyone was in bed by eight-thirty and got up early, anxious to get back to the site.

The workmen gossiped away in their villages every evening, talking about the new objects they'd found that day, and of course what the tomb might mean to Egyptology and to Luxor's tourist industry. It became a badge of honor on the West Bank to be one of the KV 5 workforce, and our workmen were easy to identify because they walked through their villages with a bit of a swagger in their step, their heads held a little higher. Some of the men exaggerated the role they had played in the new discovery, and by the end of the first week I learned that at least six of them were taking credit for being the first to crawl into the new corridor and see the statue of Osiris. Amazingly, even though virtually all the local villagers knew about KV 5, word never made it to the foreign community until February 21, when we invited two French Egyptologists, Jean-Claude Goyon and Christian LeBlanc, to see the tomb. They graciously promised not to reveal our secret.

That same day, the chief inspector, Dr. Mohammed el-Sughayyer, came by to see the new chambers. "You know, Doctor," he said, "this is the most important discovery in the valley for a hundred years. It may be more important than Tutankhamun."

I smiled broadly but said nothing. Our workmen were convinced that being too confident would invite the evil eye and court disaster and disappointment. I don't believe in the evil eye but, then, there's no harm in being careful.

DURING the next month, we continued to clear the debris from the new corridor, which we labeled corridor 7 on the plan. The debris in 7 was not as deep as it was in the chambers closer to the entrance, and so clearing it out moved along rapidly. At times, the clearing-out moved too rapidly: the workmen were so excited that we had to make sure they didn't get too carried away and overlooked or broke something. When quitting time came, many of the men complained about having to stop work. "I know there are wonderful things here, Mudir," one of them said. "Please let me find them now, not tomorrow. I know there will be more nice walls and many statues."

As we dug forward in the corridor, we found that section after section of its walls were extensively decorated with beautifully carved relief scenes, some showing the king and various royal sons standing in the presence of Osiris, Hathor, Thoth, Isis, Horus, and other deities. There were remains of paint—mainly red, blue, and white—on parts of the walls. Two cartouches of Ramesses II formed a part of these scenes, leaving no doubt about who was responsible for the work. Some of the scenes were only partially preserved in the small chambers off corridor 7, but enough remained that Susan was confident she could reconstruct them on paper. The only parts that unfortunately might not be reconstructable, she said, were the badly damaged upper parts of the walls—where the names of the sons were written. Those, of course, were the parts we were most anxious to have.

We also were finding a large number of artifacts, including *ushabtis*, the small statuettes intended magically to work as servants for the deceased in the Afterlife. Several were made of faience, a low-fired core of ground quartz or sand on which a layer of copper oxide or other impurities was laid to produce a bright blue, green, or yellow glaze. There also were hundreds of faience beads, amulets, and inlays from statues and furniture. There were ostraca, limestone chips used as memo pads; one was a receipt acknowledging delivery of two hundred oil lamps to the men cutting and decorating KV 5. There were animal bones that had been cut, sawn, or butchered, and obviously were part of the food offerings that had been placed in the tomb for the sons of Ramesses II.

By far the most common objects we found were potsherds. Thousands and thousands of them lie on the floor of corridor 7, and in the first week alone, we filled over two hundred bags with pottery, each bag weighing over three kilograms.

All the artifacts were informative, but none of them seemed to tell us what this strange tomb was all about. We could confidently say that it was the largest tomb ever found in the valley, that its plan was unique, and that it apparently functioned as a family mausoleum for several sons of Ramesses II. But we didn't know what functions its chambers and corridors might have served. And we had a long way to go before we exposed enough of the tomb to make any such analyses meaningful. I was worried that when I spoke in the United States about our work, I'd be met with questions from the audience that would cause me to shrug my shoulders and mutter, "Who knows?"

By early March, we had exposed nearly half of the north wall of corridor 7, and had discovered that it was extensively decorated in raised relief from the entrance back to the third side chamber doorway. At that point, the carved relief stopped and, beyond it, the surface was deliberately roughened by the ancient artisans—a technique known as "keying"—to ensure that a coat of plaster would adhere to it more securely. Traces of carved and painted plaster could be found on the wall beside the fourth doorway, and they continued beyond.

Why did the Egyptians change their decorative technique a fifth of the way along this corridor, abandoning relief carving in favor of painted plaster? We know that painted plaster can be produced much more quickly than elegantly carved relief. Perhaps the work in KV 5 suddenly became rushed? Could it indicate that corridor 7 was dug in two stages, meaning that the tomb was enlarged substantially at some later date in the reign of Ramesses II? This was definitely something we would have to look at closely over the next few seasons.

FILMING WITH THE BBC

A crew had been filming a television program about our project for the last year and a half, and in February 1995, they arrived at the site to continue their work. This was a co-production of the BBC in England and of ABC/Kane in America, and I could hardly wait to tell our good news to David Wallace, the program's director.

"The tomb has grown, David. We now have over sixty-five chambers. It's the largest tomb in the Valley of the Kings."

"That's very interesting," David said without a trace of emotion.

"It probably means we'll have to rethink our shooting script. And get more electrical cable and different lamps. I wish you'd made the discovery a week or two earlier. We could have brought a lot of the equipment out from London."

David is an unflappable Irishman with a reputation as a first-rate documentary filmmaker. He is a perfectionist, totally devoted to his craft, who seems to see all life through a mental camera lens. He was joined by a cameraman, an assistant cameraman, a sound man, and an assistant director, and they each traveled with at least ten large aluminum cases filled with every gadget imaginable. Our workmen were fascinated while watching them set up to film for about ten days.

Bruce Ludwig also arrived on the same day, cutting short his meetings with AUC's board of trustees in Cairo. David Wallace wanted to film Bruce and me in a sort of Carter-Carnarvon scene at the Old Winter Palace. I was supposed to rush into the hotel's billiard room, push the cues and balls aside, and spread a large plan of the new chambers across the green felt.

"Bruce, you won't believe it!" was my line. "It's the biggest tomb in the valley!"

Bruce then puts down his cue, looks at the plan, and says, "We've got it! I always suspected that there was more in the Valley of the Kings. Congratulations, Kent."

We filmed the scene about six times. David set up a beekeeper's smoke generator to make the setting more mysterious, and by the sixth take the air in the billiard room was so thick we could hardly see each other. The hotel manager was worried that the smoke alarms would be set off. Later, David decided that the scene was too hokey and he was sure the producer, Dennis Kane, would throw it out.

The next day's filming was in Luxor Temple: a scene of me with a clipboard, staring at the procession of sons of Ramesses II carved on the first court's back wall. Then, we moved back to the valley for establishment shots of the tourists in front of KV 5. David had seen some of our workmen playing football on the roadway after work and decided that we also needed a scene of them playing a match. We created a "KV 5" team that was supposedly playing a rival archaeological expedition, and a camera was set up on a level stretch of desert just behind Howard Carter's house.

The filming occupied every minute from sunrise to sunset. Shooting in the tomb was especially disruptive of the work, which I was anxious to finish. But I had to fly to Cairo with the BBC crew for two days to shoot scenes in my office. David wanted to film the computer graphics that our architect, Walton Chan, had been working on. He had seen samples of the spectacular three-dimensional tomb drawings that Walton had prepared and, understandably, he was impressed. I couldn't wait for Walton to show him the fly-through of the tomb that he had put together for the web site we were planning. Walton Chan is a Canadian with degrees both in architecture and computer science. He has a wonderful aesthetic sense as well as a complete grasp of technical matters. His maps, plans, isometric drawings, and graphics invariably have greater beauty than one usually associates with archaeological work.

Before the BBC crew left Cairo, David Wallace and I met to plan the next season of filming. "KV 5 is growing," he said. "And it has become a really fascinating story on its own. I think we will need at least one more session in Luxor, perhaps two. KV 5 should be the focus of the program, not the Valley of the Kings. I think we should delay final editing until 1997. Do you think that by then, you'll know how big the tomb is and how many sons were buried there?"

"I can't promise anything, David. The tomb is still a mystery. We've got a lot more work to do."

"Okay," he said. "Keep me informed of your progress."

WHEN I finally returned to Luxor, I was told that Mohammed, our great bear of a workman, had grabbed a falling lamp in the tomb, touched its bare wires, and received a serious shock. If Nubie hadn't knocked the wires out of Mohammed's hand with a piece of wood, there was a good possibility that Mohammed could have been killed. David Goodman and Nubie took him to a doctor's office nearby and Mohammed spent the next two days in bed. His arm was extremely sore.

Ahmed and I spent the next day checking every wire, every plug, every connection in the tomb's electrical system. I telephoned our volunteer engineering consultant, Don Richards, in Cairo and told him the problem. Don had access to several outstanding Egyptian, American, and French engineers, many of whom are interested enough in Egyptian archaeology to give us free advice and assistance. He told us we could borrow their chief electrical engineer, John Triplett. John arrived in Luxor three days later, devoted his weekend to checking the tomb, and left us with a complete electrical installation plan for KV 5. We installed the system as soon as the necessary equipment arrived from Cairo.

THE NEW YORK PRESS

On the morning of May 17, Dr. Abdel Halim Nur ed-Din and I boarded our flights to New York. The next day, the Egyptian newspapers would be given the press release that announced the discovery. A few hours later, papers in New York and Washington would break the story. AUC prepared an elaborate press release that included maps and plans, and even the names of Ramesses II and his sons in hieroglyphs. It said:

> Archaeologists have uncovered what may be the largest tomb ever found in Egypt's Valley of the Kings, it was announced today. Speaking at a press conference at the Explorers Club in New York, Kent R. Weeks, Professor of Egyptology at the American University in Cairo and Dr. Abdel Halim Nur ed-Din, Secretary-General of the Egyptian Supreme Council for Antiquities, said that the tomb was

intended as the burial place for many of the children of the Pharaoh Ramesses II. The tomb contains at least 67 chambers, with a likelihood of dozens more lying on a lower level.

As soon as the press release went out, the response was immediate and massive. Within hours, Dr. Nur ed-Din and I were sitting in the AUC office overlooking the United Nations, giving interviews by telephone. We knew that ancient Egypt was a popular subject, but we were unprepared for the high level of interest the release generated.

After several hours talking with reporters, Dr. ed-Din was taken to lunch and then to the Explorers Club. I would meet him there later, but first I had a meeting in the editorial offices of *Time* magazine. They wanted an interview about KV 5, and needed photographs and a plan of the tomb for the article they were planning. The science editor hinted vaguely that they might even devote "more than a column" to the discovery. She asked me if I'd mind leaving my tray of slides with them to look over and unthinkingly I agreed. Then I rushed out the door, already late for the Explorers Club.

The club is located in a wonderful old town house on East Seventieth Street in Manhattan. Bruce Ludwig, who is a member, had arranged that AUC would sponsor a seminar that afternoon on "The Future of Egypt's Past." The plan was for Dorothea Arnold, curator of Egyptian Art at the Metropolitan Museum of Art, Richard Fazzini, curator of Ancient Art at the Brooklyn Museum, William Kelly Simpson, professor of Egyptology at Yale, Mark Lehner, professor at the University of Chicago, Dr. Nur ed-Din, and I to each give a twenty-minute lecture on how we thought Egyptology would develop and change over the next several decades. Of course, I was expected to give a detailed talk on KV 5, but the minute I walked in the door, I realized that all my slides were at *Time* magazine. I had absolutely nothing to show the audience.

The seminar was held in a great hall on the third floor, the room filled with stuffed tigers, penguins, bears, and birds. About four hundred people were there, many of whom came up and told me how anxious they were to hear more about KV 5 and to see photographs of the tomb's interior. AUC's president opened the seminar, but I was the last to speak.

I walked to the podium and looked out at the crowd. Reporters and Egyptologists in the room leaned forward in their chairs, pencils poised, waiting for word on the new discovery. The room was silent.

"Ladies and gentlemen, because of an error, I do not have any of my slides with me this afternoon and cannot show you the interior of KV 5. Everything I was going to say about the tomb is in the press packet, copies of which you already have. Therefore, with apologies, I'm not going to talk about KV 5 at all—except to say that it truly is exciting. Instead, I will discuss the role of Egyptology in the curriculum of the American University in Cairo and AUC's role in the field of Egyptology."

The audience groaned. Red-faced, I spoke for about ten minutes, sat down, and waited to be reviled. After the seminar was adjourned, a group of editors from the *National Geographic Magazine* came by and introduced themselves.

"You certainly play your cards close to your chest," one of them said. "What is the suspense you're creating building up to? Did you find treasure?"

I apologized and again explained that the slides were with *Time* magazine; I was not trying to hide anything. The editors gave me wry looks and walked away.

The remainder of the afternoon and evening was spent talking on the phone to reporters from all over the country who had picked up the story on the wire service. I was on one line, Dr. ed-Din on another. The calls kept coming without interruption until after midnight.

The next morning, the phone started ringing at 7:00 A.M., the calls mostly from talk-radio programs. By late morning, the television reporters began calling, and that evening, I did a half-hour interview with Robert MacNeil on the PBS *News Hour*, then an interview with BBC World Service, then half a dozen network radio shows. Dr. Nur ed-Din was equally busy, giving telephone interviews to the Egyptian press, as well as background reports to U.S. newspapers. The pace was frantic.

AUC's president came by my hotel late in the evening. "Did you expect such media coverage?"

"Never. I can't understand what triggered it. Sure, people are interested in ancient Egypt, but this is almost an overreaction. It can't last. By the end of the week, it will all have died down."

That might have been the case had it not been for *Time* magazine. On May 23, five days after I met with their editors, the magazine appeared on the newsstand with a photograph of Ramesses II on the cover and a headline that announced: SECRETS OF THE LOST TOMB: THE DISCOVERY OF A CRYPT FIT FOR 50 PRINCES SHEDS NEW LIGHT ON THE EPIC LIFE OF RAMESSES THE GREAT. Inside the magazine, seven full pages were devoted to the story of our project, with color photographs and drawings of the tomb. Major articles also appeared in *Newsweek* and *U.S. News & World Report*. At the end of the week, *Time*'s science editor called and told me: "Your cover story made the May twenty-third issue the largest-selling issue we've had in over a year!" (Several months later, *Time* produced one million refrigerator magnets depicting the KV 5 cover and sent them as gifts to new subscribers.)

Calls were now coming in from reporters all over the world, and each day brought a dozen requests for television appearances and radio interviews. AUC employs a clipping service, and within two weeks they had gathered nearly a thousand articles in American dailies and news magazines alone. KV 5 also appeared on the front pages of magazines and newspapers throughout Europe, Australia, and Asia, and I was faxed stories from papers in Hanoi, Hong Kong, Tahiti, Guam, and scores of other unlikely places.

By the time we returned to work in the autumn of 1995, KV 5

View from our hot-air balloon of the mortuary temple of Ramesses II, the Ramesseum. The limestone temple is surrounded by the mud-brick walls of storerooms, offices, shrines, and a palace. (*Kent R. Weeks*)

View to the northwest from the Qurn looking over the Valley of the Kings. BELOW: David Roberts's nineteenth-century watercolor of the Valley of the Kings. The mountain peak called the Qurn sits high above the Valley in the upper right corner.

TOP: An unfinished wall in KV 57, the tomb of Horemheb, showing the several stages involved in carving and painting raised relief.
MIDDLE: Deir el-Medineh, the New Kingdom village of the workmen responsible for cutting and decorating tombs in the Valley of the Kings.
BOTTOM: Main street in Deir el-Medineh.
(*Kent R. Weeks*)

TOP LEFT: Two of the four colossal statues of Ramesses II flanking the entrance to Abu Simbel, one of his rock-cut temples in Nubia. Note the figure of Amun-her-khepeshef, the firstborn son of Ramesses II, standing between the king's ankles. TOP RIGHT: The mummy of Seti I, father of Ramesses II, in the Egyptian Museum, Cairo. BOTTOM LEFT: North wall of the Hypostyle Hall, Temple of Amun at Karnak, carved with scenes of Seti I's military campaigns in Nubia and western Asia. BOTTOM RIGHT: Figure of Mehy, recarved as Ramesses II, on the north wall of the Hypostyle Hall, which gave rise to the now-discounted theory that Ramesses II had murdered his elder brother in order to gain the throne. (*Kent R. Weeks*)

A barren rectangle in the Nile floodplain defines the now-destroyed mortuary temple of Amunhotep III. The Colossi of Memnon (*below*), monolithic figures of the deified king, flank its original entrance. (*Kent R. Weeks*)

Map of the Valley of the Kings drawn by scientists who accompanied Napoleon Bonaparte's ill-fated expedition to Egypt, 1799–1802. The entrance to the Valley lies at center right.
BELOW: James Burton's 1825 sketch plan of the first chambers of KV 5, a tomb he labeled "M." This is the only KV 5 plan made before the work of the Theban Mapping Project. (*Courtesy of the British Museum Library*)

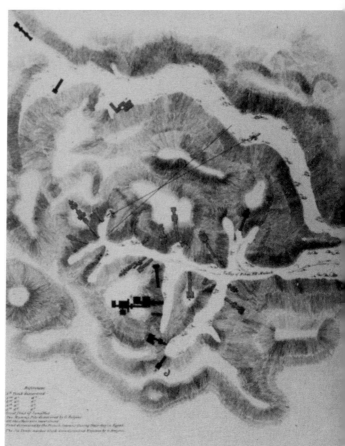

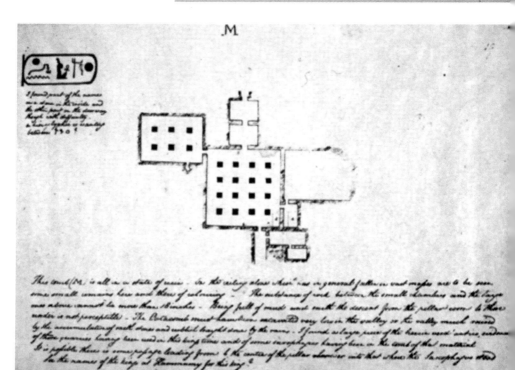

The center of the Valley of the Kings as it appeared in 1884. The entrance to KV 6, Ramesses IX, is at the left; KV 55 is to its right. BELOW: The same view in 1998. KV 6 and 55 are still visible but a rest area has been added and the valley floor widened and leveled.

TOP: Burton's name written by him with the smoke of a candle on the ceiling of KV 5's sixteen-pillared hall in 1825.
MIDDLE: Workmen clear debris from chamber 8 and the beginning of corridor 7 (*beyond doorway*).
BOTTOM: Workman Said Ali clears cementlike debris from the doorway of corridor 12.

TOP: My wife, Susan, studies the finely carved relief in corridor 7 before beginning the meticulous work of tracing the scenes.

MIDDLE: Detail of the relief in corridor 7, showing a figure of the god Horus.

BOTTOM: Detail of the relief in corridor 7, showing a figure of the goddess Hathor.

TOP: A staircase/ramp combination in corridor 11 that led us (wrongly) to expect a burial chamber beyond it.
MIDDLE: Conservator Lotfy Khaled injecting resins between decorated plaster and the limestone wall to ensure its strength and stability.
BOTTOM: Three layers of plaster cover the floor of a side-chamber off corridor 11, one of the few examples of plastered floors ever found in Egypt.

TOP: Architect Walton Chan checking environmental conditions deep inside KV 5.
MIDDLE: Photographer Francis Dzikowski taking record shots in still unexcavated sections of corridor 10.
BOTTOM: Workmen weld steel I-beams in place to strengthen the ceilings of chambers 1 and 2 in KV 5.

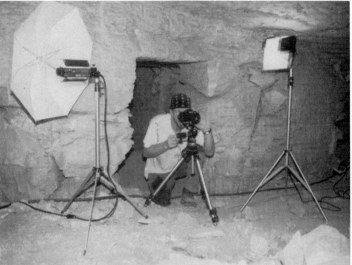

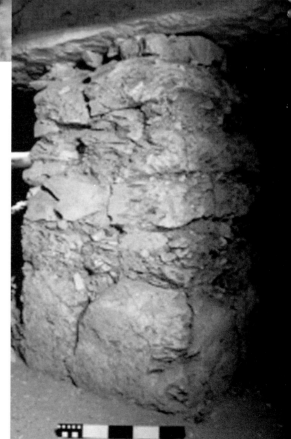

Here I analyze a layer of limestone chips topped with a thick layer of white plaster that formed a new floor in the front of chamber 3. The original floor level can be seen on the wall at left, where the smoothed limestone gives way to a rough-cut surface.

BOTTOM: One of two pillars in chamber 3, both in the center of the room, that were constructed of cut blocks instead of hewn from the bedrock. Was this done to allow a large object to be moved into the chamber?

Examining a procession of the sons of Ramesses II carved on a wall in Luxor Temple.
BOTTOM: A detail of that wall showing the firstborn son, Amun-her-khepeshef, walking into the temple.

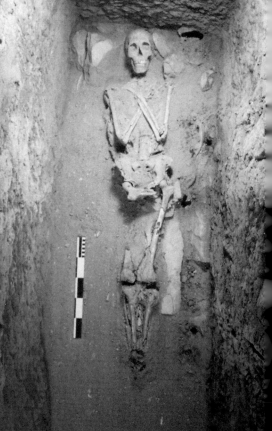

Photographs showing the excavation of a haunch of beef, three skulls, and a complete skeleton in a pit cut into the floor of chamber 2. These human bones may be the remains of the mummies of sons of Ramesses II.

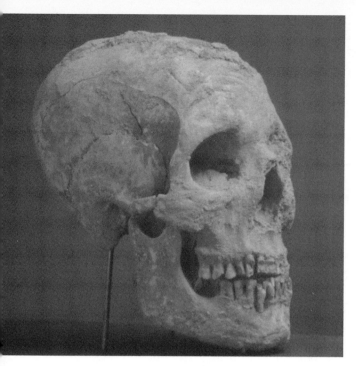

Skull number three from
the pit in chamber 2,
possibly a son of
Ramesses II.
BELOW: Detail of a
battle scene showing
Amun-her-khepeshef in
a war chariot, following
his father, Ramesses II,
into battle.

Our local workmen at the entrance to KV 5. Foreman Ahmed (*center, foreground*) holds a KV 5 sign; to the left crouches one of our inspectors of antiquity, Hamada. Workman Mohammed stands at left, to my right.

had become the most talked-about, most written-about, most photographed archaeological discovery since Howard Carter discovered Tutankhamun's tomb in 1922. Susan and I had spent months lecturing in America, New Zealand, Australia, and throughout Europe.

I found my desk piled with hundreds of requests to visit the tomb from journalists, friends, and total strangers. We turned down all of them except those from Egyptological colleagues. We were happy to meet with people outside the tomb, we replied, but our work would suffer if we allowed large numbers of people inside. Even so, at least five or six times a day, we had to stop work to entertain visiting VIPs brought by the Egyptian Antiquities Organization—foreign presidents, princes, senators, movie stars, businessmen, and journalists.

One reporter who was great fun to entertain in Luxor was Douglas Preston, who was writing an article on KV 5 for *The New Yorker*. Doug is a writer with a first-rate reputation for accuracy and readability, and because he had studied archaeology, he understood what we were doing and why. He and *New Yorker* editor Carolyn Graham stayed with us for about two weeks. We hit it off immediately and the time spent with them was delightful. The article, which appeared in January 1996, was lucid and accurate.

Also during our absence that summer, Egyptian President Hosni Mubarak had asked to visit the tomb. Of course, the EAO agreed immediately, then realized that it would be unacceptable for Mubarak to slither through the debris-filled sixteen-pillared hall. The EAO ordered that a path be dug through the rubble, even though this digging could be disastrous, both structurally and archaeologically. Fortunately, Inspector Ibrahim hired our foreman, Ahmed, to supervise the work. Ahmed has always been very conscientious and has learned a great deal about proper excavation methods. He managed to dig a passageway where it created the fewest problems, and he kept a journal of his work. Here's a sample entry that I always remember:

In the name of God the beneficent and merciful. Good morning Doctor Kent. I am sorry we digg here because I know you not want it but we must so I keep notes of the work. We digg slow and I look and watch for bots and we find none. We digg 1.30 meters inside and down 1 meter. Thank you. Good by. Ahmed.

Ramesseum. Thebes.

8

THE RISE OF RAMESSES II

THE discovery of the largest tomb in the Valley of the Kings was exciting. But what did KV 5 mean? We still did not know how many sons were buried there, or why so unusual a tomb had been hewn in the limestone hillside. Such unanswered questions were frustrating, but they certainly contributed to the worldwide interest in KV 5. Hundreds of people, from colleagues to young children, wrote letters to suggest how and where we should dig. Except for Tutankhamun, Ramesses II clearly had the highest name recognition of any pharaoh, and scores of letters outlined new theories about his life or asked for information about his reign. One thing was clear to everyone: since KV 5 had no known parallels, we would have to study the tomb minutely and look closely at the religious and political beliefs of the man who had ordered it, Ramesses II, if we were ever to explain its purpose.

DURING the early 1970s, I was appointed the director of Chicago House, the headquarters of the University of Chicago's Epigraphic Survey in Luxor, which is devoted to recording in minute detail the inscriptions and scenes on the walls of temples and tombs in the Luxor area. The survey spent over sixty years recording just one temple, that of Ramesses III at Medinet Habu, and in conclusion published over a dozen elephant-sized folio volumes of plans and drawings. Such slow and meticulous work is costly, and Chicago House only takes on scenes of great historical importance that are so poorly preserved or so analytically complex that they cannot be adequately recorded in any other, less expensive way. When I came to Chicago House, its work at Medinet Habu had been on hold for several years, and the recording of Khonsu Temple (a part of the Karnak complex) was nearing completion. It was time to look for another project.

I chose the north wall of the Great Hypostyle Hall in the Temple of Amun at Karnak, built and decorated for Seti I, father of Ramesses II. The texts here are among the most important military records written in the New Kingdom and provide a wealth of information about the geography of the ancient Near East. They're so valuable, in fact, that an analysis of them written by my colleague, William Murnane, went through two sold-out editions in five years, a record for such a specialized Egyptological study. In addition to their great historical importance, the Seti scenes are extraordinarily beautiful.

The Seti wall is one of the finest examples of monumental narrative art in all Egyptian history. "Narrative art" means simply that the wall is a "representation which tells a story"; "monumental" refers to its very large size. Indeed, the Seti wall is huge: originally about twenty-five meters high, the wall is divided into two thirty-meter-long units separated by a doorway leading into the Great Hypostyle Hall. Originally, there were over a thousand square meters (eleven thousand square feet) of carved and painted relief here, every bit of it brilliantly executed.

The carving was elegant, both technically and aesthetically. Details of hair styles and costume, the powerful muscles of the horses pulling the pharaoh's chariot, the subtle modeling of the enemies' faces, showing the tears and heartbreak of their defeat—all demonstrate an attention to detail that is unrivaled in Egyptian art. Clearly, the artisans who worked here took exceptional care to make their lines steady and sure, and to keep the layout and proportions nearly perfect. Every figure speaks of the artists' self-assurance and skill.

How ironic, then, that one of the most important pieces of evidence for the history of Ramesses II's career rests on the interpretation of scenes on this wall. At the eastern end of the wall, Seti I, the father of Ramesses II, is shown preparing to mount his war chariot and head into battle. Immediately behind him stands a young man, carved at such smaller scale that his head is no higher than Seti's knee. This figure can be found on six other scenes on this wall, and in every instance it was plastered over and a figure of Ramesses II cut in its place. The plastering and recarving was not the result of scribal error or artistic misjudgment. These were deliberate changes, the replacement of one figure with another. Fortunately for Egyptologists, much of the later plaster has fallen away and traces of both stages are visible today.

Originally, the figure on the Seti wall was a man called Mehy, whose name was derived from the phrase *em heb,* as in the names Hor-em-heb or Amun-em-heb. (Such a name is called a "hypocoristicon" by scholars; less pedantically, a nickname.) Mehy's titles include "Troop Leader" (also sometimes translated as "Group Marshaler") and "Fan Bearer." The first title apparently denotes a senior army tactician, obviously an important position and one that is appropriate for someone standing next to pharaoh in these battle scenes. The second denotes an individual in regular attendance upon the pharaoh and, consequently, someone who had the confidence of the king.

Many years ago, the American Egyptologist James Henry Breasted examined this wall and advanced a theory about why Mehy's figure had been covered over and recut. He argued that Mehy must have been the elder brother of Ramesses II and that Ramesses had Mehy murdered so that he could inherit the throne himself. In his book *The History of Egypt,* Breasted wrote:

Whether his elder brother gained the throne long enough to have his figure inserted in his father's reliefs or whether his influence as crown prince had accomplished this, we cannot tell. In any case Ramses brushed him aside without a moment's hesitation and seized the throne. . . . [This is] evidence of the bitter conflict of the two princes involving of course the harem and the officials of the court and a whole lost romance of court intrigue may still be traced by the trained eye on the north wall of the Karnak hypostyle.

This is wonderfully evocative prose, but in fact there is little evidence to support Breasted's view, although it gained a foothold in Egyptological histories and has been repeated for over seventy years. Egyptologists talked of palace intrigues, plots, and fratricide. And as a result of this, Ramesses II gained a reputation as a devious, mean, rather thick-headed villain. As recently as 1981, a leading German Egyptologist, Wolfgang Helck, argued that Mehy was definitely the heir apparent of Seti I, and the erasure of his figure proves that supporters of Ramesses II had conspired to push Mehy aside in favor of their candidate for pharaoh.

Egyptologist William Murnane, however, has an alternative explanation. He believes that Mehy was a commoner (or, remotely possible, a relative of Horemheb, last king of the Eighteenth Dynasty) who, through talent or guile, rose rapidly through the ranks of the army and played a powerful role as military adviser to the pharaoh, Seti I. Murnane argues that Mehy may have been informally considered a possible heir apparent, but only while Seti was childless or his son was still a minor. As soon as Seti's son reached puberty, Mehy's claim vanished and Ramesses II became the rightful and legitimate heir to the throne. There was no conspiracy, no poisoned wine, no dagger in the back, just a relatively normal chain of events. But Murnane does make this fascinating comment:

So uncertain of itself was the new dynasty that it first permitted the advancement of an interloper such as Mehy, then realized the danger his career might pose to a royal family whose roots also lay in the military sector. Ramesses II . . . quickly redressed the balance by promoting his own sons to an unprecedented position in public life, then maintained that policy so successfully that it became standard practice throughout the later New Kingdom.

From a very early age, Ramesses II played an active and highly visible role in his father's court. He was undoubtedly a bright child, greatly loved by his father. But it is a bit difficult to accept at face value a text from Seti's second year on the throne, when Ramesses was only ten years old, stating that the king had made his son the commander in chief of the Egyptian army:

> Everything has come to your attention since you have been governing this land. While (yet) you were in the egg you managed affairs by means of your office of child-heir. The business of the Two Lands was told to you while you were (yet) a child with the sidelock. No monument came to pass without being under your supervision. No commission came to pass without you. While you were (yet) a lad of ten years you acted as chief of the army.

Either this title was purely honorary or, as Egyptologist Claude Vandersleyen believes, the word "army" really refers to "people," and the title is only vaguely meant to help strengthen Ramesses's claim as the next occupant of the throne. We know that Ramesses probably did accompany his father on military campaigns into western Asia when he was five and six years old, but because of his age he was almost certainly an observer, judiciously placed out of harm's way, and not in the front lines commanding troops, just as he would later arrange for his young sons to travel with him and his army to witness a great battle at Qadesh.

Although some Egyptologists argue that early on, Ramesses was made co-regent with his father, sharing equally the rights and duties of kingship, most scholars now believe that he was designated "prince-regent," a title of slightly lower rank. This seems to be confirmed by an inscription from Seti's ninth year at Aswan in which Ramesses is referred to simply as "eldest son," and not by any more prestigious title. The title of prince-regent was awarded in Seti's seventh year and perhaps it was the chamberlain, Paser, who oversaw the ceremony. The event was described a few years later by Ramesses:

> When my father appeared to the populace . . . [he] spoke (thus) concerning me:
>
> "Crown him as King, that I may [see] his beauty while I (yet) live!"
>
> [He had] the Chamberlains [summoned] to set the crowns upon my brow.
>
> "Set the Great Crown upon his head"—so said he concerning me, while he was (yet) on this earth, and "he shall govern this land, he shall care for its boundaries, he shall give commands to the people."
>
> [He spoke] [of me, his eyes filled with] tears, so great was the love for me within him. He furnished me with a household (from) the Royal Harim, comparable with the beauties of the Palace. He selected for me wives throughout [the land, while] taking concubines for [me . . .].

What a birthday present! Ramesses was only fifteen years old, but already he had begun the career that would mark him as one of Egypt's greatest rulers, most energetic builders, and, certainly, most prolific fathers.

FOR about eight or nine years, Ramesses II served as prince-regent with his father before becoming pharaoh in the summer of 1278 BCE. He was about twenty years old. Ramesses was probably in residence at Memphis when he learned that his father had died at Pi-Ramesses. Whether Seti's demise was expected or not—he died at about age fifty—the death of the pharaoh would have been a terrible shock to Egyptian society, an event with the potential of bringing disaster to the Nile Valley. It was as if the god Seth had again murdered Osiris and hostile forces were poised to take control of the world. To mitigate against this danger and to ensure a safe and successful transfer of royal authority, a multitude of rules and rituals had to be meticulously followed.

Ramesses, of course, would immediately have begun wielding power as pharaoh at his father's death. But his actual coronation would not have occurred until after the seventy-day process of mummification had been completed and the former ruler was buried in the Valley of the Kings. Ideally, royal coronations were scheduled to coincide with "some new beginning in the process of nature," an indication of how closely Egyptian kingship was tied to the cycles of nature. We do not know exactly when Ramesses's coronation took place, but it might well have been at the start of the Nile's annual flood or at its recession, at the time of a solstice or an equinox, or at the start of the annual harvest.

The names and titles that Ramesses took at the time of his coronation offered clues to the future role the young ruler was laying out for himself:

The Falcon King, Strong Bull, Beloved of Ma'at
He of the Two Goddesses, Protector of Egypt, vanquisher of
    foreign lands
Horus of Gold, Rich in Years, Great in Victories
King of Upper and Lower Egypt, Usi-ma-re, ["Strong in Ma'at
    is Re"]
Son of Re, Ramesses II, Beloved of Amun

Later, on day 26 of the third month of spring in his second year of rule, he added another title, "Setepenre," meaning "Chosen of Re," or "Inheritor of Re," to this list.

The accession (not the coronation) of Ramesses II as king of Upper and Lower Egypt took place early in June, 1278 BCE, probably in the north at Heliopolis. Afterward, the new pharaoh sailed to Pi-Ramesses to oversee plans for his father's funeral. The embalming of Seti's body had already begun before Ramesses arrived, and one can imagine that, each day, a lengthy series of elaborate ceremonies for the dead pharaoh and his successor were performed by the priests. When the ceremonies were completed, the mummy was wrapped and placed inside its coffins. Ramesses and the funeral cortege then set off from Pi-Ramesses in a vast flotilla of ships bearing priests and officials, ritual equipment and funerary furniture. At Heliopolis, Memphis, Abydos, and a score of other towns along the Nile, the flotilla stopped for religious services, meetings, and meals, and at each stop its ranks undoubtedly swelled as more boatloads of mourners joined in the solemn and critical ceremonies. Peasants lined the riverbanks. Some cheered their new pharaoh; others stood in silent prayer, mourning the old. All were awed by the splendor of the funeral procession.

At Thebes, news of Seti's death had been received three months before the flotilla set sail. By the time it docked there, probably in August, priests were prepared to receive the mummy and to perform the profoundly important ceremonies in the major temples. The funeral ceremony must have been a wonderful affair. I can imagine the great procession leaving the Temple of Amun at Karnak, crossing the Nile, and sailing along a canal that cut westward through the cultivable land toward Seti's mortuary temple. There, the procession stopped, perhaps for a day or more, while more ceremonies were performed. The cortege then proceeded on foot through the barren hills to the Valley of the Kings and Seti's tomb. The mummy of the king was laid to rest in his burial chamber; storerooms were filled with the equipment and offerings he needed for the journey into the Afterlife. Ramesses II watched as priests meticulously performed the ancient rituals and sealed the tomb. This ceremony would not be performed again for another sixty-seven years.

*   *   *

RAMESSES remained in Thebes for at least another month to oversee one of the country's most important religious events, the Festival of Opet. From the New Kingdom onward, the Opet Festival, held in Luxor and Karnak temples, was one of the country's most important ceremonies. It was performed annually, during the summer when the Nile flood reached its crest, and it lasted for over three weeks. In the reign of Amunhotep III, statues of the god Amun, his wife, Mut, their son Khonsu, and representations of the king and his *ka,* were carried down a broad, paved avenue lined with ram-headed sphinxes, from Karnak southward to Luxor Temple, called "The Southern Residence." That is a distance of five kilometers, and half a dozen small stone kiosks were erected at intervals so that the priests carrying the statue in a shrine on a great model boat could stop for prayers and rest. Once at Luxor, elaborate reception ceremonies were held and musicians and dancers and singers welcomed the god and his entourage with long and enthusiastic concerts. The pharaoh then retired to the birth house, from which he later emerged, symbolically reborn and restored. Statues of his *ka* were no longer on display, because the *ka* was now thought to have taken residence in the royal body. The purpose of the festival, then, was to acknowledge and commemorate the renewal of royal authority and to celebrate and reaffirm the divine nature of the pharaoh.

We know a great deal about this procession because a detailed record of it was carved on the walls of the Processional Colonnade in Luxor Temple. The west wall shows the overland trip from Karnak to Luxor, the east wall shows the trip back, sailing down the Nile on a special bark of Amun that is tied to the king's barge and accompanied by hundreds of other vessels.

In a sense, the Opet Festival is still being celebrated in Luxor, although in a dramatically different form, not by worshipers of Amun, but by otherwise good, tradition-following Muslim and Christian Egyptians. About seven hundred years ago, a mosque was built over a part of Luxor Temple to celebrate a venerated local Muslim sheikh, Yusef Abu el-Haggag. The original mosque, surrounded by some nineteenth-century additions, is still there. Every year, during the Muslim month of Shaban (immediately preceding Ramadan, the holy month of fasting), thousands of villagers descend upon Luxor for a three-day-long celebration, the Festival of Abu el-Haggag. The city becomes a vast carnival ground: everywhere there are huge piles of dried dates, fruits, and nuts; machines that spin forth cotton candy; three-wheeled carts that sell cakes and sweet juices. Vendors sell paper hats, and strolling minstrels and magicians entertain the crowds, while horses are raced up and down the corniche. The streets are filled with people who have come from all over Upper Egypt. The high point of the Festival of Abu el-Haggag is a parade, when a large model boat is carried from the basement of the mosque on the shoulders of local men, who parade from the mosque through town, around Luxor Temple and back, accompanied by singing and dancing youths, young girls in bright-colored frocks, and children who wave palm branches from the backs of flatbed trucks. It is a remarkable scene. There is nothing Christian or Muslim about the celebration; it is a Christianized and Islamicized version of an ancient Egyptian festival.

sesame harvest near medinet habu temple, luxor   1997 8w.

9

RAMESSES II AND HIS SUCCESSOR

IN 1996, we visited Christian LeBlanc, a French Egyptologist who was working in KV 7, the tomb of Ramesses II. Alabaster fragments that Christian had found in the burial chamber are similar to fragments we found in KV 5. They leave no doubt that our fragments are pieces of an alabaster sarcophagus lid and the corner of a large alabaster box where canopic jars were stored. This is even more evidence that KV 5 was the actual burial place of the pharaoh's sons, not just a cenotaph or ceremonial center.

I am always impressed when entering KV 7, but today it seemed even more wonderful. Christian had cleared debris from the several entrance corridors, revealing parts of their superbly decorated walls. Susan was delighted and spent over an hour looking for scenes and figures that are similar to those in KV 5. With her remarkable memory, she recognized figures and hieroglyphs that we could use to restore (on paper) the damaged scenes and texts in our tomb. In terms of painting and relief carving, the tomb of Ramesses II, KV 7, and KV 5 are stylistically remarkably similar. In fact, when my colleague Egyptologist and art historian Edna Russman visited us, she thought that both tombs had been done by the same artists. The faces of the goddesses especially show the same delicate modeling of cheeks and chins, the same curvature of eyes and noses, and the same body proportions. At least part of the tomb, she said, was undoubtedly decorated during the early years of Ramesses II.

As we walked down the first three corridors of KV 7, the lamps at the far end sent an eerie yellow light through the dust-filled air. I tried to imagine what this elegantly decorated tomb might have looked like in ancient times, its fine carvings brightly, even garishly, painted. I wondered how one prepared for the burial of a man who, for sixty-seven years, had ruled over the most powerful country in the world.

KV 7: the tomb of Ramesses II.

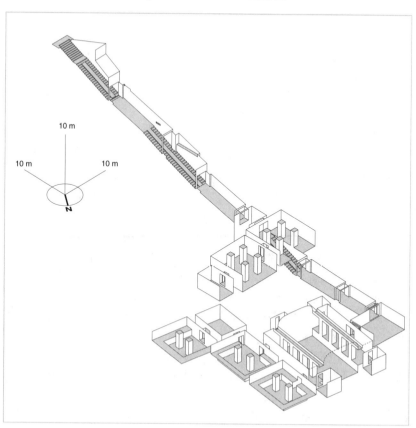

* * *

RAMESSES II was tall for an Egyptian, five feet eight inches (172 centimeters), until arthritis and spondylitis began to curve his spine, forcing him to walk slowly, stooped over, leaning on the tall staff that he always carried. He was of slight build, lean and obviously once well muscled. He had a narrow chin, high cheekbones, an aquiline profile with a large nose, and prominent ears that were pierced. His teeth pained him: he had developed periodontal disease in middle age, and his teeth were filled with cavities. But all in all, for a man in his late eighties, Ramesses II was still remarkably fit.

At the time of his death, he still had a full head of naturally red hair—a color that must have dramatically set him apart from the normally black-haired populations of Egypt and western Asia. Red hair was a characteristic feature of the god Seth, and Ramesses II may have felt an even closer affinity to this god because of it.

He was always an energetic person, a king who took great pride in his many activities and who often involved himself in their planning. One can imagine him in the last years of his life, still a forceful presence, slipping into a state of helplessness only at the very end of his life.

In the months before Ramesses II died, there must have been concern throughout the country. Messages were probably passed constantly between the king's councillors and Egypt's many temples. The High Priest of Amun, the vizier at Thebes, the officials of Memphis and Heliopolis would each have been kept informed of His Majesty's health on an almost daily basis. This would not have been an easy matter: the royal residence in the pharaoh's last days was Pi-Ramesses. Now it was July and the Nile had already begun to flood, covering the valley floor with thirty centimeters of water or more. The river's current increased from a lazy three or four kilometers an hour to more than nine. Upstream communications were slowed, and the priests and officials in Thebes and other distant towns may have had little time to complete their preparations for a royal funeral. In Egypt's palaces and temples and offices, little else was done other than preparing for the first royal funeral in over two generations.

When Queen Victoria died in 1901, after a reign of sixty-four years, no one in the British royal court was old enough to remember how a state funeral should be conducted. In exasperation, after much unsuccessful searching of records and archives, royal equerries realized that they simply had to invent a ceremony. "The historical ignorance of everyone from top to bottom . . . was beyond description," one frustrated observer wrote at the time.

I suspect that a very similar problem existed in Egypt three thousand years earlier when, in July 1213 BCE, Ramesses II died after a reign of sixty-seven years. He was close to ninety years old. After so long a reign, who of his court officials or temple priests had ever been involved in a royal funeral? In fact, none of them had probably ever known another ruler.

Egyptologists have not been able to find any detailed rules for royal funerals written down in temple archives, but it seems likely to me that they existed. Donald Redford has made a detailed study of known archival records, and he believes that temple libraries must have contained an extensive number and variety of documents: king-lists, annals, chronicles, surveys of religious buildings, geographical surveys, medical texts, wisdom literature, lists of good and bad days, dream interpretations, astrologies, hymnals, construction manuals, inventories, account books, and manuals giving festival and ritual instructions. Perhaps instructions for a royal funeral were included in that last category. If so, their form may have been similar to the instructions for the ritual embalming of the Apis bull at Saqqara, which I'll describe later.

Ramesses's death was not unexpected—because of his age—and the search for information on funerary ritual probably had been going on for months before he died. This was not simply a matter of wanting to offer the king a spectacular sendoff with lots of pomp and circumstance. The death of a pharaoh was a serious matter—perhaps the most serious any Ramesside court official or priest had ever faced. It was an event that could potentially threaten the world's very existence; order and balance had to be set right again or chaos would ensue. Prayers and offerings had to be made so that men and gods could continue to communicate. The proper ceremonies had to be performed meticulously so that the dead king would ascend to heaven and be welcomed by his fellow gods. No detail of these acts was too inconsequential to worry about: the kinds of flowers to be placed atop pharaoh's mummy, the methods used to prepare offerings of food and drink, the manner in which prayers were to be intoned, the proper knotting of the high priests' belts—all demanded careful review.

THE mortuary temple of Ramesses II—Egyptologists call it the Ramesseum—must have been a spectacular structure in ancient times. Begun early in the king's reign, it grew to substantial size: nearly 200 meters (600 feet) long and 60 meters (190 feet) wide. Its hypostyle hall is second in area only to that of the Great Hypostyle Hall in the Temple of Amun at Karnak. The temple was built near the edge of the cultivation, equidistant from the mortuary of Seti I to the north and the palace of Amunhotep III to the south. At its entrance stood a great stone pylon, decorated with elaborate relief carvings describing the battle of Qadesh. Ramesses's mortuary temple was quite deliberately patterned after that built by Amunhotep III. Like its predecessor it, too, was called the "Mansion of Millions of Years" and was closely tied to the cult of Amun at Karnak. The temple also bore the name "United with Eternity," and the form of Amun represented here was therefore described as "Amun Who Dwells in United with Eternity." At Thebes, Amun was considered the local form of Osiris; therefore, the figure of Amun in the Ramesseum represents the deceased king, Ramesses II, who had now become Osiris.

Within the enclosure walls of the Ramesseum, Ramesses II's priests had built not only a great temple to Osiris/Amun/Ramesses II, but also a small palace where the pharaoh could reside on his ceremonial visits here. Temple buildings were dedicated to Tuy,

Ramesses's mother, and Nefertari, his wife. Around the perimeter of the stone temple is a vast array of mud-brick storerooms, most of them long, corridorlike rooms with vaulted roofs. Much of this compound is just being excavated today by Christian LeBlanc.

The Ramesseum has suffered badly over time, and only a few walls and columns still stand erect. Nevertheless, it is still impressive. One of the parts that has fallen over is the largest monolithic statue ever attempted in Egypt, a gigantic block of red granite that depicts a seated Ramesses II. Even broken, lying on its back in a field of dust and weeds, it is an overwhelming piece of work. Like the plan of the temple itself, the statue was based on the Colossi of Memnon carved for Amunhotep III's mortuary temple, less than half a mile south. Giovanni Belzoni's description of this huge statue so impressed the poet Percy Bysshe Shelley that he wrote a poem about it, *Ozymandias,* the Greek form of User-maat-Re, one of the names of Ramesses II.

The Ramesseum is an impressive and architecturally fascinating structure to wander through. The most beautiful way to see—and to understand—the complex of stone and mud-brick walls, however, is to fly over it in a hot-air balloon in the raking light of a winter morning, a few hundred meters above its pillars and pylon. The temple lies exactly on the edge of emerald-green fields, then extends deep into lowland desert. Only from high up in the air can one appreciate the intricacies of its plan and the care taken in its construction. One can clearly see the layout of storerooms, the plan of subsidiary buildings, and the remarkable stonework of the temple roof. All of Thebes is beautiful from the air, but if the Ramesseum is all you see of it, it is worth the money.

Ramesses II was buried in KV 7, a tomb that remains one of the valley's great puzzles. Although it has been explored off and on by expeditions from the early nineteenth century onward, it has still not been completely cleared, and we are ignorant about much of its design and decoration. That is why Christian LeBlanc's current work there is of such importance. Most of the huge tomb is still filled with thick layers of flood debris.

When our Theban Mapping Project worked in KV 7 over a decade ago, we had great difficulty measuring the size of many of the chambers. And it was impossible to determine whether additional doorways might lead through buried walls into rooms we could not see. The debris in the corridors was so deep we were often unsure whether we were walking down sloping corridors or silt-covered stairways. In the few areas where earlier Egyptologists had picked away the debris and exposed walls and floors, it was obvious that KV 7 had been carefully dug: there were elaborate architectural details and the work was precise. The hieroglyphic texts and figures of king and gods, carved in low raised relief on the walls, were some of the most elegant to be seen anywhere. This was truly a tomb fit for a king.

We spent several weeks prodding and planning for our work in KV 7, but even after publishing the plan in one of our reports, we weren't satisfied that we had done justice to the tomb—nor could we until it was cleared. LeBlanc has now begun clearing the burial chamber and stabilizing its broken columns and cracked ceiling, and we hope to remap the tomb in a future season. In one of the small side chambers, LeBlanc found a small statue of Osiris, about half the size of the one we found in KV 5. It was badly broken but well carved and had originally been painted. The floor in front of it, like the floor in front of the niche in KV 5, was deliberately cut in a rough and irregular fashion. Neither LeBlanc nor I can yet explain this strange feature.

The tomb of Ramesses II has architectural features similar to those in the tomb of Amunhotep III. The tomb of his successor, Merenptah, on the other hand, resembles those of Horemheb and Seti I. This may reflect changes in religious and funerary beliefs during his reign.

MERENPTAH

The long reign of Ramesses II would have been a hard act for anyone to follow, and in comparison the reign of his successor,

Merenptah, seems rather dull. But the comparison is unfair. Merenptah's reign may seem inactive, but this is mainly because there are relatively few texts from his reign and these are mostly concerned with military ventures against Libyans and Asiatics. There is little information about his activities at home.

Merenptah, Ramesses II's thirteenth son, was the fourth child of Queen Isisnofret. We know almost nothing about him until the fortieth year of his father's reign, when he was appointed General of the Army. Merenptah outlived his twelve older brothers and became his father's heir apparent in Ramesses's fifty-fifth regnal year. Ramesses II was then celebrating his eightieth birthday, Merenptah his forty-eighth. Twelve years later, at age sixty, Merenptah was crowned pharaoh and ruled for nine years.

Merenptah had probably been the real power behind the throne during the last decade or so of his father's life, when Ramesses II was old and ailing. The experience he gained then most likely served him well when he finally was crowned king.

EARLY in his reign, Merenptah ordered his army into the field to fight against an invasion by a people identified as southern Libyans. A year or two earlier, the Egyptians had fought against rebellious natives in western Asia. Those battles are referred to on a stela erected in his mortuary temple at Thebes: "The princes are prostrate and cry 'Mercy!' Not one lifts his head among the Nine Bows [Egypt's traditional enemies]. Tjehnu-Land is destroyed, Khatti at peace, Canaan plundered with every ill, Ashkelon is taken and Gezer seized, Teno'am made as though it never had been. Israel is desolated and has no seed. . . ." This is the earliest reference to Israel known from a nonbiblical text. My colleague Frank Yurco, of Chicago's Field Museum, believes that he has found the first representations of Israelites in Egyptian art, carved on a wall built at about the same time by Merenptah just south of the Great Hypostyle Hall at Karnak.

Merenptah's mortuary temple lies behind the ancient Colossi of

Memnon and the modern Marsam Hotel of Sheikh Ali Abd el-Rassoul. Built of stones taken from the mortuary temple of Amunhotep III, it is currently being studied by Horst Jaritz, director of the Swiss Institute in Cairo. The fragments that Jaritz has found here include some of the best-preserved and most attractively painted wall reliefs from any temple at Thebes.

Merenptah's tomb in the Valley of the Kings, KV 8, lies only a short distance from his father's and about a hundred meters from KV 5. It has been open since ancient times, but it was not even cursorily cleared until 1903, when Howard Carter worked there. Even then, the burial chamber was left partly uncleared until the late 1980s (when American Egyptologist Edwin Brock worked there), and the side chambers off the burial chamber are still clogged with dense layers of flood debris. The tomb consists of an impressive series of corridors and stairways that descend through a pillared hall and anteroom to a large burial chamber similar in plan to that of Ramesses II. Four sarcophagi, three of red granite, one of white calcite, were intended to be placed here, each nested inside the other.

The plan of KV 8 falls within the standard range of Nineteenth Dynasty royal tombs, but it differs greatly from the plan of KV 5. We have looked in vain in the tombs of Ramesside family members for clues that might help explain the architecture or the decorative program of KV 5.

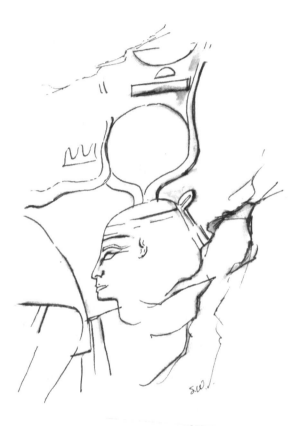

"Relief of Goddess, Chamber t, K.V.5

10

PLASTERED FLOORS

DURING our 1996 field season, I was particularly anxious to explore the T-shaped set of corridors at the rear of KV 5, hoping to learn what their purpose might have been. We had already seen traces of decoration on their walls, and we had found numerous pieces of decorated plaster lying on their floors. But nothing about the decoration told us what this strange complex of rooms had been used for. As the clearing of corridor 7 progressed, we sat each evening in our hotel and tried to devise an archaeologically testable theory, and it seemed that every evening produced a new one.

For example, Ramesses II fathered countless sons, but only two, Khaemwese and Merenptah, have known burial places: Merenptah was buried in KV 8, Khaemwese was probably buried at Saqqara or Giza. Could all the other sons named in the son-lists that Ramesses II had carved on temple walls have been buried in KV 5? Could the side-chambers off the transverse corridors be the burial chambers? There were certainly enough rooms for all of them, but for architectural reasons we decided that wasn't the purpose of the rooms. Whether the sons of the pharaoh had been interred in granite sarcophagi or in wooden coffins, the doorways of these side chambers were too narrow for them to get through.

Though the doorways leading into the KV 5 corridors are at least 1.50 meters (60 inches) wide, the side-chamber doorways never exceeded 70 to 73 centimeters in width, which is too narrow for any standard sarcophagus or coffin. If the sons were not buried in the side chambers, then where were they buried? We began to search for clues.

First we noticed that the walls between the side chambers along corridors 10 and 11—the transverse corridors leading away from the Osiris statue—were in disastrous condition, especially around their junction with corridor 7. Extending down each corridor for about five meters from the Osiris statue, the walls had cracked and shattered, and huge blocks had fallen from the ceiling to the floor. There seemed two possible reasons for this: either the great weight of bedrock above had compressed them to literally explode, or there was a void below that allowed the walls to sink. If the latter was the case, could there be another level of rooms beneath where we were standing?

We had noticed that in both corridors 10 and 11 the ceilings sloped downward. The corridors were so filled with debris that we could not see the floors, but it was unlikely that they were horizontal. In Egyptian tombs, floors and ceilings nearly always run parallel to each other. Why would KV 5 have a sloping corridor? This immediately led us to speculate that corridors 10 and 11 led to a lower level of rooms. And perhaps that was where we'd find the burial chambers.

Such a plan did have a precedent. Khaemwese, the fourth son of Ramesses II, as part of his duties as High Priest of Ptah, had supervised the burial of sacred Apis bulls at Saqqara. Originally, individual burial chambers for the bulls had been dug directly below the offering chapels on the surface above. But Khaemwese changed this plan: instead of individual tombs for each bull, he wanted a series of connected underground corridors and chambers. Later visitors called the resulting labyrinth the "Serapaeum," and in it Apis bulls were interred in burial chambers that lined the long corridors. It was possible that KV 5 was an adaptation of this

Serapaeum model, with offering chapels on an upper level and burial chambers on a lower. That meant we had to look for a lower
level of rooms. We decided to see where the downward-sloping
corridor 11 led.

First, we had to increase our workforce because we were about
100 meters (330 feet) from the tomb entrance, which necessitated
a bucket brigade of nearly forty men to cart away the debris.
Luckily, however, the debris here was only about a meter deep and
consisted mainly of fine silts. This far inside KV 5 the floods had
slowed considerably and could carry only silts, not large stones.
Digging, therefore, was relatively easy.

It took us only two weeks to dig twenty-five meters (eighty feet)
down the midline of the corridor. Then the ceiling level dropped a
dramatic eighty centimeters and ahead was a sheer face of bedrock.
An abrupt change in ceiling height in New Kingdom tomb corridors
nearly always means that the sloping floor is replaced by a staircase.
Corridor 11 was no exception. We found a finely cut staircase, the
left and right thirds of which were actual steps with risers and
treads, the central third of which was a sloping ramp. Egyptian
architects provided for this kind of ramp/staircase in corridors so
that a sarcophagus could be slid down the ramp while priests
walked along on either side, accompanying it into the burial chamber. Immediately beyond such a staircase, the floor and ceiling of
the corridor usually leveled out, was leading to a doorway into a
burial chamber. In corridor 11, the floor and ceiling beyond the
ramp/staircase were not exactly level, but sloped only slightly. The
evidence seemed clear that we were following the route of the
funeral procession, and therefore a burial chamber must lie somewhere ahead of us. I mentioned this to our workmen, who talked
excitedly among themselves about this wonderful turn of events.

"Do you think there will be gold inside the burial room?"
Mohammed asked Said.

Said turned to Ahmed. "Will it be like Tutankhamun's tomb?
Do you think it will be filled with statues?"

Ahmed was more restrained. "Of course there may not be much, but there has to be something. These are the sons of the greatest king of Egypt! He would not let them be buried as peasants."

"Don't get too excited, Ahmed," I said as the conversations got louder. "Only two tombs in the valley contained gold and jewels. The rest were nearly empty. And we know that KV 5 was robbed."

"But if we think good thoughts, maybe we will find treasure. We want you to be happy, Doctor!"

"I will be happy if we find an inscription on the wall. That will be enough."

"Then can we keep the gold, Doctor?" Said laughed.

"Don't let the inspector hear you talk about keeping the gold, Said. He'll think you're stealing."

The excitement mounted as we exposed the staircase and found that the steps were nicely cut, but with chipped and broken edges.

"The steps were broken by the weight of a stone sarcophagus!" Said declared.

"Perhaps several sarcophagi came along this corridor," said Mohammed. "Maybe even blocks of gold! Gold is very heavy; it would break steps like these." Several of the workmen nodded in agreement.

At this point, we had descended eight steps on each side of the central ramp. The debris beyond the steps was suddenly deeper, and we were digging our way through three meters of silts and fine chips. There was so little space between the debris and the ceiling that we could not see what lay ahead.

"I think we're nearing another doorway," I said to Susan, who had come down to inspect the work. "The next two or three days will show us where we might be going." I didn't want to show too much excitement because the workmen's enthusiasm was difficult to control at times like these. Even so, we had to be careful enough to record and analyze the stratigraphy and the artifacts. I also shared their excitement and their frustration, and would have loved to dig as quickly as possible. The workmen were moving nearly a cubic meter of debris every two hours, nearly double our rate at the top of corridor 11. The men could sense that a prize was almost in their grasp.

We began work the next morning at 6:00 A.M. and by breakfast time, at nine, the men had dug through the top ten centimeters of the debris and had found another vertical stone face, indicating a drop in the ceiling. However, we couldn't tell how far down it went.

"This is where the next doorway is," Mohammed said. "And there will be steps, too, just like before, God willing."

The men decided to forgo their breakfast break. I stood next to them, keeping a watchful eye on the work. About eleven o'clock, I asked Mohammed and the other workmen to stop digging. Taking a trowel, I carefully began removing the last few centimeters of silts, slowly exposing the vertical drop, moving from the left side wall across to the right nearly two meters away. I worked like this for half an hour, then had Ahmed join me. He took the left side, I the right, and for half an hour more we continued digging. We had removed twenty centimeters of debris below the ceiling, then thirty, then forty.

It seemed certain that we were following the path to a lower level. After clearing a passage down sloping corridor 11, we had dug twenty meters to a staircase, then another ten meters beyond. Slope, stairs, ramps—everything indicated that a lower level and the burial chambers of the sons of Ramesses II lay just in front of us. Ahmed and I dug another twenty centimeters of debris. As we cleared away the last bits from the vertical face, our work revealed . . . nothing! In front of us there lay only solid bedrock. The corridor simply stopped. We had hit a dead end. The men were so glum at this depressing news that I told Ahmed to stop the work half an hour early. We would go home, have a shower and some lunch, then try to rethink our ideas about KV 5.

Usually, the drive down from the Valley of the Kings at the end of the day is a noisy journey. Our two pickup trucks are bursting with twenty men each, with others hanging from the sides, another seven or eight sitting on the roof. Everyone claps and sings and jokes during the drive. On this day, there was only silence. When we reached the village of Ta'arif, the men climbed slowly off the truck and began their labored walk home. They were not looking forward to telling their wives and parents and children that yesterday's great hopes had all been dashed.

"Don't worry, Doctor," Ahmed said. "There are many other corridors, and one of them is the right one. I am sure, God willing. Maybe you should go to the bank tomorrow. It will bring us luck."

I did not go to the bank, but instead spent the morning with the workmen as they dug down to floor level in corridor 11 and exposed the rest of the blank wall we had run into. I wanted to have Francis, our photographer, take shots of the staircase before he returned to Cairo. There were surprisingly few potsherds or objects at the end of the corridor, partly because the floodwaters were not able to carry objects of any weight this far into the tomb. The few we did find were within ten centimeters of the floor and almost certainly were carried into this part of the tomb by human, not natural, agents.

By the following morning, enough debris had been removed for Mohammed to begin working with trowel and brush, cleaning the floor of the corridor for Francis's photography. Within an hour, Mohammed asked me to come over to where he was crouched, brushing the debris in front of the wall.

"What is this, Doctor?" He pointed with the brush handle at what looked like a layer of blue powder. I took the flashlight and together we swept more of the chocolate-colored silt away from the brightly colored material. I bent down, my nose nearly touching the debris.

"It's plaster, Mohammed. Be very careful. This is unusual."

We continued to brush the silt away from what indeed was a centimeter-thick coat of fine plaster, a mixture of silt and sand with wheat-chaff temper used as a binding agent. The blue surface was still bright and in remarkably good condition. By quitting time, we had exposed the entire end of the corridor, an area two meters wide and over three meters long. It was completely covered with the plaster layer, but as the floor rose behind us, toward the staircase, this disappeared. It seems to have been applied only to the last few meters of the corridor.

Plaster floors are extremely rare in Egyptian tombs—and temples too, for that matter—not only because the floors were rarely finished this way, but also because plaster was so easily destroyed by traffic, erosion, and flooding that it didn't survive in the archaeological record. The plaster floor in KV 5 was unique in the Valley of the Kings.

At 11:00 A.M., two hours before we were to stop work, Francis, our photographer, emerged from the tomb, where he'd been working since 6:00 A.M., and I don't think I'd ever seen a filthier human being. Francis is about thirty years old, a bit over six feet tall, and is rarely seen in anything but a T-shirt and baggy Indian-style pants. Today, coming out of the tomb, his clothes were soaking wet from perspiration and plastered with a thick layer of tomb dust. His long red hair, which curls into natural dreadlocks, was tightly bound in a bandanna.

For the past seven hours, Francis had been crawling into the smallest spaces imaginable, wriggling through blocked doorways into unexcavated tomb chambers, photographing the room interiors before we dug them out. This was arduous work, undertaken in hot, humid, dirty conditions. In these miserable spots, Francis and a workman who was carrying his tripods, lights, cameras, and cables, set up in spaces that were often no more than a foot high. He took photographs of each chamber as well as shots of the rubble and details of inscriptions or carvings on the walls. A single photograph often took more than an hour to set up, and a thousand things could go wrong: loss of electricity or a blown lamp, a slipped tripod clamp, a misread light meter, a leg cramp. The heat and humidity often fogged his camera lenses, and Fran sometimes had to sit for half an hour or more until the temperatures equalized. It amazes me that he does this awful work and still emerges at the end of the day in good humor, ready for the next challenge. And miraculously, even in these conditions, his photographs are superb.

Now, climbing out of the tomb, he undid his bandanna and shook limestone chips from his hair. "I had a few extra minutes and crawled into chamber five. There are some interesting sherds lying on top of the fill," he said. "Do you want me to do the room tomorrow and take detailed shots of them, too?"

I cringed at the idea. Chamber 5 was considered by our engineers to be seriously dangerous. It lies almost directly beneath the roadway where decades of buses have idled with motors running, shaking the bedrock to bits. Originally, there were about three meters of solid bedrock between the ceiling of this chamber and the roadway above. Now, there are fewer than seventy-five centimeters of limestone, and even this is in poor condition. The room is large, with several pillars, perhaps eight or ten that once held up the ceiling. But all of the pillars have collapsed, and the room is filled to within a few centimeters of the ceiling with razor-sharp limestone chips and huge limestone blocks that hang precariously from the ceiling.

"Chamber five? Absolutely not, Fran. I'd rather keep clear of five until we can get the engineers to give us a plan to shore it up."

"Okay," he said, "But I'll be happy to do it if you think it needs doing."

"Let's wait. Today, I'd like you to shoot the plaster floor we've found in corridor eleven. Tomorrow, maybe you can set up some sort of makeshift studio in chamber seven and do some test shots. Susan has a lot of small objects ready to be photographed. "

"You got it!" he said.

Two years ago, Francis walked into my Cairo office—he was well scrubbed that day—with an impressive portfolio of photographs he'd taken of historic sites in Istanbul. Simply, calmly, and with absolute conviction, he told me he was a good photographer, that he wanted to work with us, and that it was inconceivable that our project could proceed efficiently without him. He has proved himself correct on all counts.

*   *   *

FRANCIS devoted the next morning to taking more photographs of the plaster floor, and we returned to the corridor after breakfast. We also decided to clear the last side chamber on the left at the end of chamber 11. It looked as if the plaster floor in the corridor extended into this room, and I was anxious to find a clue—any clue—that might explain why corridor 11 had been dug all this distance only to stop suddenly. The room was completely filled with fine silts and limestone chips, with only an occasional potsherd visible in the fill. It took the workmen four days to clear the chamber completely and reach the floor level. There was no decoration on the walls, and only a few fingernail-sized traces of plaster still hung from their rough surfaces.

We found only fifteen potsherds and a few fragments of animal bones in the entire room, a chamber filled with thirty cubic meters of debris. That was all, except that here, too, the floor had been plastered, not with a single one-centimeter layer of colored plaster, but with three layers, one atop the other, each a centimeter thick, each a different color. The uppermost layer was dark blue, the second reddish brown, the lowest—the first to be applied—off-white.

"What is this, Doctor? What was this room?" Ahmed asked.

"I don't know," I said, repeating the line I have used over and over again while clearing KV 5. "I don't think it's a burial chamber. The door is only seventy centimeters wide. But certainly the room is something special. It is very unusual to have three layers of different-colored plaster. This may be the only monument in all of Egypt with a floor like this. KV 5 has given us something very special."

"KV 5 is very confusing, Doctor. Sometimes I go home and think about it and then I cannot sleep."

"I know the feeling, Ahmed. Believe me, I know the feeling."

wedding music

el tarif village, gurnah. 97

11

BROKEN POTS AND EVIL DUCKS

THE Antiquities Department's chief signmaker for Upper Egypt arrived at the valley unannounced on a Thursday morning late in the autumn of 1996, bringing a load of new signs to be erected in front of the tombs currently open to the public. There were already about a dozen signs in the valley, but they had been erected several years ago and give rambling and often incorrect descriptions of the tombs. Many of the stick-on letters have fallen off or faded in the sun, and the local inspectors have been trying for several years to get them replaced. Now someone—none of us is certain who—finally decided that new signs with short, catchy, English-only texts were needed. At 9:00 A.M., a truck appeared and unloaded a pile of 1- by 1.5-meter signs in front of the tomb of Tutankhamun. The inspectors talked excitedly about the signs and invited the signmaker to tea.

The signmaker is a rather arrogant and apparently myopic fellow, about forty-five years old, who I gather has been doing this kind of work for many years. But as we sat and drank tea in the inspector's office, it became clear that he did not know a word of any language other than Arabic. He painted his signs by copying whatever text was set before him and, unfortunately, the person who wrote those texts was an English-language illiterate.

The sign for the tomb of Merenptah was apparently supposed to begin "Tomb of the fourth king of the 19th Dynasty." Instead, it read, "The fourking 19th Oynesty," and then continued:

> tomb is considered one of the greatest tombs
> and is distinguished with its beautifal rema
> ining inscriptions the text oe Re Prayers
> BoookGatesBook and what is exists in the
> nether world

Later in the day, I took one of the inspectors aside and suggested that some of the signs might be improved upon (or at least made less amusing) if someone who knew English checked them over. The inspector was disappointed at first, then embarrassed, when I pointed out the errors. As we left the valley, he pointed out that if the signs were rejected, they probably would not be replaced and all we would accomplish would be to hurt the signmaker's feelings. So, the next morning, the signs went up. My favorite reads:

> The wall is Oecoratd with The Book of
> the DeadBook of the
> Book the Book BookBook.

Soon after, there was a flurry of sign installation on the West Bank. The Luxor City Council installed dozens of huge, black signs with bright yellow lettering: "Smile You Are In Luxor"; "You Are In The Embrace Of The History"; "Look You Are In The Ancient"; and "This Is Monumental Area." A directional sign that is supposed to point the way to the valley instead points away from the road and into a sheer cliff.

We worked for several weeks in 1996 in one of the side chambers of corridor 7, but were forced to stop work about 20 centimeters above the flood level. There was so much decorated plaster lying in the debris that excavation had to be done with dental picks, trowels, and brushes. In another side chamber (room 7L), we were able to reconstruct the entire wall scenes (at least on paper) from these fragments, but we had to make sure that the workmen recovered them without damaging their fragile painted surfaces. This kind of meticulous work is one of the most exciting parts of an archaeological excavation. Working to salvage plaster fragments, to identify the hieroglyph or figure of which they formed part, and then putting them together to create a complete picture of the wall is like assembling a huge jigsaw puzzle. To prepare for this, Susan and I browsed through several KV tombs, looking for winged figures with feather motifs and undulating snake patterns similar to the ones we found in KV 5. We needed comparative material to help us determine what sort of figure a painted feather might have come from. Susan worked like a detective, piecing together the clues.

The plaster fragments in chamber 8 were also interesting. On Saturday, after Francis photographed the decorated blocks in this chamber, Ahmed and I began removing other large stone fragments and found several that were vividly painted with bands of red, yellow, blue, and white, and with lines of small, cursive hieroglyphs written in black ink. The size and style of the hieroglyphs were unusual for tomb walls, and I was anxious to clean them and translate the texts.

On Monday we finally reached floor level in the northeast quarter of chamber 8. To our delight, we found a great many decorated plaster fragments and two large chunks of wall, one carved with a figure of a son wearing elaborate robes, the other with part of a hieroglyphic text. This area required some careful recording, so I stopped the work in chamber 8 until Francis could return from Cairo to photograph several large decorated blocks that had fallen from the wall onto the floor. The men were transferred to chamber 9, a mirror image of chamber 8, except that its ceiling is slightly vaulted instead of flat, which is more usual. We also found traces of plaster on the ceiling and walls as well as many marks

made by ancient surveyors in red and black ink that were apparently used to guide the quarrymen as they laid out the curvature of
the ceiling and blocked out places for side-chamber doorways. The
location of many of these marks, and the ancient plaster chinking
used to fill some of the larger ceiling cracks, indicate that a great
deal of the bedrock damage in KV 5's rear sections occurred during ancient times, not modern. That explains why so much of the
decorated plaster has fallen away: it was applied in especially thick
coats to fill deep cracks and fissures that were already there; over
the past three millennia, it simply collapsed of its own weight.

Clearing chamber 9 to floor level was a slow process that took
us over a week. The debris contained relatively few objects, and
was as hard as concrete. Once it was cleared, Susan and I spent
several hours staring at faint traces of incised decoration on the
badly fractured walls. At first, we couldn't see anything, but as we
played our lamps and flashlights back and forth across the surface,
we began to make out occasional scratches, incisions, and daubs of
paint. They were extremely faint, but there were enough for us to
reconstruct drawings of entire scenes.

The best-preserved wall section is the right jamb of the entry
door, where we discovered a relief showing the recumbent figure
of the jackal god Anubis. Anubis is a fairly common figure in
Egyptian tombs, but he is rarely found in doorways. In two other
tombs where he was shown on the doorjambs (QV 42 and 52), the
doors lead into simple, undecorated side-chambers off the main
tomb corridor. In the only other place where he is found, the tomb
of Merenptah (KV 8), the figure is carved on a jamb in the main
corridor. None of these examples suggest that Anubis's appearances on a doorjamb meant that the room has any special importance. However, in KV 5, the room beyond the Anubis jamb—
chamber 9—*seems* to be important because it has a vaulted ceiling,
which often indicates that the room was used as a burial chamber.
Chamber 9's doorway was very narrow, but even so it was worth
careful examination.

The more Susan and I stared at the chamber's walls, the more we saw. A few additional very faint traces of paint and carving became visible, and Susan thought she could make out the head of a standing figure of the king and the feathers of a winged sun disk. These traces would take patience and skill to reconstruct.

As the digging continued, we also had several men return to work in chamber 7L, a side-chamber near the Osiris statue at the back of the long corridor. Even though there were several interesting traces of decorated plaster on its walls and many plaster fragments in the fill, by and large, we were facing one of the dull and plodding periods that are so common in archaeology: for every day of exciting and wonderful discoveries, there were thirty or forty days of dirt-moving. As the workmen's routine became increasingly mechanical, it was hard to keep them from putting their brains in neutral and coasting through the day. I even found myself mindlessly brushing a chamber floor, thinking of nothing, then suddenly realizing that I was sweeping small fragments of plaster around. It's difficult to concentrate during long periods of tedious work, and so I took to moving the men—and myself—several times during the day from one task to another to help us stay relatively alert. Sometimes it worked, sometimes it didn't.

The only thing that seemed to brighten everyone's spirits was a nice find, and eventually we made a small discovery in chamber 9 that was just what we needed. It wasn't spectacular, but it was promising: a piece of alabaster with a bird's wing carefully cut on its surface—a design called a *rishi* (feather) motif by Egyptologists. It was another fragment from an alabaster sarcophagus lid.

"This means that the sons really were buried here, doesn't it, Doctor?" Ahmed said. "I knew we would find proof." He turned to the workmen who were probing around the fragment. "Keep a sharp eye out for other things, Mohammed. This is a good sign."

ON our last day with the workmen for the next several months, we finished cleaning a side-chamber (room 12K) off corridor 12 that contained a fair amount of pottery but little else. One of the sherds, small and painted, triggered Susan's memory.

"I just know I've seen this pattern before," she said as she stared at the sherd. "I know! We found another one exactly like it last year at the end of corridor seven." We went to our storeroom, rifled through boxes and bags, and, sure enough, in one of the 124 bags of pottery from that corridor, there it was. The pattern was identical, and the sherd even fit together with the one from 12K! That two sherds from the same pot lay over 40 meters (130 feet) apart shows just how thoroughly the flashfloods had tossed the debris about in the tomb.

We are fortunate that Susan enjoys pottery and is so good at studying it. Almost every area of KV 5 contains great quantities of potsherds and, even as a rough estimate, we already had several tons of them. A pot can be broken, but its fragments, called sherds or shards, never completely disappear, and for this reason are among the most common objects found in archaeological sites. The pottery from KV 5 has regularly overwhelmed us since we first began clearing chamber 1.

Potsherds demand more time than almost any other archaeological artifacts. Imagine that a sudden flood had destroyed a china shop in a foreign country and buried a million sherds in mud and silt. Now imagine that you are told to sort through the mess and to write labels on every single sherd, no matter how small; you are to glue back together any pieces that joined; and you are to draw, photograph, and analyze each vessel. Then you are expected to write a history of china manufacture, describe the uses of china, the trade in china, and the significance of china decorations and shapes. Most of us would last less than a week before simply giving up. Not Susan. Each day she works for hours, doing these very things. First, she carefully examines each sherd for painted decoration, then washes and dries them in the sun. Each sherd is labeled in ink with a reference number. For example, "KV 5 / 2 / 30" means that the sherd comes from the thirtieth bag of pottery from chamber 2 in tomb KV 5. She records detailed information on the kind of clay the sherd was made from, the treatment of its surface, its decoration, the shape and type of vessel it came from, its date, and a list of any objects or features associated with it. Then Susan attaches a photograph and a drawing of the sherd. The whole process is truly a labor of love—meticulous, time-consuming, highly skilled—and absolutely essential for the proper understanding of our tomb.

This pottery work also fascinates the thousands of tourists who pass by KV 5 each day. Some ask if we'll sell them a sherd. A few have even jumped over the rope and the Keep Out signs that surround the entrance to KV 5 and tried to steal sherds as souvenirs. Mohammed has become very good at intercepting them. Susan works in a tent directly in front of the tomb entrance, not ten feet from the main path into the valley, and her every move is watched by the hordes of tourists, some of whom stand for half an hour or more, discussing what is going on and taking scores of photographs of the scene.

Once, an American tourist watched Susan at work, then shouted to her friend, "Look at the pot washer, Ethel. My God! It's a woman! I didn't know *they* could do that stuff!" Another tourist, a German, pointed at Susan, who was trying to glue two sherds together, and said in disgust, "If your workers had not broken them, you would not have to fix them!"

On the last day of the season, we paid the workmen at noon, bade them farewell, and went back to the hotel. The next three days were going to be painful because six of our workmen insisted that we come to their homes for lunch or dinner. It's not that we don't enjoy the company, but for the next three days we would be eating two gargantuan meals daily. Susan and I knew we would have to do serious dieting between Friday and Christmas.

First, we went with Ahmed and Nubie to dinner at Mohammed's. At some point the dinner conversation turned to the numerous Late Period tombs lying among the village houses in this northern part of the necropolis where Mohammed lives. Mohammed said that none of the tombs were dangerous structurally, but anyone who entered one of them while walking behind a duck would face certain death. I laughed, thinking this was the beginning of a joke, but Mohammed was absolutely serious.

"It is true, Doctor. I swear. Everybody knows that: there are some very bad *jinns* in this village. Their spirits live inside some of the ducks here—we never know which ones, so we say prayers whenever we touch or feed or kill any of them—and the spirit is always trying to get inside a human body. If you follow a duck inside a tomb—the duck will try to lead you there—the spirit will jump out of the duck and enter your body through your nose or ear and it will take control of you. You will shake and writhe and scream and the *jinn* will speak with your voice and say terrible things—terrible things!—and will demand that you do many bad things. Then it will kill you. It is terrible."

"Mohammed is absolutely correct, Doctor," said Nubie. "I saw this with my own eyes. A boy in our village was walking here and went into the tomb and the duck jumped on his face and the *jinn* entered his body. When we found him at the tomb entrance, he was screaming and frothing at the mouth and shaking all over and his eyes were very red and very big."

Ahmed looked very excited and moved to the edge of his seat. "Yes! I remember this. We had to get the village *shaykha*, a very old, blind lady with great powers, and she came and talked to the *jinn* and said prayers and recited the Koran. After many hours, she convinced the *jinn* to leave the body and return to the duck. But it was very difficult because you must convince the *jinn* to leave from the feet and not through the eyes or nose or ears, because he will break them and the boy will be left blind or deaf."

Why would a duck be given such awesome powers? This whole conversation reminded me of a line from a prayer in the Pyramid Texts, the earliest religious texts from Egypt, dating to about 2200 BCE: "There is no one living who makes accusation against me, there is no duck which makes accusation against me. . . ."

The next day, Tuesday, we had lunch at our hotel, brought from Big Ahmed's house, and coincidentally we were served roast duck.

We often eat duck on Tuesdays because that is the market day in our village.

"How do I know this duck is not one of the *jinns*?" I asked.

Big Ahmed thought for a moment. "It may be the color," he said, "or the shape of its head. I will ask. But don't worry. This duck is dead. And it is very tasty."

IN the spring of 1997, after the holidays were over and we had completed some extensive library and laboratory studies in Cairo, Brendhan Hight, KV 5's web site manager, Francis, and I drove back to Luxor for our spring field season. Susan was in the United States, but she was going to join us in another two weeks. In the meantime, Brendhan and I were working at the Chicago House library, and Francis was photographing scenes of the sons of Ramesses II in the Ramesseum and Luxor Temple. We were planning to start work in KV 5 when our conservator, Lotfy Khaled, arrived on Saturday. We still had a lot of cleaning, conservation, and photography to do in the chambers we'd cleared and, as usual, there was a substantial backlog of pottery from the last season that needed to be labeled.

Our first day back, we went by Nubie's house to retrieve the boxes of papers, books, tripods, and other equipment we had stored there. Nubie Abdel Basset is the longest-serving member of our project, having joined the TMP in 1980 when he was only seventeen years old. Early on, David Goodman recognized Nubie's abilities and taught him rudimentary surveying techniques. He even took Nubie to Sacramento for six months to learn English and more surveying skills. Today Nubie proudly wears the title of the TMP's assistant surveyor.

As we sat in the unfinished red-brick house Nubie is building for his family, drinking tea with him, his mother, Umm Mohammed, his pregnant wife, Zeinab, and their three children (Mohammed, Mona, and Hassan), they told us in breathless tones about the horror Zeinab had experienced two nights ago. Nubie had not yet returned from Giza, where he had been working with another archaeological project. About two o'clock in the morning, Zeinab woke up and felt something on her neck. Some sixth sense told her not to move. After two or three minutes, she cautiously looked down and in a shaft of moonlight coming through the bedroom window saw a cobra, perhaps three feet long, slowly crawling across the bed and over her body. Zeinab said her heart was pounding so loudly she was afraid it would startle the snake. The reptile finally slithered onto the floor and out the door, passing under little Hassan's crib on the way. Zeinab immediately got out of bed, grabbed the baby, awakened the other two children, and rushed to her mother's house. Together, they went to find the village snake charmer.

They returned to the house—it was now about 4:00 A.M.—and the snake charmer began to search for the cobra. After half an hour, he found it behind some boxes in a storage room. He grabbed the cobra by the tail, snapped it hard against the doorjamb, and watched as its head flew across the room. Umm Mohammed and Zeinab became increasingly agitated as they told the story. By its end, I was sweating and shivering, too, sharing their fear. That night, back at our hotel, I checked every cranny of the room and closed all windows, shutters, and screens before turning in.

Snakes are not common on the West Bank, but they live in sugarcane fields because of the many small animals that live there, and houses near those fields are occasionally troubled by them. It is very rare that anyone is bitten, however.

EARLY on the first Saturday morning in the new season, I picked up Ahmed, Nubie, and our inspector, and drove to the Valley of the Kings. It was only six-thirty, half an hour before work was to begin, but already several dozen men were standing around the entrance to KV 5. This was the day we hired our first workmen.

This is always a tricky business. On many expeditions, it is customary simply to tell the foreman how many men are needed and to leave the hiring to him. But I have discovered that according to local custom, a foreman will hire only his own friends and relatives and then take 10 to 15 percent of their wages as a commission. This can mean a windfall profit for the foreman, sometimes hundreds of pounds a week, and he still becomes a hero in his neighborhood. The system is called *wasta*, meaning "it's who you know that gets you ahead." It creates problems because such nepotism can cause hard feelings. In years past, I've found myself branded as unfair or we've spent the first week of work shunned by site guards or angry workmen whose family members didn't get jobs. And on one occasion, someone shorted out our electrical system.

This time I vowed we'd do things differently. I have brought together our foreman, our two top workmen from previous seasons, the chief of the KV guards, our KV inspectors, and the man who makes tea for all of the above (an especially influential fellow), and made them a proposal. Each can bring three men of their choice to work for us. This will ensure that several families get a piece of the action, and even villagers living some distance from the valley, who normally have no chance of employment here, can earn some money. If one of the men turns out to be lazy or incompetent, his "sponsor" will bring in a replacement. But if two or more of a sponsor's men turn out badly, he will forfeit those positions for the rest of the season.

Of course, there is grousing.

"I am much more senior than Mohammed," says one guard. "He should bring two workmen and I should bring eight."

"But the guard is already a rich man," says Mohammed. "He owns two water buffalo. He should bring only one man. I am very poor and should bring ten."

And so it went for an hour, some men shouting, posturing, making menacing gestures, others whispering gossip in my ear about how lazy their neighbors were.

Still, by 8:00 A.M. we have put twenty men on the payroll who seem to be a pleasant and, we hope, hardworking bunch. And already there is good-natured teasing about whose workmen will do the best job and whose will be fired for laziness.

At the turn of the century, the great English archaeologist Flinders Petrie believed that expeditions in Egypt should only employ men between the ages of fifteen and twenty. After that, he claimed, "many turn stupid." The good ones, he continued, should be "regarded much as old servants are in a good household." There may be something in the second idea, but I certainly don't hold with the first—whatever it means. Our workmen are fine and intelligent people, and I have no qualms entrusting to them our work and, not infrequently, our lives.

All of the men are anxious to work. Some need to earn money for their families; others want to achieve some special goal. Sadat, for example (no relation to Egypt's late president), is about twenty-five years old; he's strong, bright, and wants to earn part of the several thousands of pounds he needs in order to get married. Mohammed Ahmed, who is twenty years old and whose father has died recently, is now the principal supporter of his mother and four younger sisters. Yasser is thirty years old, and his wife is pregnant with a third child—three is it, he hastens to assure us, there will be no more. Hosni, twenty-one years old, wants money to attend the hotel-management school in Luxor. Ramadan, twenty-eight years old, is a hard worker who has been with us before. He now wants money to buy the fifty thousand mud bricks needed to start building a home for his family. Hussein, twenty years old, is a very pleasant and jovial soccer fanatic who wants a television set at home so that he can watch the two most popular football teams, National and Zamalek. "I want see National to win!" he adds with a grin.

There have been some significant changes in the kinds of workmen we hire these days. Twenty years ago, archaeologists customarily hired their workmen from the village of Quft, about fifteen kilometers north of Luxor. These Quftis were descendants of workmen trained by Flinders Petrie nearly a century ago, and by tradition they were considered the best workmen available.

Unfortunately, their skills have not kept pace with the dramatic changes in archaeological techniques. Egyptologists no longer consider the Quftis necessary, and most have moved on to work in other fields. Archaeologists today prefer to hire from villages near the excavation site and to train the workmen themselves.

Another change has been in the education of the men. Even fifteen years ago, very few were literate, but today all but six of the twenty men we employ can read and write. They also take an active interest in the work we do, asking questions about Ramesses II, discussing with each other the significance of the artifacts we find, offering suggestions about the progress of the work. Several have even asked if there are Arabic-language books on ancient Egypt, and I am only too happy to encourage this interest.

In contrast to the common stereotype of Upper Egyptians, I have found them to be hardworking, intelligent, and kind. Upper Egypt—the Nile Valley between Assiut and Aswan—is to Lower Egypt as the Deep South is to the rest of America. It is dirt-poor; it has virtually no industry and depends almost entirely upon agriculture for income. It has the country's lowest literacy rate (about 22 percent); and for years it has been utterly ignored by a government that happily lavishes money and training schools and projects on governorates in the north. Whenever there is a nitwit in a television comedy, he is called a Sa'idi (an Upper Egyptian), as is also any lout in a drama. Sa'idis are always the brunt of jokes: how do you identify a Sa'idi's luggage at the airport? His is the bag labeled "Portland Cement." The poverty and illiteracy and economic hardships are indeed a reality, but to label Sa'idis stupid or oafish is simply wrong. Our workmen are excellent examples. They are a pleasure to work with.

By 8:00 A.M., all the men were happy and anxious to begin work. We had turned away a great many who had been hoping for a job, but we took their names and promised they'd be first on the list if we increased the size of our workforce. None of them had asked what the wages would be. They had a vague idea, but that was irrelevant. The important thing was to be employed. God knows, these people badly need whatever income they can get. Jobs in this area are scarce and an average *family* earns less than a hundred dollars a month. Yet a kilo of meat costs about six dollars a pound; a donkey costs about fifty dollars; a water buffalo, over seven hundred; a wedding, five or ten thousand. The few jobs that are available, mostly as agricultural laborers, offer about a dollar a day. We pay five dollars a day, a respectable wage, and this year, as in years past, our foreman, Ahmed, and I will be constantly implored by villagers to give them or one of their relatives a job—any job—even if only for a short time.

WE put the men to work in chamber 3, the sixteen-pillared hall. Clearing through the entrance of this chamber, then north and south along its west wall, was crucial to determine why KV 5 has so unusual a plan. The sixteen-pillared hall appeared to be the center of this enigmatic complex, and its decoration should play a significant role in any interpretation. We were now ready to clear a one-meter-wide section alongside the west wall down to floor level, avoiding any of the chamber's pillars, as we had been instructed. Now, we hoped we would be able to see what would happen with the recut floor of chamber 3; with the date of the carvings in corridors 12 and 20; and with the recutting of the doorways at the tomb's entrance, between chambers 1 and 2, chambers 2 and 3, 3 and 7, 3 and 12, and others. This information would be extremely helpful in tracing the growth of KV 5.

The small trailer given to our project by Santa Fe International came down from Cairo today and was now installed beside the entrance to KV5. This would undoubtedly make our work and our lives this season quite different from past years. This twenty-two-foot caravan was freshly painted an unobtrusive desert tan, scrubbed inside and out, fitted with electricity, a photo studio, computer desk, drafting table, and shelves. Now we would not have to stand at a worktable, swatting flies in the blazing sun before an audience of thousands of photograph-taking tourists asking over and over in a dozen different languages: "Find any-thing interesting?" "What are you doing?" "Do you like doing this?" "Do you sell bottled water?"

It was an enormous relief to escape the crowds, but not fifteen minutes after we had moved into the trailer, the tour guides began knocking on the door to complain. One told us that our work had become a major tourist attraction and he was sure that if we deprived his clients of a photo opportunity, he'd take home fewer tips. We offered to erect a small sign with a plan of the tomb and photographs of objects and decorated walls. This seemed to satisfy him.

Our new field office turned out to bring us good luck, because early in the day it arrived, we found three pieces of a single canopic jar inscribed with the name of the ninth-born son of Ramesses II, Sethy. They lay in the doorway between chambers 2 and 3, surrounded by several good-sized fragments of mummified tissue, fragments of wooden statues or furniture, and several faience "wiglets," parts of a wig worn by small statues. There also were huge quantities of pottery. It took Susan ten days or more to study the backlog we'd already amassed.

We also had been finding large quantities of animal bones. At our invitation, a few weeks into the season, Duke University professor Elwyn Simons flew down from his paleontological work in the Fayum to identify some of our faunal material. Several days later, my colleague at AUC Dr. Salima Ikram also examined the bones. We have collected hundreds of bird and animal bones from the debris in KV 5, and hope that their identification may indicate what some of the rooms were used for. The distribution of the faunal remains is intriguing: there are human bones in chambers 1, 2, and 3; cow bones in 4, 7, and 12; hyena and jackal bones in 13; and pig in chamber 3. Some of this material had been washed in, of course, but much of it may have been part of the original offerings placed here for the sons' funerals. In chamber 8, for example, dozens of cow bones were certainly a part of ancient offerings, since they have the saw and cleaver marks of ritual slaughter. The jackal, on the other hand, might have crawled into the tomb and died there. Its bones had been scattered about by floods, but we have found almost enough of them to assemble the entire skeleton.

DAVID Wallace and his BBC film crew arrived yesterday, for the third season of filming. He also brought along a representative of ABC/Kane Productions in Washington and an ABC still cameraman. As usual, things turned chaotic the moment their bus pulled up at the entrance to the valley. The filming this time would be brief—only five days—but David already warned me that we would be shooting from 7:00 A.M. until 5:00 P.M. daily, and that I should be on call at all hours. We were joined later in the morning by Hugh Downs of ABC News, who hosted the American version (not the BBC version) of the final program. He was very pleasant, and surprisingly knowledgeable about ancient Egypt. We filmed a couple of sequences on the hillside above KV 5, and Hugh made the climb to the top with less puffing and panting than some of David's film crew, most of whom were at least two decades younger.

WHEN we were able to get back to our work, it took several weeks to clear the debris from along the west wall of chamber 3. Susan was delighted, because there are traces of very large scenes that are mirror images of each other, on either side of the central door. Each appears to show four life-sized, seated sons of Ramesses II, facing a standing priest wearing a panther skin. Two of the sons' faces are well preserved and beautifully carved. The rest of the wall must have been equally dramatic before the various floodings took their toll. Susan needed many days to draw the faint scratches, all that was left of what originally was an elegantly carved and painted wall.

While Susan worked on that, I began clearing a part of chamber 2 that we had ignored for over a year. We had left the northern third of that chamber undug, because two huge stones had fallen from the ceiling many years ago and lay atop the debris. Breaking and removing them was a major chore, but it had to be done before we could excavate. However, the decoration and texts on the other walls of chamber 2 had been so interesting that we wanted to look at the room's northern wall, too. First, Francis photographed the deep layers of silt that filled the northern third of the chamber. Then, for the rest of the week, the men worked to break the stones into manageable pieces and carted them out of the door. Ahmed slithered into the tiny space between the ceiling and the fallen blocks and wielded his hammer and chisel to break them up. Then he slid the pieces down onto the shoulders of Mohammed or Said or Mansour, who then carried them out the door. Some of the pieces weighed nearly two hundred pounds. The work was dangerous and nerve-racking, not so much because the men were in danger, but because if a stone were to fall it could seriously damage the plaster decoration on the chamber walls.

Once the stones were gone, we were able to clear the northern third of the room. Our goal was to learn whether other sons of Ramesses II were mentioned on the decorated walls hidden by the rubble, and we spent nearly a week digging out the debris. This task was more time-consuming than we'd anticipated, since dozens of pieces of decorated plaster had fallen off the walls during several floodstages and now lay in very friable condition in the rubble. Fortunately, we were able to salvage these fragments, piece them together, and reconstruct on paper a substantial part of what had once been a beautifully carved and brilliantly painted wall. In one scene, Ramesses II is shown presenting his sons to various gods, and in another he stands before a table of offerings and a large canopic box.

On Sunday, we reached floor level. The debris here was filled with scores of objects, and throughout the morning, a beaming Ahmed regularly climbed out of the tomb to hand Susan fragments of inscribed canopic jars, alabaster *ushabtis*, amulets, fragments of wooden coffins, beads, and fragments of mummified human remains, as well as overflowing baskets of potsherds. It was quite a haul and we were all busy cleaning, drawing, photographing, and transcribing this incredibly valuable material.

As the workday was winding down, while Ahmed, Mohammed, and I were troweling more of the debris from the floor, we noticed what appeared to be a crack in the bedrock. Brushing away more of the silt, we saw that it was, instead, a deliberately cut edge.

"It looks as if there might be a pit in the floor, Ahmed," I said. "Or at least some kind of rectangular depression."

"Maybe it's a staircase leading to some lower level," he mused.

"Maybe there will be statues in it," said Mohammed. "Or treasure!"

We didn't have time to explore this at that time, but the next morning we went right back there. After another hour of digging, we found that the breaks formed a large rectangle, about eighty centimeters (thirty-three inches) wide, that extended horizontally over four meters (thirteen feet), the entire length of the chamber. Originally, the depression had been covered over by several large, flat slabs of limestone; one of those slabs still lay in place at the western end. We had dug only about twenty centimeters below the floor of chamber 2, but it seemed likely that the depression was, in fact, a pit. I had no idea how deep the pit might be or what it might have been used for.

Whatever it was, it was potentially very exciting, and the workmen groaned when I said that we'd have to wait before clearing more of the pit . First, we had to deal with the plaster decoration on the wall behind it. If we made a careless move while digging, when removing the debris that was holding some of the plaster to the wall, then the decoration would be lost. I told a disappointed Ahmed to halt the work until our new conservator, Lotfy Khaled, arrived from Rome in two weeks.

The men sighed, and instead went to corridor 12, the steeply sloping passageway we had found at the front of the pillared hall. Last November, we had already cleared about twenty meters of its length, exposing the doors of twelve side chambers. On Saturday, we began digging here again, hacking with picks through the cementlike debris that filled the corridor from floor to ceiling. It was slow going—we could move only about fifty centimeters (twenty inches) forward each day—and given the height and width of the corridor, that meant we were moving about six cubic meters (seventy square feet) of rubble daily. Still, our progress was respectable when you realize that the material had to be carried in small baskets by a bucket brigade extending nearly a hundred meters (three hundred feet) from the dig to the dump site.

After two hours of work, we had gone only about twenty centimeters (eight inches) forward. There was a void at the top of the debris, not more than fifteen centimeters wide, seven centimeters high. When we peered through it, we spotted what looked like a doorjamb about two meters ahead of us. After another six hours of digging, we peered through the opening again. We could see that the door led into a large chamber.

Mohammed and the other workmen apologized for having acted so disappointed when we stopped work in the pit. "This is much, much better, Doctor," said Mohammed, his broad smile showing tea-stained teeth. "I will dream about this tonight."

Early the next morning, I found the workmen excitedly discussing this new door and the room beyond. We immediately started cutting into the debris, and by 9:00 A.M., we had dug through the top of the debris and created a channel large enough for thin Ahmed to crawl through. He was ready to start right away, but I asked him to wait until the breakfast break, when the workmen would be outside and the dust would have settled.

In the meantime, another workman, Saleh, was unfortunately lying in the tent in great pain. Several years ago, in the army, a large piece of equipment had fallen on his knee, and since then he had been having frequent attacks of throbbing pain that were only made worse by operations at the army hospital in Assiut. I drove him to the local clinic, but the doctors were so rude and unhelpful that after twenty minutes we left. I bought some medicine at the local pharmacy, took him home, and told him to rest for a few days. I would send our doctor to see him later.

The last time I had been to that clinic was about a year ago. Driving one morning down to the inspector's office, I found two Danish students lying in a pool of blood alongside the road to the valley. Their motorcycle had skidded on a sandy stretch of asphalt, and they had been thrown head over heels into a field of boulders and sharp limestone fragments. The girl's head wound was bleeding profusely. The young man had a badly scraped arm and was in tears. He knelt over her, sobbing, "It's my fault, I'm sorry, I love you." I drove them to the clinic, took them inside, and discovered a single fly-covered bed with no sheets, a sink with no water, an empty refrigerator, and a doctor with a cigarette dangling from his lips who acted as if he'd never seen blood before and wasn't about to look at it now. This was the "new" clinic, built only a few years ago and still the closest source of medical care for about twenty thousand people on the West Bank. I packed up the two students and drove them across the river to Luxor, where there is a hospital with basic amenities and doctors who, though only slightly better equipped, do care. In Cairo we have access to some of the finest physicians, surgeons, and dentists in the world. What a pity that, once again, the people of Upper Egypt are left to suffer.

I didn't return to the site until 10:00 A.M. Breakfast had ended half an hour earlier, and Ahmed wanted to crawl into the new chamber. We each grabbed hard hats and we went inside.

The crawl space between the debris and the ceiling of the room was extremely small—only about thirty centimeters high. But Ahmed simply lay down and slithered across, pausing every few meters to check his bearings and look around. I, on the other hand, had difficulty finding a path I could move along. But when I finally got there I saw that the room was large. Three pillars were equally spaced along its north–south midline and the room itself appeared to be about five meters (sixteen feet) wide and more than ten meters long. What excited us most, however, was the presence of two doorways cut into the south wall. Crawling over to one door, Ahmed peered through the narrow gap between debris and ceiling.

"This leads to another corridor, Doctor," he said. "I cannot tell for sure, but I think it very long and there are many doorways in its walls."

Another corridor like 7, 10, and 11? If these corridors were like the others in the tomb, then they probably had about twelve side-chambers each, which meant that the total number in KV 5 was not 97, but over 124. If, as seems likely because of its location, the corridor parallel to chamber 12 (corridor 20) is a mirror image of it, then KV 5 has *at least* 150 rooms!

Ahmed and I went topside to tell Susan the news. She smiled and said, "We won't live long enough to dig it all," and returned to washing potsherds. Susan has always been the realist in our family.

OVER the next several weeks, we continued clearing the extremely hard, dense debris in this new corridor, which was heading directly into the center of the valley, toward the tomb of Tutankhamun. The work was slow, and before closing down in March, we had proceeded only about three meters down the corridor, exposing the doorways into four side-chambers along the path.

On the last day of the season, one of our youngest workers, Mostafa, who was only eighteen years old and was working with us for the first time, found a fragment of a large *ushabti*, nicely painted with cursive hieroglyphs. It lay in the fill about two meters along the corridor and bore the cartouche of the pharaoh Setnakht, the first king of Dynasty 20. Setnakht's tomb, KV 14, lies in the very back of the valley, so the statuette must have washed into KV 5 at the end of the New Kingdom or after. That flood must have been fairly powerful to have carried a heavy alabaster fragment so far into the tomb. Mostafa was ecstatic and spent the remainder of the day telling his more blasé co-workers how his careful digging and alertness had produced the discovery.

*   *   *

THE other excitement of the week was a full moon, a partial lunar eclipse, *and* a spectacular view of the comet Hale-Bopp, which hung directly over the Qurn and the Valley of the Kings. It was a marvelous sight, and Ahmed decided that it was a good sign for our digging in KV 5.

The last time this comet was seen on Earth was 4,200 years ago, when Egypt's Sixth Dynasty ruler, Pepi I, sat on the throne. One of the Pyramid Texts carved on the walls of his burial chamber in his pyramid at Saqqara refers to a comet, very possibly the earliest reference to Hale-Bopp itself: "I see what the *nhh*-stars do, because so fair is their shape; it is well for me with them and it is well for them. I am a *nhh*-star, the companion of a *nhh*-star, I become a *nhh*-star, and I will not suffer for ever."

Virginia Lee Davis, a former classmate of mine at Yale, was the first to note that in the hieroglyphic original of this text, the word "*nhh*-star" was written with the drawing of a star followed by the hieroglyph for long hair—a delightful way, she believes, of representing a star with a wispy tail—that is, a comet. (The word "comet" derives from the Greek word for hair, a confirmation of this idea.)

WHEN our conservator, Lotfy Khaled, arrived at KV 5 from Rome in autumn 1997, I immediately asked him to start work stabilizing the north wall of chamber 2, the wall above the pit. This was delicate work. There were traces of the name of the person buried in the pit painted on the plastered wall, but the plaster hung precariously and even a strong breeze could have dislodged it. Lotfy carefully pushed the plaster against the wall and injected epoxy resins to bond it in place. Several days later, he gave us the go-ahead to continue removing debris from the pit. Almost immediately, we began finding artifacts. In the center of the pit, thirty centimeters below the chamber floor, we uncovered a large fragment of burned wood with bits of mummified tissue adhering to it. It was almost certainly part of a coffin, because a tiny piece of gold foil lay beside it, perhaps a part of the gilding of the coffin's lid.

Beside the coffin fragment, we found two inscribed pieces of an alabaster canopic jar bearing the name of Mery-Atum, the sixteenth son of Ramesses II. Actually, there are only two reed-leaf hieroglyphs—which together represent the Egyptian letter *y*—preserved on the fragments, but [Mer]y[Atum] is the only son of Ramesses II whose name contains that letter in such a position within a name. And several of Mery-Atum's titles are carved on the pieces. The canopic jar fragments certainly offer the clearest evidence yet that Mery-Atum, too, was buried in KV 5, but they were not the first clues we had found.

IN 1902, Howard Carter found a Nineteenth Dynasty ostracon lying in debris at the entrance to the Valley of the Kings, apparently close to KV 5. Its text described the location of several KV tombs and other features of the valley. The ostracon was first published by Elizabeth Thomas, who described it as being "like a pirate's chart to buried gold, full of clues we cannot interpret." We do not know the purpose of the ancient text, but its scribe seems to have been intent on precisely recording the locations of several KV tombs:

From *tr(t)yt* to the general-in-chief *(p3 imy-r ms' wr)*
30 cubits; (and to) the tomb of the Greatest of the Seers
    Meryatum,
25 cubits. From *Tr(t)yt* (and? to?)
the tomb of the oils to my Greatest of the Seers, 40 cubits.
Downstream on the northern path where the old tomb is,
30 cubits to the general-in-chief.

On the ostracon's other face:

[From?] the tomb of Isisnofret to the
[tomb of] my Greatest of Seers Meryatum, 200 cubits.
From the end of the Water of the Sky
to the tomb of Isisnofret
445 cubits.

The text is difficult to interpret, but Thomas, and more recently Egyptologist Nicholas Reeves, have made several important suggestions about its content. First, they believe that the title "general-in-chief" *(p3 imy-r ms' wr)* is a reference to Ramesses II. If this is correct—and I think it likely—then the *tr(t)yt* (the Egyptian name for the willow tree), lay 30 cubits (15.7 meters) from the tomb of Ramesses II. The *Tr(t)yt* is also said to lie 25 cubits (13.1 meters) from the tomb of Mery-Atum—that is, from the entrance to KV 5.

The two references in this text to Isisnofret are also important, because if they refer to the Isisnofret who was one of the principal wives of Ramesses II (and not, for example, to the Isisnofret who was married to Ramesses II's son and successor, Merenptah), then they provide a major clue to the location of her tomb. That tomb has never been found, but the ostracon indicates that it lay in the valley— 200 cubits (104.6 meters) from KV 5 and 445 cubits (232.8 meters) from the "Water of the Sky." That phrase refers to those parts of the sheer cliffs surrounding the valley over which floodwaters pour during heavy rainstorms. If we can determine which part of the cliff is the "Water of the Sky," then it shouldn't be too hard to determine roughly the spot referred to. I asked our architect, Walton Chan, to draw a sketch plan of the valley using these data in order to show the places where some future Egyptologist might dig in a search for Isisnofret's tomb. The solid black dots seem the most likely spots.

Finding Isisnofret's tomb would be an important discovery. We know a bit about the other principal wife of Ramesses II, Nefertari, but Isisnofret remains a mystery. Yet both of them seem to have held significant positions in the royal court. It's worth looking briefly at what little we know of the lives of these two women. After all, four of their sons were buried in KV 5.

ISISNOFRET

Isisnofret was the second principal wife of Ramesses II. She presumably married the pharaoh at about the same time he married Nefertari. And when Nefertari died a quarter-century later, Isisnofret appears to have ascended to Nefertari's courtly position. That is all we know about this woman except that she was the mother of at least two of the pharaoh's principal sons. Some

Possible locations of the tomb of Isisnofret. Circles are possible tomb locations, and those near KV 10 and KV 8 seem the most likely.

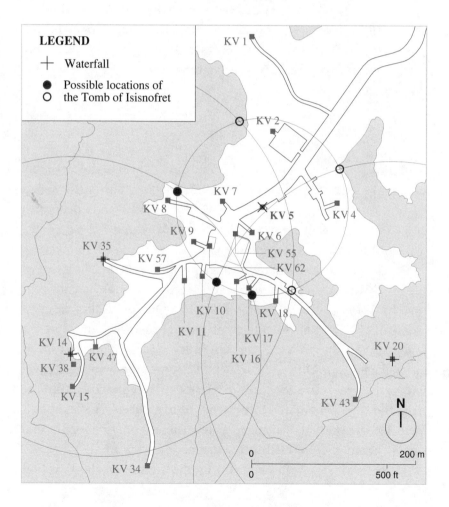

Egyptologists believe that there was a degree of enmity between her and Nefertari, but to me this seems to be based on imaginative interpretations of vague and badly broken texts.

However, possibly there was a geographical division in the authority of Isisnofret and Nefertari and in the duties of their sons. Nefertari is invariably referred to in Upper Egyptian inscriptions, while Isisnofret's name appears in those of Lower Egypt. Could there have been spheres of influence in the roles of these two women—Nefertari's influence having been in the south and Isisnofret's in the north? And was each queen authorized to perform certain of the principal royal and religious duties in one part of the country but not the other? However their roles were divided, they both bore sons who rose to positions of great prominence in Egyptian society. Surely this shows that Isisnofret's role in the royal court was as significant as Nefertari's.

NEFERTARI

Nefertari is the most famous of Ramesses II's wives and arguably one of the most famous women in ancient Egyptian history. Her current reputation is based largely on the magnificently decorated and amazingly well-preserved tomb that was dug for her in the Valley of the Queens, designated QV 66.

The Valley of the Queens, in ancient times called "The Place of Beauty," was given its modern name in the early nineteenth century by Jean-François Champollion. The Queens' Valley lies just south of the workmen's village at Deir el-Medineh and about a mile south of the Valley of the Kings. Its modern name is a bit of an exaggeration. Only a few of its eighty tombs belong to royal wives; the others are for those of various royal children. All date from the New Kingdom. Only twenty of the Queens' Valley tombs have decoration that has survived; few tombs contain more than a single chamber. Nefertari's is the dramatic exception.

QV 66 was discovered in 1904 by the curator of the Egyptian

Museum in Turin, Ernesto Schiaparelli, who had begun work in the Valley of the Queens only a few months earlier, in 1903. It was the most spectacular of the thirteen tombs he discovered in his seventeen years of work there. The brilliant colors on its walls and the superb quality of its paintings guaranteed that everyone wanted to see the tomb, making it an immediate must-see tourist destination. At the urging of the government and travel agents, Schiaparelli worked quickly, and QV 66 was opened to visitors less than a year later, in 1905.

Unfortunately, even then the tomb was in precarious condition. There were two very serious problems. First, the hillside where the tomb was dug consisted of very poor-quality limestone, and the ancient artisans could not prepare the fine, smooth wall surfaces that painted decoration requires. Instead, they were forced to cover the rough-cut, sometimes crumbling chamber walls with thick layers of coarse plaster, which they then covered with a heavy coat of whitewash. After that they painted the scenes and texts. Second, the tomb lay in the path of flashfloods that occurred whenever a rainstorm fell here every century or so. Though these floods never filled Nefertari's tomb with debris as they did in tombs in the Valley of the Kings, the water seeped through the cracked and fractured bedrock, forming puddles on the floor, raising humidity to dangerous levels, and weakening the plaster on the walls. The water and high humidity caused salts that occur naturally in limestone to migrate toward the surface of the stone. At the surface, exposed to air, these saline solutions crystallized and grew in size, pushing the thick plaster layer forward until it hung, suspended, free of the wall itself. Of its own weight, this unsupported plaster—and with it the superbly decorated surfaces—simply collapsed and fell to the floor.

Even in 1904, Schiaparelli saw that serious damage had occurred to many parts of the tomb, and opening it up to tourists only made matters worse. By 1905, 20 percent of its decorated walls had already disappeared. By 1934, even more had vanished, and the problem of protection was now obvious enough and serious enough that the government belatedly closed the tomb to the public. Unfortunately, this did not stop the deterioration.

Not until 1986 was there a plan to protect Nefertari's tomb. It was submitted to the EAO by the Getty Conservation Institute, who proposed a joint EAO-Getty venture to bring in the most qualified conservators possible and work to stabilize the tomb's plastered walls. It took courage even to suggest such a project: the techniques needed were extremely delicate, some of them experimental, and if anything went wrong, the EAO and Getty staff would face the wrath of not only governmental agencies but the world at large. A team of about twenty conservators and photographers, supported by several dozen consultants and headed by the Italian conservators Paolo and Laura Mora, spent a year studying the tomb, photographing it in detail, analyzing plaster and pigments, and noting the pattern of changes in its environmental condition. The following year, they began to clean the paintings and, as much as was possible, they strengthened and stabilized the plaster with special resins and acrylics.

The work was meticulous and demanding. Lotfy Khaled, who was one of the conservators on the Nefertari project, said that nothing had ever made him as nervous—or had given him greater satisfaction. With every stroke of a brush, every dab of a cotton swab, another section of fragile decorated plaster might collapse; but there was also the hope that the work would preserve these rich paintings for the future. The project took six years to complete, the results were a great success, and it stopped the deterioration of decorated walls in some areas of the tomb, and dramatically slowed it in others. Equipment was installed to help maintain temperature and humidity at safe, constant levels.

But the Getty emphasized that Nefertari's tomb would remain stable only if it remained closed to tourists. In 1995, against the recommendations of many conservators, the EAO decided to reopen Nefertari's tomb. They agreed, however, to limit the number of tourists who could visit: not more than ten persons at a time in the tomb, no group to stay more than a quarter of an hour, a

The Theban Necropolis covers 10 square kilometers (6 square miles) and extends from the Nile west across 3 kilometers (1.8 miles) of rich farmland to the dry Theban Hills beyond. It is possibly the richest archaeological zone in the world. BELOW: My wife, Susan, and I show ancient artifacts to television personality Hugh Downs (*left*) at the entrance to KV 5.

TOP: One of the Theban Mapping Project's hot-air balloons hovers on a photographic mission above the mortuary temple of Queen Hatshepsut at Deir el-Bahari at Thebes. BOTTOM: Project surveyor David Goodman setting grid markers on a Theban hillside.

Project benefactor Bruce Ludwig stands in the entrance to KV 5, two days after its rediscovery in 1989.

BELOW: Even the smallest fragments of objects and organic remains provide clues to the purpose of the tomb's many chambers.

I crouch with the workmen atop the debris filling the sixteen-pillared hall, clearing a doorway in its rear wall. That door led into a long corridor lined with dozens of chambers and suites of rooms.

Chamber 7, lying beyond the sixteen-pillared hall, led to more corridors, over sixty rooms, and a statue of Osiris, discoveries that stunned archaeologists.

Nubie Abdel Basset and I survey the transverse corridors at the rear of KV 5.

A carved figure of Osiris, Egypt's most important god of the Afterlife, stands in a niche at the rear of KV 5. The limestone statue is about 160 cms. (5 feet 3 inches) tall. BELOW: Close-up of the missing face of the statue, showing the *shebyu*-collar around its neck, an indication that the figure is the deified Ramesses II shown as Osiris.

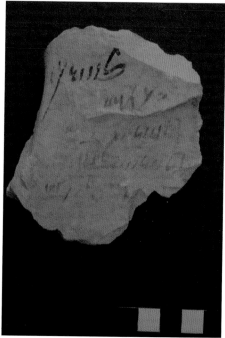

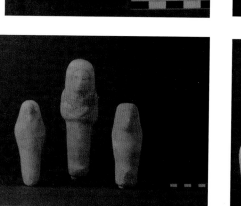

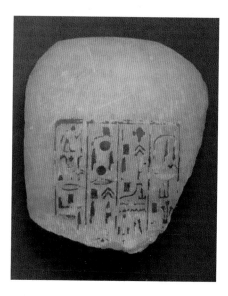

Some of the many objects found in KV 5. The tops of alabaster jars and finials from the harnesses of war chariots (*top left*); ostraca, such as this limestone fragment on which a delivery receipt for oil lamps was written in hieratic (cursive hieroglyphic) in the Nineteenth Dynasty (*top right*); alabaster *ushabtis*, statuettes intended to magically serve the deceased in the Afterlife (*middle left*); pieces of alabaster canopic jars inscribed with the names and titles of sons whose mummified organs were sealed inside (*middle right*); a fragment of the canopic jar of Amun-her-khepeshef (*bottom*).

Susan Weeks's water-color copy of the south wall of chamber 2. The scenes show Ramesses II presenting a deceased son to gods in the Afterlife, and a figure of the goddess Hathor, shown as a cow standing on a barque.

BELOW: Susan cleaning artifacts at the entrance to KV 5.

Corridor 12 extends downward beneath the roadway, away from the entrance to KV 5 into a still-undug complex containing at least two dozen more corridors and chambers. BELOW: The skeleton of an adult male mummy found in a pit in the floor of chamber 2 and possibly the remains of one of the sons of Ramesses II.

maximum of 150 visitors daily. The admission price was set at LEg. 100 (about thirty dollars), ten times the cost of regular Valley of the Queens tickets. Nevertheless, from the beginning, the demand for tickets was incredibly heavy. The law of supply and demand took hold: tickets were scarce and therefore tourists considered them prizes and gave highest priority to visiting the tomb. Tourists and tour guides lined up at the ticket office at 5:30 A.M. with the determination of teenagers who wanted to attend a major rock concert. At first, police had to be called in to quell riots among the ticket buyers, and fights between travel agents and the ticket seller were common. Twice in 1995, shortly after the tomb's reopening, police fired their guns into the air to quiet the unruly crowds.

Because of this chaos, some in the EAO are now arguing that QV 66 be opened to everyone, with no limit on the number of visitors. "We do not limit the number of people who visit Tutankhamun's tomb," one inspector told me. "Why not let thousands in here, too, and make money?" I hope this plan withers, because if unlimited numbers of tourists visit Nefertari each day, the Getty Institute's dire predictions will surely come true, and this masterpiece of Egyptian art will disappear forever. As the Getty staff noted, "Monitoring has shown that a single individual exhales and perspires between one-half and two cups of water per hour as well as carbon dioxide. So every day [under the new rules for limiting visitors] between five and twenty liters of water are deposited in the tomb. This moisture must go somewhere. What is not reabsorbed by people's clothing or extracted by the ventilation system is sucked up by the plaster and paint of the tomb."

Making matters worse, such humidity encourages bacterial growth. The tourists also present a physical threat to the walls, inadvertently touching or brushing against them, carrying dust into the tomb. And tourism requires artificial lights that may have a bad effect on ancient pigments.

One alternative to opening the tomb might be to construct a full-sized model of it for visitors, similar to what has been done at other fragile archaeological sites, such as the Paleolithic caves at Lascaux, in France. A Swiss team is studying this possibility.

Nefertari's tomb is the largest and most elaborately decorated tomb in the Valley of the Queens, but its plan is fairly standard. Two staircases and an intervening offering hall lead directly to a burial chamber. The chamber is typical of New Kingdom design: two rows of pillars divide the chamber into three sections; the floor in the center section is cut lower than the other two. Three small side rooms serve as offering chambers. The chambers are decorated with brilliantly colored scenes of fairly standard subject matter—though they are considered to be some of the finest examples of painting ever executed in Egypt. They show Nefertari with Osiris; Nefertari with Hathor and Nephthys; Nefertari with Isis. The tomb's entrance has her names and titles: "Hereditary Noblewoman; Great of Favors; Possessor of Charm, Sweetness, and Love; Mistress of Upper and Lower Egypt; the Osiris; the King's Great Wife, Mistress of the Two Lands, Nefertari, Beloved of Mut, Revered Before Osiris."

Other than this, we know little about Nefertari herself. Indeed, we know little about any of ancient Egypt's queens; custom dictated that biographical details of royal wives went virtually unrecorded. For years, Egyptologists have suspected that Nefertari came from Thebes and perhaps was the daughter of a nobleman's family. One of Nefertari's names was Mery-en-Mut (Beloved of Mut), a reference to the goddess Mut, wife of Amun and a member of the Theban triad. This hints at a Theban connection, but it's slim evidence at best.

We also do not know when Nefertari and Ramesses II were married; it seems likely that she was one of the first women he wed at age fifteen, and we believe that she died in the twenty-fourth year of her husband's reign, when the two of them were in their forties. Most Egyptologists do agree that in the Nineteenth Dynasty, Nefertari's combination of high status as principal royal wife and her great authority within the royal court, together with her apparent beauty, charm, intelligence, and guile, earned her a reputation few Egyptian women ever equaled. Like Queens Tiy and Ahmose-Nefertari before her, she was deified during her lifetime. A text carved on a wall in Luxor Temple offered this description of her:

> greatly favoured, possessing charm, sweet of love . . .
> Rich in love, wearing the circlet-diadem, singer fair of face, beautiful with the tall twin plumes, Chief of the Harim of Horus, Lord of the Palace; one is pleased with what(ever) comes forth concerning her; who has (only to) say anything, and it is done for her—every good thing, at her wish (?); her every word, how pleasing on the ear—one lives at just hearing her voice. . . .

It is impossible to say what Nefertari actually looked like; we do not have her mummy, and Egyptian art was not concerned with photographic-like portraiture. Still, when QV 66 was decorated, an effort was made to show that she was an especially beautiful Egyptian woman. Her skin color, for example, instead of being the usual pale yellow that characterizes females in nearly all other Egyptian painting, is a rosy hue and her cheeks are heavily rouged. Like the descriptions of her in the texts, representations of Nefertari in QV 66 set her apart from other women and, clearly, placed her above them.

Nefertari is not shown in KV 5, but it is possible that the decoration there, in Ramesses II's tomb (KV 7), and in QV 66 was done by the same group of artisans. There are several stylistic similarities. But hewing the first part of KV 5 was done long before either Nefertari or Ramesses II ruled Egypt, perhaps a century earlier.

BOULGAS AT BACKDIRT PILE. KVS

12

KV 5 BEFORE AND DURING THE

REIGN OF RAMESSES II

EARLY in our excavation of KV 5, while we were still clearing chambers 1 and 2 and studying their stratigraphy, we laid out a history of the tomb during the three millennia that followed the reign of Ramesses II. I outlined that history in Chapter 6, and we labeled the various intervals Phases Three (starting after the reign of Ramesses II) through Seven (the most recent phase). But what happened before Phase Three? What was the story of KV 5 from the day an ancient quarryman first began cutting it deep into the hillside until the last of the sons of Ramesses II had been interred and the tomb closed for the final time? Though I'm sure the picture will become clearer as we continue our work, we have already started to collect and examine clues that have allowed us to piece together a general picture of KV 5's history during the first centuries of its existence.

Some of those clues were confusing at first. We knew that KV 5 dated to the reign of Ramesses II, because we found his cartouche carved on several walls throughout the tomb. Yet certain features of KV 5—its location, design, and size—just did not fit within the range of attributes typical of Nineteenth Dynasty tombs. As we worked our way farther into the tomb, those features began to

show a pattern in their distribution. We wondered: were the quarrymen and artisans of Ramesses II the first men to dig KV 5? The
more we looked, the more we decided that they were not.

I cannot prove it yet, but it seems likely that a stage in KV 5's
history predated the reign of Ramesses II. During his reign, KV 5
was used as the burial place of royal sons; we now call that period
Phase Two. But I think there was an earlier stage, which we will
call Phase One.

Evidence for Phase One is largely circumstantial, and is the least
well-documented period in KV 5's long history. There is no hard
archaeological or epigraphic proof for it—yet—but studying the
tomb's architectural details suggests that a part of KV 5 was originally dug fifty to a hundred years before Ramesses II came to the
throne, and was then usurped by him early in his reign. The reasons I believe this are: the location of KV 5, the plan of its entrance
and first two chambers; and the dimensions of its doors.

Location is perhaps the weakest of these factors, but it's not
irrelevant. KV 5 lies in a small, rectangular area of the Valley of
the Kings, about 150 meters (500 feet) long and 20 meters wide.
In the rectangle is a cluster of four late Eighteenth Dynasty tombs.
At the rectangle's southern end there is KV 62, the tomb of
Tutankhamun; at the northern end is KV 46, the tomb of Yuya
and Thuya; and near the tomb of Tutankhamun lies KV 55, the
tomb of Queen Tiy. KV 5 is in the center of this area. Elizabeth
Thomas recognized the shared geography of KV 5, 46, 55, and 62,
and suggested that "by situation and location . . . it is possible [to
date KV 5] to the end of Dyn. 18, as well as [to] the reign of
Ramesses II. . . . "

Tombs of the Nineteenth Dynasty—that of Seti I, for example,
or Ramesses II—basically consist of a series of long, narrow corridors, cut one after the other, that together form a tunnel leading
toward a burial chamber. These tombs so strongly resembled long
tubes, in fact, that early Greek travelers called them "syringes," or
Pan pipes. The only variations in their syringelike plans are the
right-angle turn found in the plan of Ramesses II (which harks

back to the tomb plan of Amunhotep III), or the jog in the main axis in Seti I's.

But KV 5 is not syringelike. It has a central sixteen-pillared hall with doorways leading off it in all directions. Nothing in any of the known tombs in Thebes—in the Valley of the Kings, the Valley of

Plan of KV 5 as of April 1998. Numbers are the currently used chamber designations.

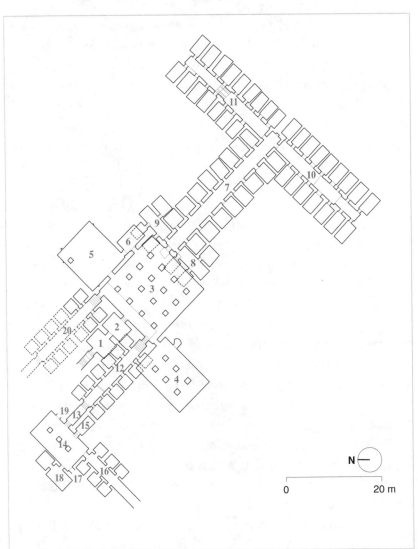

the Queens, and the Tombs of the Nobles—is remotely similar to this. Nor is there anything similar in tombs at any of Egypt's other principal sites, such as Giza, Saqqara, or Amarna. Even though its plan is unique, KV 5 does, however, show one element that, according to Elizabeth Thomas, is characteristic of late Eighteenth Dynasty tombs: its entrance leads directly into a rectangular chamber, not into a syringelike corridor. This feature can be seen in the tombs of Tutankhamun (KV 62), Yuya and Thuya (KV 46), and KV 55—the tombs in the KV 5 rectangle—and three other tombs, KV 12, 27, and 28, which are also thought to be of later Eighteenth Dynasty date. (KV 12 was re-used in the Dynasty 19). In addition, entrances to these Eighteenth Dynasty tombs were cut deep into the floor of the valley immediately at the base of moderately sloping hillsides.

But the dimensions of the tomb's doorways are perhaps the most convincing reasons to believe that the tomb's first few chambers were dug during the late Eighteenth Dynasty. Entrance doorways of Dynasty 18 KV tombs are *never more* than 200 centimeters (78 inches) wide, and royal tombs average 150 centimeters wide. Entrance doorways of Nineteenth Dynasty tombs in KV are *never less* than 200 centimeters wide; royal tombs average 211 centimeters. The difference between the doors of the two dynasties is half a meter. KV 5's entrance doorway is only 110 centimeters wide—at the far lower end of the Eighteenth Dynasty range—and even that measurement is of the doorway *after* it had been widened by more than 15 centimeters sometime during Ramesses II's reign. Originally, it was only about ninety-five centimeters wide.

When you consider each of these elements—the location of the tomb, how it is laid out, and the width of the doorways—they may not be convincing individually, but taken together all features are compelling. They mean that a part of KV 5 was originally dug in the late Eighteenth Dynasty, then usurped by Ramesses II thirty to a hundred years later.

Which parts of KV 5 constituted the original tomb? Perhaps only chambers 1 and 2, including the pit cut into the floor of chamber 2 where the original occupant was buried. Perhaps it also included part of chamber 3. Since KV 5 lies in the Valley of the Kings, it was most likely dug for a pharaoh or a senior member of the royal family.

A number of other elements tie KV 5 to the late Eighteenth Dynasty. Perhaps the most important was Ramesses II's frequent use of Amunhotep III's political and religious views as the model for the dramatic changes that he wrought in Egyptian concepts of kingship and government administration. Nothing explains the purpose of KV 5 better than our knowledge that Ramesses II used these views as a way of having himself declared a god before his death. To understand how and why Ramesses II did this and what it meant for his many sons, we must leave KV 5 and walk to the edge of the cultivable land south of the Ramesseum, to the mortuary temple of Amunhotep III.

ABOUT three hundred meters east of the Antiquities Department office, beyond thick stands of sugarcane, and five hundred meters west of a huge public school and the local police station, stand two of Thebes's most majestic figures. They are called the Colossi of Memnon. Their location on the rich soil of the Nile Valley, rather than at the desert edge, give them a certain pride of place today: they are the first ancient monuments seen by West Bank tourists, and they always make a deep impression. These monolithic statues, cut from two blocks of extremely hard quartzite, are among the largest pieces of sculpture ever produced by man. Each stands over eighteen meters (sixty feet) high, weighs over seven hundred tons, and depicts the Eighteenth Dynasty pharaoh Amunhotep III seated formally on his throne.

Originally, the two Colossi flanked the central doorway of the entrance pylon of Amunhotep III's enormous mortuary temple. But that temple was made largely of mud brick and lay in the zone of cultivated fields that flooded every summer when the Nile overflowed its banks. That wasn't bad planning by ancient engineers;

it was intentional. Parts of Egyptian temples were meant to represent places traditionally associated with original creation. The hypostyle (meaning columned) hall of the temple, for example, a forest of columns with lotus and papyrus capitals, represented a primeval swampland. In some temples, such a hall was actually expected to flood each summer, when the Nile rose. But by the end of the New Kingdom, when the Temple of Amunhotep III was abandoned and maintenance work on its foundations had ceased, its walls began to dissolve in the annual flood and the building melted into oblivion.

Today, the temple has all but disappeared except for a large stela at the rear of the ancient building, a few foundation stones, and fragments of statues of Amunhotep III. There is also a peculiar-looking sphinx with the body of a lion and the tail of a crocodile. Several impressively large acacia trees stand in a field of barren, brown silt, and goats graze where the hypostyle hall once stood. A recent brushfire, started when a taxi driver flicked a cigarette out of his car window, has caused some serious cracks in the statuary, and the area looks even more forlorn than usual.

The Colossi are impressively large, but the temple is an archaeological has-been. Few tourists even realize that these imposing statues were originally part of a larger funerary complex. In fact, it was the largest mortuary temple built at Thebes, a spectacular complex of columns, pylons, and walls. Amunhotep III described it with obvious pride in a text carved on one of its stelae:

He made (it) as his monument for his father, Amon, lord of the thrones of the two lands, making for him a splendid temple on the right of Thebes; a fortress of eternity out of fine white sandstone—worked with gold throughout. Its floors were purified with silver, all its doorways were of electrum. It was made broad and made very large and inscribed for eternity. . . . Its storeroom was filled by servants from among the children of the chiefs of every foreign country out of the plunder of his majesty. . . .

Undoubtedly the Colossi of Memnon made a deep impression on Ramesses II, a century later. The statues gave him an example to follow when he built his own mortuary temple, the Ramesseum, a few hundred meters to the north. There, he erected a single colossal statue of himself, similar to the Colossi of Amunhotep III but even larger. Amunhotep III had called his Colossi "Ruler-of-the-Rulers," and Ramesses II used this same name (together with the variant "Re-of-the-Rulers") for his.

The purpose of such huge statues, Professor Lanny Bell of the University of Chicago argues, was to make a religious, not a political impression: "the largest statues found in Egypt (at Abu Simbel, the Ramesseum, and the Colossi of Memnon) are of deified kings, rather than non-human deities, as though their function is to convey to the viewer the impression that the union of king and godhead has created a superdeity on earth."

Only a decade ago, the Colossi gazed eastward across thousands of acres of fertile, green fields toward the rising sun. Today, they stare into an asphalt parking lot filled with buses, a portable toilet, a fake-papyrus shop, and the lenses of thousands of tourists' cameras. A busy east–west highway passes not more than ten meters south of the site, and just across the road there is a hotel for backpackers that has been closed for several years since the owner died. There is an ongoing argument over who should inherit the property. There is also a long line of wilting cardboard cartons where hawkers display clay cooking pots, fake scarabs, bottled water, and postcards.

Travelers to Thebes in the eighteenth and early nineteenth centuries nicknamed the two Colossi "Shammy" and "Tammy." I have often wondered how they got such odd-sounding names. For more than a century, Egyptologists have dismissed the terms as gibberish, with no known hieroglyphic, Arabic, or European source. But a possible etymology recently occurred to me. Imagine a European traveler visiting Thebes in the early 1800s. He knows virtually no Arabic. He stands before the Colossi and asks a local villager about the statues. He points to the colossus on the left and asks, "Who is that?" Then he points to the colossus on the right and asks, "Who is *that*?"

The villager, not understanding the question but trying to be helpful, responds: *"Di, il shamaal. Da, il yameen."* This is the one on the left, that is the one on the right. To the traveler's unpracticed ear, *shamaal* was heard as "Shammy;" *yameen* was misremembered as "Tammy," and the two words were taken to be the names of the statues themselves. It's certainly possible because tourists regularly mishear Arabic words.

The more traditional name for the statues, "The Colossi of Memnon," is scarcely more appropriate. In 27 BCE, a major earthquake struck Thebes, seriously damaging the northern of the two Colossi. Its upper part broke off and each morning, as the air temperature rose and the humidity dropped, the statue could be heard emitting a strange sound, like a musical note, just after sunrise. The Greeks who visited here believed that the statue was a figure of their folk hero Memnon, the son of Eos, goddess of the dawn. In legend, Memnon had been killed by Achilles at the battle of Troy. The sound made by the Theban colossus was therefore explained as Memnon's sad cry to his mother as she arose each day on the horizon. His mother was so moved by her son's sorrowful cry that each day she was driven to tears, and it was said that these tears fell as dew on the fields of Thebes. Hundreds of Greek travelers came to Thebes to hear the colossus, and the bases of both statues are covered with graffiti carved by Greek tourists commenting on the quality and purity of the sound. Early in the third century CE, however, the statue's upper part was rebuilt in stone on the order of Septimius Severus. He thought he was doing a very good thing, undertaking a long-overdue job of preservation. Once the colossus was patched, however, Memnon was never heard from again.

AMUNHOTEP III ruled Egypt for thirty-eight years. He was only about eight years old when he was crowned king in 1386 BCE.

During the first several years, of course, he was too young to be pharaoh in anything but name, and actual power was probably wielded by his mother, Mutemwia, and senior court officials. Young Amunhotep would have spent much of his time studying under court tutors. Judging by his later career, he was undoubtedly a precocious and talented student: his reign is considered by Egyptologists to have been one of the grandest and most aesthetically glorious periods of Egyptian history.

Its glory was not due to military activity, however: Amunhotep came to the throne when Egypt was already in control of a great empire, so there was little need for wars or skirmishes. Instead, its greatness was measured by its art and architecture, by its court life, and by a complex set of rapidly evolving beliefs about the relationship between gods and pharaoh that then dramatically affected every facet of Egyptian society. Many of these beliefs had unintended consequences and, in several ways, nearly brought parts of Egyptian society to the brink of disaster. It was Ramesses II, seventy years later, who tried to straighten things out.

During his reign, Amunhotep III said that he wanted to build monuments "the like of which never existed before since the primeval time of the two lands." Because of his pursuit of this goal, he was given a nickname, *menwy*, meaning "the monument-man."

HE built several temples south of Egypt, in Nubia, that were in part intended to be shows of royal Egyptian authority. But they also had serious religious function and many contained scenes of the king's deification and of his Sed-festivals. Several of these temples established patterns that Ramesses II would later use as models for his own temples. For example, Amunhotep III constructed a temple at Soleb that showed him in self-adoration, as king honoring himself as god. Fifteen kilometers north, at Sedeinga, he built a smaller temple dedicated to his wife, Queen Tiy, as the goddess Hathor. Ramesses II later followed this pattern at Abu Simbel. Both Abu Simbel and a temple at Soleb were dedicated to Amun-Re of Karnak and to the pharaoh as god. They identified Amun-Re as the solar eye and pharaoh as the lunar eye, the two eyes of Horus. At Sedeinga, and at Abu Simbel, the queen was honored as a form of the solar eye of Ra or Hathor. The temples of Ramesses II and his wife, Nefertari, at Abu Simbel were similarly dedicated.

Amunhotep III expanded upon a tradition that had been common in a few Old Kingdom reigns, but largely ignored from then until the Eighteenth Dynasty, of giving important government posts to members of his immediate family. Each of his daughters held several titles, and it seems that not only his children by Queen Tiy, but also those of other principal wives, were regularly rewarded in this manner. In fact, as French Egyptologist Nicolas Grimal observed, "family ties dominated the national political scene." The prominence given to the royal offspring became even more significant in the Nineteenth Dynasty reign of Ramesses II.

ONE of Amunhotep III's most ambitious projects was the excavation at Thebes of a great basin, covering over two and a half square kilometers. Today it is called Birket Habu, which is Arabic for "The Lake of Habu," a reference to the nearby site of Medinet Habu, where Ramesses III's mortuary temple is located. It lies about 2 kilometers (1.2 miles) south of the Colossi of Memnon and immediately east of the great royal palace built by Amunhotep III.

Birket Habu was once described by members of Napoleon's expedition to Egypt as a race course—a "Hippodrome"—where horses were run and troops exercised. Several early visitors called it a "pleasure lake" for Queen Tiy. Others referred to it as a harbor, used to receive shipments of foreign trade goods and tribute. More recently, however, British Egyptologist Barry Kemp has argued that Birket Habu and the royal palace adjacent to it, called Malkata, were constructed specifically for the first Sed-festival of Amunhotep III in regnal year 30.

The Sed-festival was an important religious milestone in a king's reign. It was closely tied to Osiris, Horus, and Seth, and, especially, to the solar god, Re. For some reason, its importance diminished after the Old Kingdom and did not again achieve prominence until the reign of Amunhotep III. During his reign, many elements of the Sed-festival ceremony were moved from land to water, perhaps as a way of mimicking the journey of the sun in its solar bark. When the pharaoh symbolically replicated this same journey, he was triumphing over death, just as the sun did when it set each evening, traveled through the dark Netherworld, and was reborn at sunrise.

Kemp believes that after the first Sed-festival had been performed, Malkata and Birket Habu were abandoned. Then, a few years later, the basin was enlarged and made ready for a second festival in regnal year 34. The palace was completely destroyed by the basin's enlargement and had to be rebuilt a short distance away.

The enlargement of Birket Habu and the rebuilding of Malkata were projects of gargantuan proportions that clearly show how important the Egyptians felt the Sed-festival was. Birket Habu lies about 2.5 kilometers west of the present Nile and measures 2.4 by 1 kilometers, or an area of 2 million square meters. Kemp, along with Egyptologist David O'Connor, made a careful study of the size of the mounds surrounding this ancient excavation and calculated from the amount of dirt the mounds contained that the lake had originally been dug to a depth of about six meters. This works out to a total of 14.4 million cubic meters of silt—360 million basketsful—that had to be dug out, carted off, and dumped up to a kilometer away from the site. If we assume that five thousand men worked on this project and each moved a basket of dirt every five minutes ten hours a day without interruption—a wildly optimistic figure—it took them over two years of continuous work to complete the digging of Birket Habu. It is the largest earthworks known from ancient Egypt. Even more remarkable is the fact that a second "Birket," equal in size to this one, was dug on the East Bank, across from Birket Habu and south of Luxor Temple. It was also enlarged for the second Sed-festival.

Today, Birket Habu is filled with Nile silts that are under intensive cultivation. Fields of sugarcane, wheat, sorghum and vegetables cover the landscape. It is rich soil here, well watered, and the fields are brilliant green. But the harbor can still be easily recognized, especially from the air or from a vantage point atop the limestone cliffs two kilometers to the north. It is surrounded by huge mounds of chocolate-colored silts dug in ancient times and piled around the perimeter of the harbor. These mounds were too high and steep to be used for agriculture, and for centuries they have been thickly covered with villages. Several of our workmen live there.

Malkata, the palace of Amunhotep III, lay on the western shore of Birket Habu, beyond the cultivation on a wide, flat sandy plain that continues west to a series of rugged limestone hills and valleys about four kilometers away. It covers over 80 acres, 227,000 square meters and, in ancient times, it was covered with a vast and splendid array of buildings. According to Barry Kemp, Malkata's plan was similar to that of an Egyptian temple, a design intended to reflect the increasingly strong belief that Amunhotep III was both king *and* god, that the line between kingship and divinity had become blurred.

Today, Malkata resembles a lunar landscape. Antiquities thieves have dug here for centuries, looking for pottery, papyri, statuettes, and amulets, and they were often richly rewarded. The Arabic word *malkata* means, literally, "the place where there are things to be picked up." Thousands of painted potsherds still litter the churned-up surface, faience beads surface after a strong wind, and badly weathered traces of mud-brick walls run like dotted lines across the plain.

After the eleventh year of Amunhotep III's reign, virtually all knowledge of royal activities disappeared. We were left with the material remains at Malkata, texts inscribed on temple walls, and inscriptions from the tombs of royal courtiers, but in spite of their high aesthetic standard, the material offers few historical facts. This is especially disappointing because I believe that information about the last decade of Amunhotep III's life, the period when he was deified and ruled as a living god, is crucial to understanding the career of Ramesses II and his children.

During the Old Kingdom, Sed-festivals were apparently major and highly significant events; during the Middle Kingdom, their importance dwindled and they became rather cursory affairs, little more than a brief service followed by a short announcement that it had taken place. Under Amunhotep III, however, great pains were taken to perform the ceremony in the most proper (in other words, most ancient) form possible. An inscription in the tomb of Kheruef suggests that research had been conducted to ensure its purity: "It was his majesty who did this in accordance with the ancient writings. Generations of men since the time of the ancestors had never celebrated *sed*-festival rites, but it was commanded for . . . the son of Amen. . . ."

The festival took place here in Malkata, and to commemorate the event, it was called "The House of Rejoicing." All three of Amunhotep III's Sed-festivals, in years 30, 34, and 37, took place here; each lasted two months. The entire court took part—the queen, the royal family, officials, priests, foreign ambassadors—and festivities included elaborate parties with dancing, singing, drinking, and gift-giving.

Amunhotep III was also responsible for extensive building activity throughout Egypt and Nubia. But none of his monuments can rival his Luxor Temple, on the East Bank of the Nile at Thebes, in importance. This was Amunhotep's triumph: not only was the temple a monument of impressive architectural and artistic merit, but it revealed a dramatic shift in the way Egypt viewed its pharaoh and pharaoh's relationship to the gods. As one Egyptologist described it, "Luxor Temple seems to have been the mythological and theological power base of the reigning monarch from the New Kingdom onwards." Luxor Temple also had a significant effect on the reign of Ramesses II, who considered it of such importance that he devoted substantial time and wealth to its enlargement.

THE TEMPLE OF LUXOR

Luxor Temple has always excited visitors. Even in the last century, when it was still buried deep under mounds of garbage and sand, when its walls were covered with modern dovecotes and mud-brick houses, European travelers spoke of it in romantic terms. In 1881, when it was finally cleared of debris, the temple was immediately dubbed "the most beautiful monument which remains from the XVIIIth Dynasty." It certainly must have been impressive in ancient times. With obvious pride, Amunhotep III described it as being built: "out of good white stone, it being broadened, made very large, and its beauty being exaggerated. Its walls are of electrum, its floors of silver, all its doorways being worked on their thresholds. Its pylons approached heaven, and its flagstaves were in the stars."

Luxor Temple was a beautiful structure, but its setting is hardly likely to inspire such praise today. It lies beside the noisy and heavily traveled corniche, in the heart of the modern city. The stark, 1950s-style New Winter Palace Hotel lies a hundred meters to its south, separated from the temple by a dismal concrete shopping mall; the Luxor police station, surrounded by a field of leaking sewer pipes, and the Brooke Hospital for Animals lie to its north. Luxor city center, with its warren of houses and tourist bazaars, lies to the east. The headquarters of President Hosni Mubarak's National Democratic Party, a turn-of-the-century villa that lists slightly and is badly cracked, stands directly atop a part of the archaeological site.

Thousands of tourists pass through the temple each morning, but I advise visitors to wait until after sunset before visiting. It is less crowded then, its urban surroundings are hidden by darkness, and well-placed spotlights transform its courtyards and sanctuaries into the romantic building our Victorian ancestors saw, filled with scenes of ancient kings and gods, dancers, musicians, and acrobats, where priests and courtiers, servants and slaves, parade eternally through the temple's grand courts and colonnades.

When Ramesses II enlarged Luxor Temple and placed statues of his divine self before its huge entrance pylon, he boasted that he did so only after consulting historical records, perhaps dating from the reign of Amunhotep III, to ensure that his work would be acceptable to the gods. On the temple pylon, Ramesses II said he had ". . . researched (in) the office of archives, and he unrolled the writings of the House of Life. He (thus) knew the secrets of heaven and all the mysteries of earth. He discovered that Thebes, the Eye of Re, was a primeval mound which arose in the beginning (?), since this land had existed, and Amen-Re [had functione]d as King—he illumined the sky and lit up the sun's circuit, looking for a place (whereon) he might allow the rays from his Eyes to alight."

SEVERAL years ago, a former director of Chicago House, Professor Lanny Bell, made a study of the inscriptions in Luxor Temple and argued that the temple was specifically dedicated to "the divine Egyptian ruler or, more precisely, to the cult of the royal *ka*." The royal *ka* was that element of a king's nature that joined him to the gods and to his royal ancestors. The *ka*, shown as the king's twin, was depicted with the pharaoh in scenes throughout the king's life as proof that the king had the potential to become divine. But, according to Bell, the pharaoh "actually *becomes* divine only when he becomes one with the royal *ka*, when the human form is overtaken by this immortal element. This happened at the climax of the coronation ceremony," and that ceremony took place in Luxor Temple.

A century and a half after Amunhotep III's coronation, Ramesses II erected gigantic statues of his *ka* before the first pylon of Luxor Temple. There, in the presence of family, priests, officials, and the god Amun, he declared himself to be a living god. From the reign of Amunhotep III onward, such a ceremony was considered an essential part of the process to legitimize one's claim to the throne and to establish the divine nature of one's rule. The way this came about during Amunhotep III's reign has been documented by Ray Johnson, the current director of Chicago House, who has been studying the reign of Amunhotep III for two decades.

According to Johnson's studies, the representations of Amunhotep III can be divided into four phases, each of which spans roughly a decade of the pharaoh's reign. In each, his figure was changed in subtle ways. The first phase was little different from that which preceded it in the reign of Thutmosis IV. But in Phase II the pharaoh was deliberately depicted as a youthful and vigorous man, handsome, muscular, well proportioned, the physical ideal of what an Egyptian pharaoh should be.

Then, in Phase III, Amunhotep III's features changed. He was no longer as handsome and youthful as in earlier phases, but instead became more mature, with a double chin and large, pierced ears, his eye painted but not carved.

Phase IV can be seen in Luxor Temple's long, narrow, twenty-two-meter-high colonnaded hall, which had been built in front of the solar court and was entered through a large pylon. Its two rows of seven papyrus-capital columns each created a grand processional route that the king and his entourage walked down during the celebration of his year 30 Sed-festival. Here, the king was "foppishly attired"; representations again emphasize a degree of youthfulness, but this time they are strained and heavy-handed, not naturalistic but highly stylized characterizations of youth. For example, the eye of the king is far too large for his face; his body is shorter and fatter than normal proportions would dictate; he bends slightly forward instead of standing erect; and a paunch strains against his wide belt. These representations date to just after Amunhotep's first Sed-festival, and were intended to show that the pharaoh had undergone a transformation. They were a visual affirmation that the "rejuvenation process of the Sed-festival" had done its job.

Amunhotep III had not, however, suddenly been reinvigorated, as his reliefs imply, into a young man in good health. In fact, we know from several pieces of evidence that by his thirtieth regnal year the pharaoh was in bad shape. Contemporary paintings and reliefs show him to be seriously overweight. The mummy that some Egyptologists (but not all) believe is his, exhibits severe and painful dental abscesses. His health was a serious enough problem that he ordered seven hundred statues of Sekhmet, a goddess of health and healing, to be installed in his mortuary temple.

The changes in Amunhotep's style reflected a basic shift in how the divine status of Egypt's pharaoh was perceived. In Phase IV representations, Amunhotep III wore two or three strands of large gold beads around his neck, like a choker necklace. These beads formed what was called a *shebyu*-collar. Prior to the reign of Amunhotep III, this collar was worn by figures of *dead* pharaohs who, at death, were united with the sun god, Re. Ray Johnson explains the significance of this:

> The presence of a *shebyu*-collar, generally associated with transformed but deceased kings, on figures of the living Amunhotep III is a statement that this transformation has miraculously occurred before death. For the last eight years of his reign Amunhotep is represented in a timeless, youthful form, more cult image than actual man. The changes in the representation of the king, when read correctly, actually proclaim his deified state as the sun god's "living image on earth." . . .

This *shebyu*-collar is also found on the statue of Osiris at the end of corridor seven in KV 5. When he visited KV 5, Johnson suggested to me that the statue we discovered there therefore might not be a representation of Osiris but one of the deified, living Ramesses II *as* Osiris. Some Egyptologists believe that, no later than his first Sed-festival, Ramesses II had been declared a god. He was henceforth represented in the same manner as Amunhotep III, and for the same reasons.

The significance of this is that Amunhotep III and Ramesses II did not wait until they died to assume divine status. Each was made a god while he was still alive. Betsy Bryan, my colleague at Johns Hopkins University, describes the result:

> Thus, we find that at the end of his reign Amunhotep's constructions from the Delta to the Sudan express his desire to solarize the major cults of Egypt and to identify himself with the creative aspects of the sun god in the process: encircling the earth as the sun, bringing fertility to the earth as the creative sun disk, and keeping universal order as the eye of Ra . . . the result brought Egyptian religion to the brink of Akhenaten's theology of the sole god Ra-Horakhty in the sun disk (Aten).

There can be no doubt, then, that Amunhotep III became a god in his own lifetime—in fact, he seems to have been obsessed with the idea of his own divinity—and that priests and officials of the court devoted much of their time after year 30 to the reaffirmation of this belief.

Throughout Egyptian history, pharaohs had always been considered divine. The king was both the divine "them" and the mortal "us," dying as we mortals die, but then reborn as only gods could be. One of his most ancient titles, *nesu-bity*, sometimes translated as "King of Upper and Lower Egypt," probably more correctly refers to this duality—the king's two bodies, as it were—*nesu*, the undying, divine king, and *bity*, the individual, mortal pharaoh. One of the pharaoh's principal duties emphasized this dual nature: he was expected to perform annual ceremonies that would ensure the continued existence of humankind, and these ceremonies were also meant to ensure the rejuvenation of the gods.

With Amunhotep III's first Sed-festival, in year 30, the perception of pharaohs as both mortal and divine changed. Instead of being a change to something new, New Kingdom priests believed it was a restoration to what it had been in the Old Kingdom.

The first flourishing of the solar cult in Egypt dates to the Fifth Dynasty at the important Lower Egyptian site of Heliopolis, about twenty-five kilometers north of Memphis. The city was called Iunu by the Egyptians and in the Bible, it was On. In the Old Kingdom, the city of Heliopolis was as important as Memphis. A huge temple was erected there to the sun god, Re-Harakhty, and the creator god, Atum; in the Middle Kingdom, the temple was greatly enlarged; and in the New Kingdom, thanks to renewed interest in the solar cult, it grew even larger and wealthier.

During his Sed-festival, Amunhotep III was joined permanently with Atum and Re-Harakhty. This, Ray Johnson believes, was the original, Old Kingdom reason for the Sed-festival: it was "the ritual death of the king and his assimilation with the sun after thirty years of rule." Amunhotep III returned to this position, uniting himself with the solar deity. In Egyptian theology, when a pharaoh died he became every god and could be worshiped in many forms. But Amunhotep III sought to become one deity above all others: the solar god, Re-Harakhty. The epithets he took for himself describe this: "Re-Harakhty, who becomes active from the Akhet [the zone between the horizon and the Netherworld] in his identity as the light that is in the sun disk," as well as Atum, who is often joined to the solar deities as Atum-Re, or Atum-Re-Harakhty.

The plan of Luxor Temple differed from earlier New Kingdom temples in several ways, but especially in its emphasis upon wide courts open to the sun, where intensely bright sunlight confirmed the renewed emphasis upon solar cults. Indeed, one of the principal reasons for building Luxor Temple was to show Amunhotep III *as actually being* the sun god. And this holds true for the designs of his other temples as well. Betsy Bryan sums it up: ". . . Amenhotep's constructions from the Delta to the Sudan express his desire to solarize the major cults of Egypt and to identify himself with the creative aspects of the sun god in the process: encircling the earth as the sun, bringing fertility to the earth as the creative sun disk, and keeping universal order as the eye of Ra."

Under Amunhotep III, the idea that there were as many deities as there were forces in nature was replaced with the view that one god stood out from all the rest, a god of light, whose symbol was the disk of the sun. In regnal year 30, Amunhotep III *became* that disk: he was Aten Tjehen, the "Dazzling Aten," the solar disk of Re, "the sole god, with no other except him."

Early on, however, implementing these Atenist religious views posed a problem. If Amunhotep III was now a living god, the Aten, the living form of Re-Harakhty, how could he also serve in the role of the living pharaoh? Presumably, someone still had to attend to the many secular activities of pharaoh—serving as arbiter in legal disputes, conducting foreign relations, overseeing Egypt's economy and its agriculture and irrigation. Perhaps some of these matters could safely be entrusted to court officials. But others had to be performed by a person with the magico-religious connections that only a pharaoh possessed. After Amunhotep III's new divine duties began to keep him principally at Malkata, his other, secular duties now had to be performed by his son, Amunhotep IV.

THE REIGN OF AKHENATON

Amunhotep IV is arguably the most-discussed pharaoh in all Egyptian history, but his story is also the most problematic. He has been labeled everything from a religious genius to a mentally deranged, physically deformed zealot. He has been the subject of a study by Sigmund Freud, an opera by Philip Glass, a novel by Mika Waltari, and a film by Darryl F. Zanuck. Thousands of articles have been written about him, ranging from the profoundly scholarly to the profoundly ridiculous. Part of the reason there are so many conflicting ideas about Amunhotep IV is that we have almost no solid facts to go on; and in the absence of fact, many writers have let their imaginations soar.

Over the last half-century, the story that traditional Egyptology has woven about Amunhotep IV and his reign has changed very little until recently. Basically, it goes like this:

Raised in Egypt's luxurious royal court at Thebes, leading a pampered and effete life, young Amunhotep IV was crowned pharaoh when his father died. Although physically deformed, the young pharaoh married a lovely woman, Nefertiti, with whom he was deeply in love. The two eventually had five daughters. During the early years of his reign, Amunhotep IV had developed a great dislike for the priests of Egypt's traditional gods, especially the priesthood of Amun, because he thought they were a political and economic threat. As the young pharaoh brooded, his distrust of the religious authorities grew stronger. Finally, in his sixth regnal year, he ordered his family and his court to move with him to an uninhabited strip of desert on the Nile's east bank, three hundred kilometers north of Thebes. Amunhotep IV had been dreaming of a new religion that would replace the standard beliefs of Egypt's priests with the notion that there was only one god in the universe, the sun's physical disk, called the Aten. Upon moving to Amarna, which he called Akhetaton, "The Horizon of the Aten," Amunhotep IV changed his own name to Akhenaton, "Agreeable to the Aten." He immediately issued a decree closing all the temples of Egypt and declared that he would now worship no god but Aten. He remained at Akhetaton until his death, outliving Nefertiti, and in the later years of his reign seems to have entered into a relationship with Smenkhkare, a young man of unknown origin, whom he is shown embracing affectionately. Smenkhkare became pharaoh upon Akhenaton's death. He ruled for only two years, replaced by the young son (or brother or nephew) of Akhenaton, Tutankhaton. Only a child at his accession, and ruling under the guidance of an official called Ay, Tutankhaton changed his name to Tutankhamun, issued an edict reopening the traditional temples of Egypt, restored the priesthoods, and declared that the ideas of Akhenaton were heretical and therefore null and void. Immediately, armies of men were sent throughout the country to destroy any evidence of Akhenaton's reign: his temples were razed and his name was omitted from later king lists. He was declared a criminal, and it became anathema to admit that he had ever existed.

Most recently, several Egyptologists, especially Ray Johnson, have proposed a more convincing outline of Amunhotep IV's life, to which I've added some embellishments of my own.

We don't know anything about Amunhotep IV until, in the twenty-eighth year of his father's reign, two years before Amunhotep III's first Sed-festival, he was made his father's co-regent. Actually, we do not even know that with certainty, but Ray Johnson makes a compelling circumstantial case for it.

During the Middle Kingdom, six centuries before the reign of Amunhotep III, pharaohs from Amunemhet I on were concerned about ensuring that their legitimate heir and not some interloper followed them on the throne. To achieve this, a pharaoh, during his lifetime appointed his rightful heir, normally his eldest son, to share the duties of kingship. When the pharaoh died, his son was already in place on the throne, thus making any attempt at a palace coup more difficult.

I am convinced by Ray Johnson's argument for a co-regency between Amunhotep III and his son Amunhotep IV. However, in this case, the reason for the co-regency was not a desire to ensure a peaceful transition between rulers but, rather, it was due to Amunhotep III's evolving views of the relationship between king and gods. Throughout much of his reign, Amunhotep III was intensely preoccupied with the solar theology of the priests of Heliopolis, particularly with two of its principal deities, Atum and Re. The god Atum was a creator god. The priests of his cult believed that either by masturbating or (in another version) by spitting, Atum had created Shu, god of the air and supporter of the heavens, and Tefnut, Shu's sister and consort. From this pair came all the other gods and goddesses in the Egyptian pantheon. When Amunhotep III was deified at his first Sed-festival, he became that living creator god in his several manifestations as Atum-Re-Harakhty. The pharaoh had become the "living image" of the god—indeed, of all the gods—and the *shebyu*-collar that he wore from year 30 onward indicated this divine status.

For at least two years before the Sed-festival, Amunhotep III had been making plans for his divinization. Throughout Egypt and

Nubia, he instructed that his temples be remodeled to include a large solar court similar to the one he was building at Luxor Temple. On the walls of several solar courts—in his Theban mortuary temple, for example—scenes were carved and painted of the forthcoming Sed-festival. Also, the king's decision to make his son co-regent in year 28 was likely a necessary part of his plans for deification.

At the same time that Amunhotep III was changing the way he appeared in art, showing himself with exaggerated and timeless youthfulness, Amunhotep IV's appearance was also being altered. In a temple dedicated to Re-Harakhty at Karnak, built by Amunhotep IV shortly after being made co-regent but before his father's year 30 Sed-festival, he was depicted with his father's features: large, almond-shaped eye, double chin, thick neck, and straight nose. After year 30, Amunhotep IV's style changed. Some have labeled it more naturalistic; others describe it as an exaggerated, even grotesque, parody of the human form. Egyptologists have termed it the "Amarna Style," and it is the most obvious feature of Amunhotep IV's reign.

In the Amarna Style, Amunhotep IV and Nefertiti are depicted with such a confusing mixture of sexual attributes that it is sometimes difficult to tell them apart. Both have feminine hips and breasts, long, thin arms and legs, and protruding stomachs. Both have narrow, almost gaunt, faces with long chins, sunken cheeks, thick lips, huge, narrow eyes and large, pierced ears. Both appear to be hermaphrodites. These attributes have been called "naturalistic," though they are anything but. They are the attributes of fecundity figures. However the Amarna Style is described, one of its purposes apparently was stylistically to distinguish pharaoh from co-regent: Amunhotep III was now the idealized, living solar god, and Amunhotep IV, the physical, mortal pharaoh.

During his early years as co-regent, Amunhotep IV lived at Malkata with his parents and his wife, Nefertiti, and already was showing a "predilection" for the god Atum-Re-Harakhty. Interest in solar gods in Egypt dates back to the Old Kingdom, and during the Eighteenth Dynasty there was a substantial renewal of interest in Re and particularly in the solar disk itself, the Aten. Beginning in Amunhotep III's thirtieth regnal year, the name Aten was written in a cartouche, just like the name of a pharaoh. In texts dating to that time, it is clear that Amunhotep III had actually become the living manifestation of the Aten, the living Atum-Re-Horakhty. Thus, when Amunhotep IV was shown adoring the Aten, he was actually adoring his divine father. In one contemporary text, Akhenaton was described as "the son . . . who came from the disk, effective for the one who is effective for him." As Amunhotep III had become the living Atum-Re-Harakhty, so his son, Amunhotep IV, had become that god's offspring, Shu, and Nefertiti, his wife, had become Shu's sister/consort, Tefnut.

During these years, Amunhotep IV continued building at Karnak, not for Amun, but for the "new" solar gods. In addition to a temple for Re-Harakhty, he also began work on a huge temple to the Aten that would cover thirty thousand square meters. It lay immediately east of the Temple of Amun at Karnak.

These temples differed significantly from other New Kingdom temple plans. Earlier temple buildings shared several features in common: they were built along a single axis; they were almost bilaterally symmetrical; and along their main axis, the floor gradually rose, the ceiling dropped, rooms became smaller, and chambers grew darker. By the time one reached the sanctuary where the statue of the god was kept, one stood in a small, totally dark chamber. Obviously, such darkness was inappropriate for the temple of a sun god, so Akhenaton's temples consisted of large rooms and courtyards all open to the sky. With their whitewashed floors and walls that blocked the wind, they were stiflingly hot and blindingly bright.

Amunhotep IV's buildings at Karnak—there were intended to be as many as six—made use of small, easily manageable blocks of limestone we call *talatat,* measuring about 53 by 23 by 26 centimeters, instead of the huge blocks traditionally used in Egyptian temples. It is thought that these smaller stones made it possible to construct buildings more rapidly. According to Amunhotep IV's chief sculptor, a man named Bak, the idea of using *talatat*—and, indeed, all of the innovative styles of art and architecture that characterize the king's co-regency and reign—came from the pharaoh himself. Amunhotep IV's temple was destroyed shortly after his death, and its stones were used as fill in the construction of later pylons. Ironically, this perfectly preserved the very scenes and texts that his successors were trying to destroy. Over 45,000 *talatat* have been recovered from Karnak. In the scenes here, Amunhotep IV and his wife are shown in poses of adoration beneath the Aten, the sun's disk, from which extend rays of light. The rays immediately in front of the two royal figures end in small hands that hold out *ankh* signs, the symbols of life.

Many of the elements of Amunhotep IV's so-called Amarna Revolution are already in place in these temples, but clearly there must have been ongoing discussions in the royal court about what, precisely, the pharaoh and his co-regent had to do to ensure the proper functioning of kingship in its new form.

One dramatic result of these theological musings was the decision to move away from Thebes.

AKHETATON

Shortly after Amunhotep III's thirty-fourth regnal year, the sixth year of Amunhotep IV's co-regency—and very shortly after the celebration of the second Sed-festival—Amunhotep IV, his family, and an entourage of officials and artisans left Thebes and moved north to found a new city. As he departed, Amunhotep IV announced that he was changing his name, abandoning its reference to the god Amun. Amunhotep, "Amon Is Satisfied," was to be known as Akhenaton, "Agreeable to Aton." And Akhenaton claimed that they were moving to a site that had been chosen by the sun god himself. It was christened Akhetaton, the "Horizon of the Aten."

Every time I've visited Akhetaton over the years, I've been amazed at what an awful place it is. The cultivation along the river's edge is only a few meters wide. Beyond it, to the east, there is nothing but a barren sand-covered plain, about three kilometers wide and ten kilometers long, shaped like a half-moon, and lined with high limestone cliffs that curve from north to south. Usually, the site is hot and windless, and when the wind does blow, sand and silt swirl across the landscape. Most tourists are anxious to get away from the heat and flies and choking dust, and usually head quickly for the tombs cut into the cliffs east of the plain. Bouncing uncomfortably in an open wagon pulled by a noisy tractor, they are oblivious to the fact that they are being driven over the site's most interesting part, the ancient town.

Akhetaton, whose modern name is Tel el-Amarna, is not a pleasant place and we have no clear explanation why Amunhotep IV chose it. One theory is that it was a virgin site where no earlier temples had been built; therefore, it could be considered pure and unblemished. Another is that he was drawn by the lush fields and the important Middle Egyptian town site of Hermopolis lying west across the Nile.

THE word "revolution" has been badly overused in Egyptology, but it does appropriately describe the changes wrought by Akhenaton and his father. They declared that there was only one principal god in the universe, the living Atum-Re-Harakhty, the Aten, who manifested himself in Amunhotep III. Then, they established two royal courts, sister cities where this new religion operated. One city, Malkata in Thebes, the "Palace of the Dazzling Sun Disk," was home to Amunhotep III, the living god of creation. The other, Akhetaton, was home to "the beautiful child of the sun disk," Akhenaton, the living manifestation of the god Shu, who was responsible for bringing light and life to the world. Both Malkata and Akhetaton complemented each other. Akhetaton, on the East Bank, was where the Aten, the sun's disk, rose on the horizon each morning; Malkata, on the West Bank, was where Atum-Re, the setting sun, traveled into the Netherworld each night. Both Malkata and Amarna were divine enclosures. They were not just parts of Egypt, but timeless places from which pharaoh and co-regent, Atum-Re and Shu, ensured the continuing operation of the universe. Both cities, both persons, were necessary to make certain that pharaoh and the gods could function properly.

Amunhotep III celebrated a third Sed-festival in year 37. Two years later, he was dead. For reasons we do not understand, he was not buried in the main (or East) Valley of the Kings, but in the larger and somewhat more remote West Valley. His tomb, designated as WV 22, had apparently been begun and abandoned by Thutmosis IV.

Architecturally, WV 22 is generally similar to other Eighteenth Dynasty royal tombs: alternating stairs and ramps lead to a small pillared hall, more stairs and ramps lead off the hall at right angles to the first set, and a six-pillared hall is followed by a sarcophagus chamber with a floor that was dug at a slightly lower level. A series of small storerooms lie off the burial chamber. Also, there are two somewhat larger rooms that were dug off the king's burial chamber, one at the rear intended for Queen Tiy, another through the left wall for their daughter Sitamun, who was declared a royal wife near the end of Amunhotep III's reign. The only objects from the tomb which we have records of today include *ushabti* statuettes, jewelry, canopic jars, fragments of wooden coffins and chests, pottery, and a pair of papyrus sandals. This particular tomb plan would not be followed again until the reign of Ramesses II.

AFTER twelve years as co-regent, Akhenaton became sole ruler of Egypt. Almost immediately, he dramatically issued a decree closing the Temple of Amun and those of several other gods around the country. Given the important role Egyptian temples played in Egypt's economy, closing them must have had serious and far-reaching consequences. He banned any references to Amun, and even the writing of the word "god" in the plural was prohibited.

Soon after his father's death, Akhenaton possibly appeared in reliefs wearing the *shebyu*-collar, although it has also been suggested that a figure at Amarna shown with the *shebyu*-collar might be Amunhotep III, not Akhenaton. If it is Akhenaton, he had then declared himself to be the living sun god, and if so, he presumably needed a co-regent to serve him as he had served his father. We have no hard evidence for this and no indication of who that co-regent might have been, but I think that it was his wife, Nefertiti.

The argument is shaky, but for the dozen years of Akhenaton's co-regency, Nefertiti played an unusually prominent role in Egypt's religious and political affairs. She was even represented in poses traditionally reserved for the pharaoh—shown, for example, wielding a mace and smiting the enemies of Egypt, or standing like a mighty conqueror, with (female) prisoners-of-war kneeling at her feet. Over and over again, Nefertiti shared center stage with her husband, performing religious rituals and overseeing political events, sitting in loving partnership with Akhenaton and their daughters as they received the gift of light and life from the Aten. But after regnal year 12, except for a few scenes in the royal tomb at Amarna, references to Nefertiti simply disappear.

At precisely this moment, however, a new figure appears in the record: a male figure named Smenkhkare, "He Whom the Spirit of Re Has Ennobled." We know nothing about Smenkhkare's origins or his career. He is represented in a few scenes with Akhenaton's eldest daughter, Meritaten, but nothing suggests that he was her husband. Smenkhkare bears the same epithet that Nefertiti bore: Nefer-neferu-Aten, "Exquisite Beauty of the Sun Disk," an odd epithet for a man. Several relief scenes show Akhenaton and Smenkhkare in such affectionate poses that some Egyptologists have suggested a homosexual relationship between the two.

It is also possible that Nefertiti, who was already prominent in court life and well versed in the new solar religion, was transformed into her husband's co-regent when he became sole pharaoh. Perhaps Nefertiti and Smenkhkare were the same person. A number of Egyptologists think so. The shift in gender, from female Nefertiti to male Smenkhkare, simply meant that instead of being the manifestation of the goddess Tefnut, the sister of Shu, Nefertiti now took Akhenaton's former role as Shu, while Akhenaton replaced his father as Atum-Re. Completing this picture, perhaps Akhenaton's eldest daughter, Meritaten, then became the new Tefnut.

Amunhotep IV was attempting to return to the solar cults of the Old Kingdom. But of course he was not able to duplicate what came before, and created instead a hybrid form that blended the modern perceptions of the old with the necessities of contemporary life. Even so, if this was all he was trying to achieve, Akhenaton might have set a pattern of religious beliefs for the rest of dynastic history. But unfortunately, he carried his father's ideas to an extreme. Canadian Egyptologist Donald Redford has likened what Akhenaton did to a fanatical Christian priest throwing aside Christ, the Trinity, and all the saints, and declaring that the cross was not just a symbol of salvation but the one, true God himself. Therefore, it's little wonder that when Akhenaton died in the seventeenth year of his reign, his successors tried to destroy every trace of him—although the cult of the Aten lived on in a much subdued form until its temples were finally closed by Ramesses II.

Akhenaton had a tomb dug for himself and his family in the hills east of Akhetaton. Neither his body nor those of his family members have ever been found, and most of the decoration in the tomb was completely destroyed as part of the campaign to rid Egypt of any traces of Atenism. Prior to his move from Thebes to Akhetaton in year 6, work was most likely begun on a tomb for the then-co-regent at Thebes. One candidate for that tomb is a West Valley sepulcher, WV 25, an unfinished stairway and corridor cut at the far end of the valley, although its dating is not certain. Other candidates thought by some to be Akhenaton's Theban tomb include WV 23, KV 55, KV 57—and KV 5.

*   *   *

THE evidence is slight, but many Egyptologists believe that, like Amunhotep III, Ramesses II also declared himself a god fairly early in his reign. Scenes and texts at Abu Simbel intimate as much. In doing so, he encountered the same problem his predecessor had faced: how to handle the secular duties of pharaoh after being declared a god. If they weren't performed by pharaoh, who could do them? With both Amunhotep III and Ramesses II, I think the answer was the pharaoh's son, his heir apparent. In a sense, the pharaoh's duties were divided, and the divine responsibilities were handled by the deified pharaoh, while the more secular responsibilities were taken over by the eldest son of his principal wife. This notion of shared responsibilities had first been established in the reign of Amunhotep III, but his son, Amunhotep IV/Akhenaton, had carried the idea to an extreme. Ramesses II again tried to allocate duties to his heir apparent and his attempt, I believe, may explain why KV 5 came into existence.

Ramesses II outlived many of his children, so several of his sons became heirs apparent and shared aspects of the kingship with their father during his lifetime. In the new scheme of things, these sons held positions of greater responsibility and authority than any ordinary crown princes had in the past. They actually *shared* aspects of kingship with their father. Thus, when these sons predeceased him, each was given a funeral and a tomb that was more elaborate than ordinary royal princes had received in former times. Just as their role had been somewhere between that of a pharaoh and crown prince, the form and function of their tomb lay between those of a pharaoh and his sons.

Ramesses II may have buried those sons who died early in his reign in the first chambers of KV 5. After his deification, when his heirs apparent had taken on new responsibilities because of their father's deification, those who died were interred in other parts of a much enlarged KV 5, created to acknowledge their new roles in court life and religion. Perhaps the tomb was enlarged several times to provide suites of rooms for the sons' burials. Each son may have had a burial place consisting of several offering chambers with elaborately decorated walls, quantities of funerary goods, and, of course, a burial chamber. Deep inside the tomb, watching over the bodies of his now dead heirs, stood the figure of Ramesses II wearing the *shebyu*-collar, the figure of Ramesses II as Osiris.

KV 5 DURING THE REIGN OF RAMESSES II

Lacking any evidence to the contrary, I assume that KV 5 was not actually used as a burial place during Phase One (its late Eighteenth Dynasty stage) and was abandoned. Therefore, when Ramesses II decided to usurp KV 5 for his own purposes, he was confronted with an empty, perhaps undecorated, two-chambered tomb. The broad picture of what happened next seems clear.

When Ramesses II's workmen set out to enlarge and remodel KV 5, their first task must have been to redecorate chambers 1 and 2, then cut and decorate chambers 3, 4, 5, and 6, all of which lie on the same level in the tomb. But when did that occur? On the ceiling of the sixteen-pillared hall, very close to the spot where James Burton wrote his name in lampblack, there is an unfinished graffito that was very graciously examined for us by our French Egyptological colleague Yvan Konig. Written in black ink, in hieratic (a cursive form of hieroglyphic), and clearly of Nineteenth Dynasty date, it reads: "Year 19, the completion of. . . ." Then it stops. Almost certainly this text refers to the nineteenth year of the reign of Ramesses II, but what was "completed"? Was it the cutting of the chamber from the bedrock? Decorating its walls? Filling it with funerary equipment? We don't know. (I have not yet been able to determine, by the way, if the chamber had always been a sixteen-pillared hall. Possibly it started out as a narrow chamber beyond chamber 2 or as an eight-pillared hall that was later doubled in size.)

We do know that Ramesses II's workmen were busy doing

something in KV 5 in regnal year 19. We can prove that much of the work in the tomb was undertaken during the first two decades of his reign. We know this because of the way the names of the pharaoh were written on the tomb's walls. The cartouches of Ramesses II appear several times in KV 5: on the doorjamb at the tomb entrance, on the walls of chambers 1 and 2, in the beginning

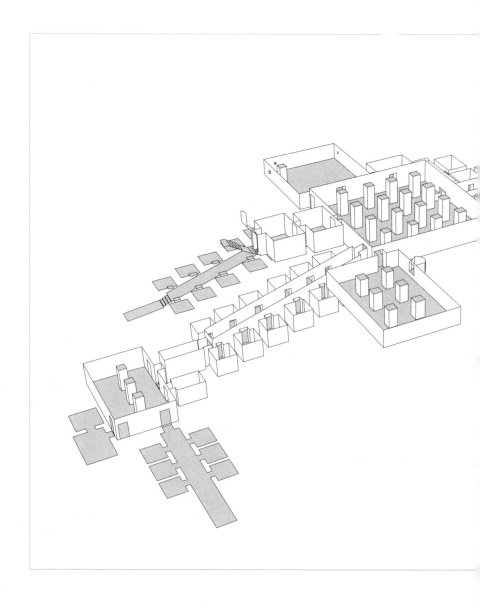

of corridor 7, and on the wall of corridor 13. In every case, the name is written "Ra-messes," *not* "Ra-messu." Ramesses II changed the spelling of his name in regnal year 20, though we do not know why. But in KV 5 his name is written in its preyear 20 spelling, and that means that the corridors and chambers where the name appeared—1, 2, 7 (part), and 13—were all decorated before

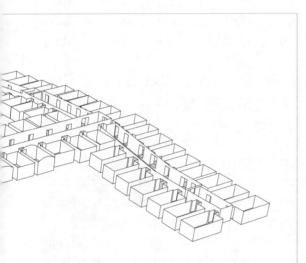

Perspective drawing of KV 5 as of April 1998. Corridors and chambers shown in plan have been seen but not yet surveyed.

year 20. And, of course, chamber 3 must also date to no later than the year 19 graffito on its ceiling. Chambers 4, 5, and 6 may also be of this date.

During the first two decades of his reign, the workmen of Ramesses II undertook the following work in KV 5: they decorated chambers 1 through 6; they cut and decorated the first part of corridor 7 and possibly chambers 8 and 9, together with the small chambers off them that are cut beneath chamber 3. They changed the floor level of chamber 3; and they hewed corridors 12 to 13 and perhaps those corridors' mirror images, corridors 20 to 21.

I include only the first part of corridor 7 in this phase of the work. The decoration on the first three meters of wall here (from the entrance door between corridor 7 and chamber 3 to the doorways that lead into sidechambers 7b and 7o), was carved in very fine low relief directly on the limestone walls. Beyond this, from side chambers 7b and 7o onward, the wall was "keyed" for plaster, been deliberately roughened so that a coat of plaster would adhere more firmly to it. Then, the decoration was carved and painted on a thick layer of plaster applied to the roughened wall. There was no geological reason to change the decorative style: the quality of the stone beyond doorways 7b and 7o was just as good as that of the stone preceding them, and the artisans could just as easily have carved it instead of using plaster, as they had done the first part of the corridor. Perhaps this change in technique occurred because it sped up the work. It's a lot easier to paint on plaster than to carve limestone delicately.

It's not known exactly how much time elapsed between the cutting and decorating of the first part of corridor 7 and its extension farther into the hillside, but it may have been a decade. In the cartouches of Ramesses II in KV 5, he spelled his name in its preyear 20 form. At the back of corridor 7, the statue of Osiris—or more correctly, the statue of the divine form of Ramesses II as Osiris—wears the *shebyu*-collar. I don't believe the king wore this collar until after his divinization, sometime before his first Sed-festival in year 30.

We cannot yet determine if work on the first part of corridor 7 was done at the same time as the work in corridor 12 (and corridor 20), but I suspect that corridor 7 came first. The stairs leading from the sixteen-pillared hall into corridor 7 were cut into the hall's original floor. The doorway into corridor 12, however, was not cut until the floor at the front of the sixteen-pillared hall had been lowered by nearly a meter. The sequence seems to have been as follows: the sixteen-pillared hall was dug, either as a single unit, in two 8-pillared stages, or in three stages if, in the Eighteenth Dynasty, a small corridor or niche lay beyond chamber 2. The walls of the pillared hall were then decorated and, finally, a section of the floor, about 150 centimeters wide, extending along the length of the hall's front wall, was cut lower. The lowering of the floor left about 80 centimeters of bare wall below the ground line of the decoration on the west wall. After the floor had been cut lower, *then* the doorways into corridors 12 and 20 were dug. One explanation for this extra work was that it enabled the workmen to add side chambers along corridors 12 and 20 that could extend beneath the floors of chambers 2, 4, and 5. Had they started the corridors at the original chamber 3 floor level, they could not have hewn the first four side chambers without breaking through the walls of the chambers above and beside them. Clearly, KV 5 was not based on a single plan that was carried out at one time. There were several stages.

Perhaps at this time, too, the main doorways of KV 5 were widened. These doorways lead into corridors rather than side chambers. The jambs of the entrance door into chamber 1, the doorways from chambers 1 into 2, 2 into 3, and 3 into 7 were each recut to make them fifteen centimeters wider, even though this meant cutting into figures and text that had already been carved on the chamber walls. (The walls presumably then had to be plastered and recarved.) Again, an explanation can only be guessed at: such recutting allowed some object wider than the original doors to be

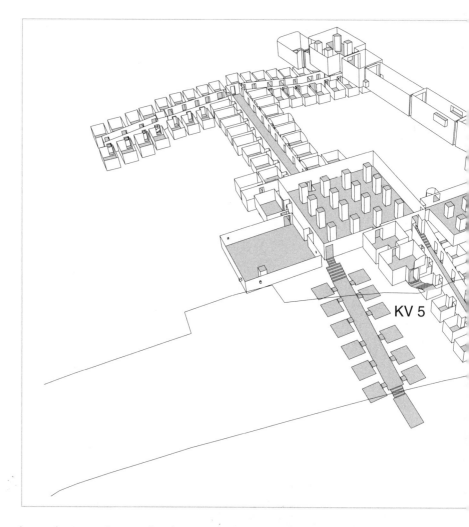

KV 5

brought into the tomb, the most obvious such object being a sarcophagus. There is no evidence for this, but if correct, we have to
ask ourselves where this sarcophagus was placed. I suggested earlier that a sarcophagus could not fit through the doors into the
tomb's side chambers. It could only have been dragged along the
corridors that have wide doorways to places in the tomb as yet
undiscovered.

All of this confusing information just shows how much of a puzzle KV 5 is. Changes were made to the tomb's plan over several

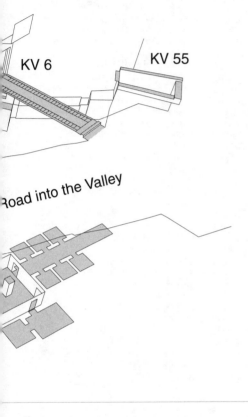

KV 6

KV 55

Road into the Valley

Perspective drawing showing the geographical relationship between KV 5, KV 6 (the tomb of Ramesses IX), and KV 55 (a tomb of the Amarna Period).

decades, and never did the tomb come even close to evoking the plan of a standard tomb. Things become even more obscure when we ask who (plural) Ramesses II ordered to be buried in KV 5 and in which order their bodies were interred. On the walls of the eight chambers we have so far cleared, we have found over two dozen representations of sons in paintings and reliefs. However, in nearly every case, the names have been destroyed by flooding and salt damage.

If KV 5 was intended for all of the principal sons of Ramesses II except Khaemwese and Merenptah, then we can expect to find more than forty different figures on the wall and forty burial chambers in the tomb. If fewer than that were buried here—perhaps as few as the four sons whose names we have found on objects and walls—then how were they chosen and what happened to the others? Our four sons lack a common mother, their titles differ, and they are of significantly different ages. Perhaps they only shared a common residence. Perhaps the sons buried in KV 5 all lived in Thebes while other sons lived in Memphis or Pi-Ramesses. Anything seems possible with this perplexing tomb.

Remesseum . 97 . silo .

13

THE SONS OF PHARAOH

THE knowledge we have of the sons of Ramesses II—and his wives and daughters—is meager, but it is more than we have about the families of other pharaohs. We know that Ramesses II had at least thirty sons by his principal and secondary wives, but that list includes only sons who survived infancy and takes no account of children by minor wives and concubines. There were undoubtedly many of those, but nothing about them is known. The sons of the principal queens were called "King's Son of His Body," meaning that they were biologically related to Pharaoh and born to a prominent wife, and we know their names from various temple inscriptions.

With few exceptions, the kings of Egypt left very few written records of their children. Except for the son who succeeded to the throne, they usually did not even mention the names of their offspring. This does not mean that pharaohs were uncaring fathers, but rather that kingship was perceived and represented in religious contexts in such a way that specific details were not given about royal family members. Among the few exceptions to this are texts from the Fourth Dynasty reigns of Cheops and Chephren, who left behind enough detail about their sons that fairly accurate genealogical tables are possible.

During the reigns of Thutmosis IV and Amunhotep III, New Kingdom pharaohs first referred to their children in monumental inscriptions, and Ramesses II included extensive (if not complete) lists of his principal sons and daughters. Unlike earlier rulers, Ramesses II had numerous processions of the princes and princesses carved on his temple walls. There are at least nine such scenes, inscribed in five different temples. Three of the temples lay in Nubia, two in Thebes:

- Abu Simbel: eight sons and nine daughters represented in procession
- Temple of Derr: identical to the Abu Simbel procession
- Luxor Temple: (a) seventeen sons depicted, fifteenth son omitted, sons 9 and 10 have their order switched
  (b) the same, but fifteenth son included
  (c) twenty-five sons represented
- Ramesseum: (a) twenty-three sons represented in procession
  (b) eleven sons in procession
- Wadi es-Sebua: (a) thirty sons, eight daughters
  (b) twenty-five sons, more than eight daughters
- Abydos, Seti I temple:
  (a) twenty-nine sons, sixteen daughters
  (b) twenty-seven sons, twenty-two daughters

Farouk Gomaa, an Egyptologist now at Tübingen University in Germany, has made a careful study of these lists. He notes that they all (with the exception noted in the scene at Luxor Temple, section a) always give the sons' names in the same order, and he believes that this is an indication of their birth order. The difference in the number of names depends on when in Ramesses II's reign the list was written: later lists include more sons because by then more sons had been born. The lists rarely indicate who each son's mother was, and so we have to learn that from other sources.

The lists name the children, male and female, of the pharaoh's principal wives, including not only living children but also those who died. Gomaa believes that only the children born to Nefertari and Isisnofret were ever in line to inherit the throne, but others, at least those of some other primary and some secondary wives, were shown in the procession as well. As Gomaa remarked, "If he [Ramesses II] had left one out, it would have meant that he cast him out and did not want to let him partake of the gods' mercy." Indeed, that was the very essence of the processional scenes. "Ramesses II did not commission these representations on the temple walls to boast about the large number of his children, but rather to recommend his children to the mercy of the gods. . . . The depiction of people on temple walls who were not kings was a rare favor which secured the person depicted eternal life with the lord of the temple. . . ."

In addition to the processions of sons and daughters carved on the temple walls, there are also partial lists or scenes that show only two or three offspring. Some of these representations might be called "action scenes":

- At Abu Simbel, a scene shows sons 1, 2, and 3 in war chariots, following their father into battle.
- In another Abu Simbel scene, two sons are shown standing.
- Also at Abu Simbel, four sons—numbers 1, 2, 5, and 6—are shown with daughters 3, 4, and 5.
- At Karnak, twelve sons bring prisoners-of-war back to Egypt.
- In Luxor Temple, sons 1 to 4 and 7 to 14 accompany prisoners-of-war.
- In the Ramesseum, two sons climb storming ladders, two are shown slaying enemies, and four stand behind shields.
- A colossal statue from Tanis shows sons 4 to 8.
- At Beit el-Wali, at least two sons are shown, son number 1 and another standing in war chariots.
- Inscriptions carved at Aswan and (perhaps slightly later) at Gebel es-Silsileh by Khaemwese show Khaemwese and sons 2 and 13 and daughter Bint-Aneth, all children of Isisnofret.

In tabulating the various lists, we are able to determine the names of Pharaoh's first sixteen male children born to his principal wives. The ones whom we have found named on objects or walls in KV 5 (as of 1988) are marked with an asterisk:

*1. Amun-her-khepeshef ("Amun Is with His Strong Arm"). Until the coronation of his father as pharaoh, he had been known as Amun-her-wenemef, ("Amun Is on His Right Hand"). He was the son of Nefertari and crown prince from regnal years 1 to 40. He died between age forty and fifty-five.

*2. Ramesses, whom we call Ramesses Junior to avoid confusion with his father, was a son of Isisnofret. He lived at least to Ramesses II's fifty-second regnal year and was heir apparent from regnal years 40 to 52.

3. Pa-Re-her-wenemef; son of Nefertari; probably died before regnal year 30.

4. Khaemwese; son of Isisnofret; lived at least until regnal year 55; heir apparent from regnal years 52 to 55.

5. Montu-her-khepeshef (called Montu-her-wenemef in Luxor Temple)

6. Neben-kharru

7. Mery-Amun

8. Amun-em-wia (probably the same son as the one called Seth-em-wia in some lists)

*9. Sethy (not to be confused with his grandfather, Seti I). This Sethy spells his name differently, more like the early writings of the name in the Eighteenth Dynasty. It is possible that this Sethy was named after an Eighteenth Dynasty ancestor, the father of Ramesses I, who lived and worked in the court of Amunhotep III and/or Akhenaton, but the evidence for this is not firm. He probably died before regnal year 30.

10. Setep-en-Re

11. Mery-Re I; son of Nefertari; probably died in his twenties

12. Hor-her-wenemef.

13. Merenptah; son of Isisnofret; succeeded his father Ramesses II as pharaoh; heir apparent from regnal year 55 on
14. Amunhotep
15. Itamun
*16. Mery-Atum

Of the thirty sons of Ramesses II, we have the most significant evidence about his fourth son, Khaemwese, and his thirteenth son, Merenptah.

KHAEMWESE

Khaemwese held the position of High Priest of Ptah at Memphis, and was most likely buried either at Giza or Saqqara. His brother Merenptah succeeded his father as pharaoh and has his own tomb in the Valley of the Kings, KV 8. Khaemwese and Merenptah are the only two sons we are certain were not buried in KV 5. Even so, their lives may give us a few clues about the lives of their brothers and half brothers interred there.

During his lifetime, Khaemwese's administrative skills, his knowledge of religious matters, his intelligence, and common sense made him one of the country's most respected individuals. A thousand years after his death, he was still regarded as one of the greatest scholars and magicians Egypt had ever produced. Several stories were written about him. One tale in "The Stories of Setne Khaemwese," for example, recounts how Khaemwese tried to possess a book of magical incantations written by the god Thoth, and another tells of how he once traveled into the Netherworld to see firsthand how the good were rewarded and the evil were punished. A part of the latter tale is so similar to the account in the New Testament of Lazarus and the rich man (Luke 16, 19–31) that some scholars believe that the biblical story was derived from it.

The second child of Ramesses II's second wife, Isisnofret, Khaemwese was probably born shortly after their marriage, perhaps while Seti I was still alive and Ramesses II was still a teenager. Khaemwese bore several titles and epithets: "King's Son of His Body, His Beloved, the Divine Essence Issuing from Ka-nakht [the Strong Bull, meaning Ramesses II], Khaemwese, True of Voice." While still a young prince—he may barely have been in his teens— Khaemwese and his older half brother, Amun-her-khepeshef, accompanied Ramesses II on a military campaign in Nubia. Records of this campaign are carved on the walls of the temple at Beit el-Wali. In one scene the two boys are standing with their drivers in war chariots, following their father onto the field of battle. In another, Khaemwese is taking part in a military campaign at Tunip in western Asia.

Unlike several of his brothers and half brothers, Khaemwese bore no military titles in these or any other scenes. He earned his formidable reputation not as a military leader, but as a cultured and erudite gentleman whose rapid rise through the ranks of the priesthood of Ptah at Memphis was due, ancient texts claim, to his talent, intelligence, and keen administrative skills. Khaemwese apparently was that rare breed of royalty—an individual admired and honored even more for his personal talent than for his royal blood.

In an inscription in the Serapaeum at Saqqara, Khaemwese wrote that he had joined the Memphite priesthood of Ptah at an early age and, not long after, had been made a "sem-priest of Ptah." The title of sem-priest can be traced back to the beginning of Egypt's history when, even then, it was regarded with significance. Whenever possible, the post was held by an elder son of pharaoh who, as sem-priest, played a major role in royal funeral ceremonies and who was therefore closely affiliated with the cult of Osiris. Sem-priests can be identified in Egyptian art by the elaborately painted panther skin they wear draped over their shoulders.

Khaemwese's appointment as sem-priest seems to have taken place just prior to his father's sixteenth regnal year. About a decade later, perhaps in regnal year 25, when he himself was about twenty-five years old, Khaemwese was promoted again, this time to the pre-eminent position of High Priest of Ptah. (For convenience, Egyptologists call holders of this title HPPs.) Over twenty-eight individuals in dynastic times bore this title, and all of them came from important Egyptian families: eighteen were sons of HPPs, two were sons of viziers, three were sons of pharaohs. The post was first given great prominence during the reign of Amunhotep III, who became the first pharaoh to give the title to his son. When Ramesses II made Khaemwese his High Priest of Ptah, he was following Amunhotep III's example. Some Egyptologists have argued that the High Priest of Ptah gained special prominence under Ramesses II because, like Amunhotep III, he thought that strengthening that position would effectively counter the potentially threatening powers of another priesthood, that led by the High Priest of Amun (the HPA) at Karnak.

Certainly, under Ramesses II, the High Priest of Ptah was at least equal in power to the High Priest of Amun. As the HPP, Khaemwese was responsible for all sculptors, jewelers, and artists working on royal commissions; he oversaw all royal architectural projects; he was in charge of religious ceremonies not only for Ptah but for Sokar, Osiris, Re, Apis, and other deities; and he was responsible for arranging the king's Sed-festivals.

We know that Khaemwese supervised the building of his father's mortuary temple, the Ramesseum, at Thebes; directed construction in the Great Hypostyle Hall at Karnak; and supervised temple-building at several sites, including Pi-Ramesses, the Ramesside capital city in the eastern Nile Delta. These were all major undertakings, not only as engineering works, but because each was for major deities at major sites. Khaemwese also oversaw the design and construction of the Great Temple of Ptah at Memphis. He is depicted on two colossal statues of Ramesses II that stood in front of that temple, his small figure barely tall enough to reach his father's knees. The figure is badly eroded, but the Egyptologist Farouk Gomaa has been able to make out a short inscription: "The King's Son, *Sem*-Priest and Servant of the God in the Temple of

Ramesses-miamun [Ramesses II] in the Temple of Ptah, Khaemwese." On a fragment of a stone column now in the Royal Scottish Museum that also came from Memphis, he is described as: ". . . Your beloved son . . . [the Greatest] of the Leaders of the Artistic Crafts, the *Sem*-Priest and King's Son, Khaemwese."

Being an architect of some talent and a priest concerned with tradition and form, Khaemwese took an active interest in the monuments of earlier pharaohs and boasted about it. Certainly, at Memphis he had ample opportunity to study Egypt's heritage: the great necropolis of Saqqara lay only a few kilometers to its west, that of Giza only a few more kilometers to its north. While examining the many earlier temples, shrines, pyramids, and tombs at these sites, Khaemwese said that he was astonished that scores of the structures were crumbling and on the verge of collapse. By Khaemwese's time, these monuments were already over a thousand, even fifteen hundred, years old, most were covered with sand, some had fallen over, and others had been used as quarry sites, torn apart to provide stone for a later pharaoh's buildings. Their appearance was embarrassing, and Khaemwese determined to do something about it. After consulting with Ramesses II, he began a program of cleaning and consolidation that resulted in the restoration of over a dozen pyramids, temples, tomb-chapels, and statues. In each case, Khaemwese carved inscriptions on the monuments proclaiming his good work:

His Majesty decreed that the Chief directing artisans, *Sem*-priest and King's Son, Khaemwaset, should restore the name of [here were carved the names of the pyramid of Unas or Shepseskaf or Sahure or Djoser or Userkaf, as appropriate] . . . Very greatly did the *Sem*-priest and King's Son Khaemwaset wish to restore the monuments of the Kings of South and North Egypt, because of what they had made, (of) which their solidity was falling into decay. He has established a decree for its (the pyramid's) sacred offerings . . . with its water . . . endowed with a land-grant, together with [its] personnel. . . .

On a statue of an Old Kingdom prince, Khaemwese wrote that the reason he undertook such restoration was because "so greatly did he love antiquity and the noble-folk who were aforetime . . . " This sounds noble, but there were doubtless other reasons. Of the eight or so monuments on which Khaemwese carved such restoration inscriptions, six were pyramids, symbolic of the cult of Re, and four dated from the Fifth Dynasty, when the cult of Re was especially strong. Perhaps Khaemwese believed that earlier forms of the solar cult of Re were purer. His restoration of early buildings might not have been an act of religious piety or archaeological concern, but instead an opportunity to learn more about a cult's earlier beliefs. One could then adjust contemporary practices accordingly.

At Memphis, the god Ptah, whose cult Khaemwese oversaw, was made manifest to mankind in the form of a living bull called the Apis. The bull that represented Ptah was chosen from among all the cattle of Egypt and housed in an elaborate sanctuary within the Precinct of the Temple of Ptah at Memphis. Selecting the Apis bull was a major undertaking. Upon the death of an Apis bull (they had a life expectancy of about twenty-five years), priests scoured the countryside searching for a replacement that possessed all the special markings that religious beliefs said the new Apis had to have. According to Herodotus, the bull must be "black and is known by these markings: he has a triangular white spot on his forehead and the likeness of an eagle on his back; the hairs of his tail are double and he has a 'beetle' under the tongue." When a new bull was selected and brought to Memphis to be declared the living manifestation of Ptah, its mother was brought, too. It was believed that the Apis was conceived when a bolt of lightning impregnated his mother, and she was therefore considered a manifestation of the goddess Isis.

As High Priest of Ptah, Khaemwese played a significant role honoring the Apis bull during its lifetime and supervising the bull's funeral at its death. These ceremonies were important because, when it died, the Apis was transformed into Osiris, just as the deceased pharaoh was believed to do. The dead Apis was called Osiris-Apis, or Osorapis, a name similar enough to that of the Greek god Serapis that the two gods became joined in the Ptolemaic period.

Osiris was one of the most important gods in Egypt, a god of vegetation, fertility, and the Afterlife. He was usually shown in the form of a mummy, arms crossed over his chest, holding the crook and flail, symbols of Egyptian kingship. It is quite possible that Osiris was originally a foreign god (perhaps from western Asia) adopted by the Egyptians, but by the Fifth Dynasty he had clearly become a part of the Egyptian pantheon. Osiris was considered to be the grandson of Shu, the god of air, and of Tefnut, the goddess of water; he was the son of Geb, the earth god, and of Nut, the goddess of the sky. From these ancestors, Osiris had inherited the title of king of Egypt, and he taught the foundations of civilization to his subjects. His consort was Isis, who was both his wife and sister, and the two of them ruled over Egypt during an age of peace, goodness, and wealth. Osiris was an extremely popular god in Egypt, especially in the New Kingdom, because he, above all other deities, could offer worshipers a fair hearing when they sought entry into the Afterlife. In addition, he held out the promise of resurrection and eternal life once they got there. His principal cult centers were Busiris, in Lower Egypt, and Abydos, in Upper Egypt, where he (or at least his head) was believed to have been buried. The cult of Osiris played a significant role in the Egyptians' concept of kingship. At death, a pharaoh was joined with Osiris, and, especially in the early Ramesside period, kings erected great monuments at Abydos in his honor.

Osiris had a brother, Seth, who was, in almost every way possible, his antithesis. In an act that Egyptian priests believed had shaken the foundations of divine existence, Seth grew jealous of his brother's great power as king and in a fit of anger murdered Osiris, then dismembered his body and scattered its pieces throughout Egypt. Seth immediately declared himself king of Egypt.

Isis, distraught at the death of Osiris, scoured Egypt to find her husband's body and restore it to life. Aided by Nephthys, the wife/sister of Seth, she finally located parts of the body at Abydos and other religious centers, gathered the pieces together, and magically made Osiris whole again. Fanning the corpse to give it the breath of life, Isis momentarily brought Osiris back from the dead, for just enough time that the two could have intercourse. Isis became pregnant, and nine months later, in a town in the northeast Nile Delta, she gave birth to a son named Horus. Meanwhile, Osiris journeyed into the Afterlife, where he became the Lord of Eternity. By restoring him and allowing him to become ruler of the Netherworld, Isis enabled Osiris to complete a cycle of life, death, and rebirth—the same cycle of life, death, and resurrection that Osiris symbolically offered to human beings. (Because of her role in this story, by the way, Isis gained an enduring reputation in Egyptian culture as a magician and healer. Her name means "She Who Has Power," and she was regularly invoked in ancient Egypt, and later in Graeco-Roman times, as protector against poisonous bites, dangerous animals, and evil acts in general.)

After Osiris left this earth to become the Lord of Eternity, Horus succeeded him as king of Egypt. Henceforth, Horus was closely associated with kingship, and every pharaoh in turn was believed to be his living manifestation. Then, at death, every pharaoh was believed to journey to the Netherworld to become Osiris. At death, or more precisely, at the coronation of the dead king's successor, the divine aspect of a king, his royal *ka*, passed to his legitimate heir. As the Swiss Egyptologist Erik Hornung put it, "Osiris is buried but his son Horus takes over the reins of world government; in his role as the sun god Re, Horus is 'tomorrow,' whereas Osiris is 'yesterday.' " Or, Horus is life in this world, Osiris is life in the next.

WHEN an Apis bull died, all of Egypt went into mourning, and an elaborate mummification ritual lasting seventy days was performed by the priests. We know about this ritual in considerable detail thanks to a papyrus bought in Alexandria in 1821 from "an unscrupulous dealer in antiquities," and now in Vienna's Kunsthistorisches Museum. Today known as "pVindob. 3873," the papyrus dates to the second century BCE. It measures forty-three centimeters high and nearly two meters long, and was written on both sides in a strange combination of demotic and hieratic scripts, two late forms of the Egyptian language. The papyrus describes the Apis embalming ritual in elaborate detail. It notes that the priests were expected to wear special costumes for seventy days of mourning, to let their hair grow long, and to avoid bathing. They were expected to wail loudly throughout each day, to fast completely for four days, and to avoid meat or milk for the remaining sixty-six.

The body of the dead Apis was carried from the stall it had spent its very pampered life in, to an embalming house within the Precinct of the Temple of Ptah. This building was cleared several years ago by a young British Egyptologist, Michael Jones. Inside the small stone structure, there was a rectangular chamber with a huge, magnificent alabaster platform in its center. The platform was carved to resemble a bed, its feet like the paws of a lion and a lion head at each corner. The Apis bull was laid on the platform, and the elaborate embalming process then began. A system of channels and basins caught the bodily fluids as they were drained off during washing and purification. These were saved and buried with the embalmed bull.

The section of pVindob. that describes embalming the Apis bull's tongue indicates how complex the process was:

> He begins the embalming of his tongue. They anoint it with the warm medicament. He cuts up a *sj.t*-cloth, which measures 3 palms in length and 6 digits in width. He swaths it at its front with 3 wrappings, while the *sj.t*-cloth is soaked in the warm medicament. He pulls up his tongue. He places the *hbs*-cloth under it. He pulls the edges of the *hbs*-cloth up until his tongue reaches in front of it upwards. He makes go . . . the left one to the right . . . the right one to the left; the (bandage)

in the midst goes upon them. The great *bnt*-cloth up, the little *bnt*-cloth and the *swt-mtr*-cloth like . . . for it upwards.

For each part of the animal—face, eyes, nose, ears, teeth, horns, and beyond to the tail—the papyrus describes procedures that had to be followed precisely if the Apis was to be transformed in the Afterlife into Osiris. These were important and complex undertakings, and even the pharaoh played a role.

An inscription from Saqqara describes Ramesses II's visit to the Apis embalming house to participate in such a ceremony during the king's thirtieth regnal year: "On this day, the majesty of Apis proceeded to heaven and to repose in the embalmery with Anubis, he who is in the embalmery. He embalmed his corpse, he removed his fluids (of decay), he banished his blemishes, for his rebirth, upon the pure alabaster in the Mansion of Gold, and to open his mouth with natron and incense. . . . "

The mummified Apis bull was buried at Saqqara in an underground complex called the Serapaeum. The Apis cult dates back to the earliest period of Egyptian history, and undoubtedly there was a sacred Apis necropolis at Saqqara from the Early Dynastic Period or even before. The earliest evidence we have of Apis burials dates only from the Eighteenth Dynasty reign of Amunhotep III, when individual Apis bulls were interred in single subterranean chambers entered along a short, sloping corridor. A small chapel was built aboveground, directly above the burial chamber. Between the reign of Amunhotep III and year 30 of Ramesses II, records show that a total of eight Apis bulls were buried, one every decade or so, and all followed this single-interment pattern.

But in year 30, the same year as his father's visit to the Apis embalming ritual, Khaemwese, who had been appointed HPP only a few years earlier, altered the pattern of Apis burials. Instead of interring each bull in a separate tomb, he dug a great catacomb, a subterranean gallery consisting of a long corridor and, off it, a series of burial crypts. When a bull died, it was mummified, placed in a huge stone sarcophagus (some weighed over eighty tons),

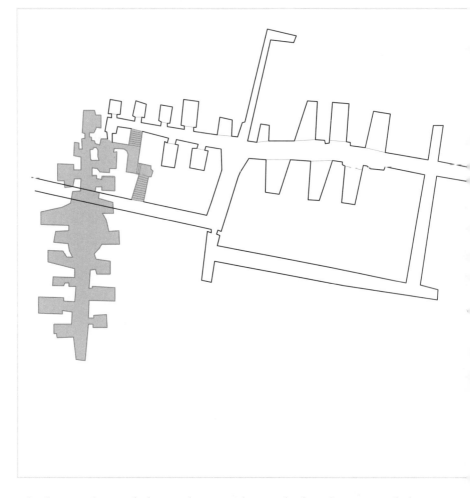

which was dragged down the corridor and placed in one of the crypts. The crypt was then walled up. When the next bull died, the Serapaeum was enlarged if necessary, more crypts were hewn in the bedrock, and the burial procedure was repeated.

In Khaemwese's time, the Serapaeum was over one hundred meters long. By Ptolemaic times, the complex had grown to include over 350 meters (1150 feet) of corridors, each 3 meters wide and 6 meters high, with several dozen crypts along them in which the sarcophagi were placed. A great temple to the Apis was built directly above the catacomb. The New Kingdom part of the

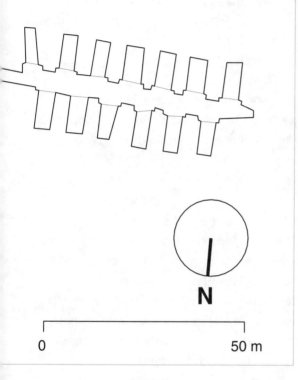

N

0   50 m

The Serapaeum, burial place of the Apis bulls. It was Khaemwese, fourth son of Ramesses II, who was responsible for its plan. For a time, we thought it might have inspired the plan of KV 5, but as KV 5 grows more complex, that now seems less likely.

Serapaeum attributable to Khaemwese is not accessible today. Tourists who visit the site can see only the later corridors, constructed in Late Dynastic and Ptolemaic times. At least in general plan, the Serapaeum that Khaemwese designed bears a resemblance to the plan of KV 5.

Khaemwese was especially proud of the construction of the Serapaeum. In a dedicatory inscription at the site he wrote:

The *Sem*-priest and King's Son, Khaemwaset, he (also) says: "O you *Sem*-priests, High Priests ('Chiefs directing artisans'), and worthies of the Temple of Ptah, God's fathers, priests in charge of sacred domains, prophets, lector-priests of this Temple, all who are [. . . . . .], and every scribe proficient in knowledge through the great god [who open the door-leaves of] heaven, who are before the god, and who shall enter into this Temple which I have made for the living Apis—and who shall see these things which I have done, engraved upon the stone walls as great and unique benefactions:

Never has the like been done, set down in writing in the Great Festival Court before this Temple. . . .

It will indeed (seem) to you a benefaction, when (by contrast) you look upon what the ancestors have done, in poor and ignorant work(s); there is none who should act [against] what is made for the repose of another. . . .

Remember my name, when decreeing [future such works . . .] . . . .

One of Khaemwese's other principal duties was to plan his father's Sed-festivals. The Sed-festival, sometimes called a jubilee, was usually first celebrated by a pharaoh in the thirtieth year of his reign, then at two- or three-year intervals throughout the remainder of his life. We don't know why this interval was chosen, partly because few pharaohs reigned long enough for these performances to be a common occurrence. In the Eighteenth Dynasty, only Thutmosis III and Amunhotep III held more than one jubilee. Ramesses II set a record. His first was in regnal year 30; then there were thirteen more, in years 33, 36, 39, 40, 42, 45, 48, 52, 54, 57, 60, 63, and a last festival in year 66, only a few months before his death. During these celebrations, Egypt reaffirmed the allegiance of the Two Lands to the pharaoh and paid tribute to the living king.

The Sed-festival was far more than a jubilee or a tribute. It was one of the oldest ceremonies in ancient Egypt. It had special importance in the Old Kingdom, and the way it was performed remained little changed for seventeen hundred years, from the First Dynasty until late in the Eighteenth Dynasty. Then, Amunhotep III made some significant alterations. One of the most dramatic was transfering the jubilee ceremony from temples on land to boats on the waters of a great lake, Birket Habu, which he had dug adjacent to his palace at Thebes. This may have been a way of mimicking the journey made by the sun in its solar bark through the Netherworld, thereby giving greater prominence to the solar cult. In Ramesses II's day, the festival was probably performed at Pi-Ramesses, with other major celebrations held at Memphis and Thebes.

Khaemwese organized the first nine of his father's Sed-jubilees. On a cliff at Gebel es-Silsileh, a site just north of Aswan, he carved an announcement of this great event: "Year 30, First Occasion of the Sed-festival of the Lord of Both Lands, Usimare Setepenre [given life forever. His Majesty decreed that] the jubilee-festival should be proclaimed in the entire land, by the King's Son and *Sem*-priest, Khaemwese, justified." To say that the festival was a joyous occasion seems an understatement. Khaemwese's text continues: "Father Amun has made for you your goodness in his mind; every god and goddess, their hearts are satisfied with your goodness, they spend all day, telling of your goodness, their hearts are (so) satisfied by your goodness."

IF Khaemwese was declared crown prince during his father's lifetime, it was only for a very brief period. We know from a shipping manifest from Memphis harbor that one of Khaemwese's elder brothers, Ramesses Junior, was still crown prince in regnal year 52. We are almost certain that his younger brother Merenptah was crown prince in year 55. Khaemwese must have died late in year 54 or year 55, which means that he could have been crown prince for no longer than three years and perhaps for only one.

We have not yet found any reference to Khaemwese in KV 5, and I doubt that we will. Egyptologists believe he was buried in the north, and many once thought he was buried in the Serapaeum.

They pointed out that Auguste Mariette—the French archaeologist who discovered the Serapaeum in 1851—found the mummified body of a middle-aged male lying in one of the side niches, accompanied by necklaces of semiprecious stones and amulets, wearing a gold mask. But Mariette found this material only after he had set off explosives to blow his way through the bedrock above the crypts. The mummy and its equipment might literally have been blown into the niche from a nearby tomb. No objects or texts were found proving definitely that the body was Khaemwese's. Later, Mariette decided that Khaemwese's tomb was most likely at Giza. Some Egyptologists have argued that he was buried within the Precinct of Ptah at Memphis, yet others he was first buried in North Saqqara, then reinterred six centuries after his death, in the Serapaeum.

Recently, during work at North Saqqara between 1991 and 1993, an expedition of Japanese Egyptologists from Waseda University uncovered the remains of a limestone building a kilometer north of the Serapaeum. On the building's east side they found a six-meter-wide, twenty-five-meter-long portico whose ceiling was originally supported by at least ten lotiform columns. Inside were several small chambers. Throughout the building, limestone blocks were scattered about, carved with the name and figure of Khaemwese. Over 2,500 objects were found here, all of them dating to the New Kingdom or later. But the architectural style of the building seemed to have been based on Old Kingdom models. Project directors Izumi Takamiya and Sakuji Yoshimura believe that the building was erected by Khaemwese. They say he modeled the structure on earlier monuments, that the building was deliberately archaizing in plan, that Khaemwese sought to follow here what he thought to be a much purer (because ancient) architectural form. After Khaemwese's death, the structure was dismantled; later still, it was restored. Now Egyptologists wonder: is this peculiar building a religious shrine or could it in some way be connected to the burial place of Khaemwese?

AMUN-HER-KHEPESHEF

We know something about the lives of Khaemwese and Merenptah (Merenptah was discussed in Chapter 9), but the processional lists indicate Ramesses II had perhaps thirty more sons and at least thirty daughters. Until the Theban Mapping Project discovered in 1995 that there was decoration on the walls of over a hundred chambers in KV 5, we knew little about those children. Now, perhaps, we can look forward to putting some flesh on the bones of the sons of Ramesses II. One of the most interesting and important is the firstborn son, Amun-her-khepeshef.

Amun-her-khepeshef's life could be one of history's most fascinating—if only there was more information available. *If* the Bible is correct and a series of plagues actually brought about an exodus of Jews from Egypt, and *if* the Exodus took place in the reign of Ramesses II, *then* Amun-her-khepeshef may have been killed by the tenth plague that God visited on Egypt. Amun-her-khepeshef was buried in KV 5, and medical studies may prove that one of the bodies we have found there may be his.

Amun-her-khepeshef was a son of Ramesses II and Nefertari. During his father's co-regency, the young prince had been called Amun-her-wenemef, "Amun Is on His Right Hand." At his father's coronation, however, his name was changed to Amun-her-khepeshef, "Amun Is with His Strong Arm." We do not know why this change occurred, but other sons of Ramesses II also had name changes at various times during their lives.

Amun-her-wenemef may have had other names, too. Egyptologists now believe that he was the same person as the Seth-her-khepeshef who had once been thought to be yet another son of Ramesses II. It was not unusual for a member of Egypt's royal house to have had several names; depending on what part of the country the individual resided in, a reference to one god was replaced by another. For example, when the young man was at Thebes, center of the cult of Amun, he was called *Amun*-her-khepeshef, but when he went to Pi-Ramesses, where the principal god was Seth, he might very well have been called *Seth*-her-khepeshef.

Amun-her-khepeshef bore several titles: "Fan-bearer on the King's Right Hand, Heir, Hereditary Prince, Royal Scribe, Generalissimo (of His Majesty), Eldest and Bodily King's Son, First King's Son, Commander of the Troops, Effective Confidant, Beloved of Him." If Amun-her-khepeshef and Seth-her-khepeshef were the same person, then an inscription on a stela from the eastern Delta site of Qantir gives us several other titles: "Chief of the Secrets of the King's House, Lord in Charge of the Entire Land, *Sem*-priest of the Good God, Delegate and Judge of the Two Lands, Controller of Lands Far-flung."

The titles borne by Amun-her-khepeshef are rarely the same as those held by the three other sons buried in KV 5. "Heir" and "Prince" are common to all; "Fan-bearer on the King's Right hand" is held by all but Sethy; "Royal Scribe" is given to all but Mery-Atum; "Beloved of Him" is given to all but Ramesses Junior. The title "First of His Majesty" is held only by Mery-Atum. And several titles, including "Effective Confidant" and "Commander of the Troops," are held only by Amun-her-khepeshef.

That last title is particularly interesting, because it indicates that Amun-her-khepeshef, of all Ramesses II's sons, played a significant role in the army. Indeed, the only evidence we have of Amun-her-khepeshef's activities are records of him taking part in battles in Nubia and western Asia early in his father's reign.

These battles were frequently depicted on temple walls. According to some Egyptologists, the young prince could not have been more than seven or eight years old at the time the battles were fought, so the scenes are polite fictions intended to give Amun-her-khepeshef a reputation as protector of Egypt. Other Egyptologists think that Amun-her-khepeshef was already a teenager and could very well have played a military role.

No deeds caused Ramesses II to boast more fulsomely than his military campaigns in western Asia. He devoted more wall space to battle accounts than any other pharaoh. These boasts are odd: many of the military activities of which he was proudest seem to have been tactically inept and even disastrous. His accounts have led many Egyptologists to accuse him of vanity and ostentation. The late American Egyptologist John A. Wilson found the military accounts of Ramesses II to be nothing more than "blatant advertising." In the king's accounts of the battle of Qadesh, says Wilson, "Ramses II doth protest too much. . . . It is all too clear that he was a stupid and culpably inefficient general."

The battle he fought in year 5, in the northern part of what is now Lebanon, was the most important of his reign and certainly the one of which he was the proudest. Amun-her-khepeshef took part in it. It was the battle of Qadesh, today considered one of the most famous military engagements of ancient times, partly because it is the first battle in history for which we have detailed records. Ramesses II recorded the story in huge scenes that sprawl across hundreds of square meters of walls at the Temple of Amun at Karnak, at Luxor Temple, at the Ramesseum, at his Abydos Temple, and again at Abu Simbel. The crucial location of Qadesh made its control essential if Egypt was to have access to Asian trade routes and prevent foreign armies from launching attacks against Egypt and the Levantine countries under its control.

During the reign of Seti I, an Egyptian campaign had been sent "to destroy the land of Qadesh and the land of Amurru." Although temporarily successful, Seti's control of Qadesh was short-lived (he relinquished the town in a treaty later signed with the Hittites), and Ramesses II, from early in his reign, seems to have looked forward to its recapture. The desire for conquest and for enlarging the Egyptian empire, which had been pounded into Ramesses since his youth, and the promise of booty, tribute, and prisoners to be used in great building activities all spurred Ramesses to action. In the fifth year of his reign, Ramesses assembled his army at Pi-Ramesses. The town became the staging area for an expedition that was set to recapture Qadesh and then control Hittite territory.

Egypt's army had four corps of about six thousand men each at Pi-Ramesses, and each was named for a principal deity. There was the Amun corps, raised principally at Thebes; the Pa-Re, raised at Heliopolis; the Seth, from the eastern Delta; and the Ptah, from Memphis. Each corps included about four thousand infantry, divided into twenty companies, and one thousand chariots. The chariots were light, fast, and highly maneuverable. Each was manned by a charioteer and an archer, whose lethal composite bow could be effective against enemies over a hundred meters away. We have found such bows in the tomb of Tutankhamun, and copies of them have actually been tested for range. The infantry was armed with battle-axes, swords, and daggers.

One can imagine the excitement in Pi-Ramesses as soldiers trained, supplies were organized, and tactics were discussed. There can be no doubt that Ramesses II himself played an active role in all aspects of the planning. Then, in April, 1274 BCE, Ramesses II, accompanied by Amun-her-khepeshef and Khaemwese, stood in his chariot at the head of the army and gave the order to move eastward. Logistics prevented the entire army from leaving at once. More likely, each corps moved out separately, perhaps at two- or three-day intervals. Their supplies were carried in slow-moving oxcarts, but food and the fodder for their horses had to be scrounged from the villages through which they passed.

Over the next month, traveling about twelve miles a day, they crossed the northern plain of the Sinai Peninsula, through Gaza and Canaan. Late in May, they arrived near the town of Qadesh. Ramesses and his sons traveled with the Amun corps, and they made camp about a day's march south of the town itself. The Ptah, Pa-Re, and Seth corps each lay farther south, separated from each other by gaps of about ten kilometers. Over the next few days they would move forward and join the Amun corps before the attack began.

The question was where the enemy was located. The Hittite army, led by King Muwatallish, was certainly heading toward Qadesh—no one doubted that the battle would be fought there—but when and from where it would arrive was unclear. As Ramesses and his generals pondered the situation, Egyptian sentries spotted two bedouin lurking near the encampment. Brought before the pharaoh, the two men were interrogated. They claimed that Muwatallish and his army were still many miles to the north and could not possibly arrive at Qadesh for several more days:

> Then said His Majesty to them: "Where are they, your brothers who [se]nt you to speak of this matter to His Majesty?"
>
> Then said they to His Majesty: "They are where the despicable Chief of Hatti [Muwatallish] is, "for the Fallen One of Hatti is in the land of Aleppo, to the north of Tunip. He feared Pharaoh too much to come southward, when he heard that Pharaoh was coming northward."
>
> Now, these Shashu said these things, and lied to His Majesty. (For) it was the Fallen One of Hatti who had sent them, to find out where His Majesty was. . . .

The two bedouin had been sent into the Egyptian camp by the Hittites to mislead Ramesses, and amazingly, Ramesses and his officers gullibly accepted the story without confirming it, and even released the two bedouin. The two men then raced back to Muwatallish and told *him* where pharaoh was located and where he was heading.

Convinced that the Hittite army was still several days away, Ramesses ordered the Amun corps to continue to move toward Qadesh. Here they established another camp, dug a defensive embankment around its perimeter, and set up a shrine to Amun and a huge tent with an electrum throne for the pharaoh in its center. Clearly, no one expected that a battle was imminent. But the next day, two other men were found by Egyptian sentries and were brought to Ramesses's tent:

> Then said His Majesty to them: "What are you?"
>
> What they said: "We belong [to] the Ruler of Hatti—he it is who sent us, to see where His Majesty is."

His Majesty said to them: "Where is he [Muwatallish]? . . .
"They said [to] His Majesty: "See, the despicable Ruler of
Hatti has (already) come, along with the many foreign lands
that accompany him, whom he has brought with him as allies.
. . . They are furnished with their infantry and chariotry (bearing their combat-weapons); they are more numerous than the
sands of the sea shore. See, they stand equipped, ready to
fight, behind Old Qadesh.

Under torture, the men claimed that Muwatallish and his army
were in fact just on the other side of Qadesh, only a few miles
away. Ramesses was stunned. It was clear to the Egyptians that
their position was extremely dangerous, even catastrophic, and so
the king directed his vizier to send urgent messages to the Seth,
Ptah, and Pa-Re corps, urging them to come forward immediately.
The Pa-Re corps appeared the next day at midmorning. Tired from
their fast march, disorganized and strung out for several miles, the
Pa-Re corps immediately found itself in a battle its soldiers were
not prepared for.

Even before all the Egyptian infantry and chariotry had arrived,
the Hittite army burst from the forests around Qadesh. With loud
cries and great clouds of dust, their huge chariots and lathered
horses thundered across the plain directly into the Pa-Re infantry,
slashing and stabbing with spears and swords, crushing the fallen
beneath their wheels, turning the brown landscape into a bloody
carpet of dead and dying soldiers. Egyptian soldiers in the rear
panicked and ran. The Hittites cut through the Pa-Re corps and
continued their headlong rush toward the encampment of the
Amun corps and Ramesses II.

At the Egyptian camp, the Amun corps received news of the disaster when the few surviving Pa-Re chariots raced into the enclosure. The Hittites were immediately behind them. The Egyptian
soldiers, utterly unprepared for the assault, raced through the
camp seizing any weapons at hand, desperately lashing out at the
enemy through blinding clouds of dust, deafened by the screams of

the dying and the thunderous roar of horses and chariots. Officials swirled around the pharaoh and his young sons, and hastily led them to comparative safety at the far end of the camp. Ramesses himself was giving orders to the chariotry for an attack. Once Amun-her-khepeshef and Khaemwese were safe, the pharaoh mounted the royal chariot and led his archers into the battle. The Egyptian chariots, lighter and more maneuverable than the Hittite vehicles, gradually began to repel the rout.

In one of the principal records of the battle, Ramesses is described as singlehandedly turning certain Egyptian defeat into glorious victory:

> His Majesty appeared (gloriously) like his father Montu, he took his panoply of war, and girded himself in his coat of mail; . . . The great (chariot)-span which bore His Majesty was (named) *Victory in Thebes*, of the Great Stable of Usimare Setepenre, Beloved of Amun, of the Residence.
>
> Then His Majesty set forth at a gallop, he plunged into the midst of the forces of the Hittite line, entirely on his own, no-one else with him.
>
> So, His Majesty went on to look around him; he found 2,500 chariot-spans hemming him in, all around him, even all the champions of the Hittite foe, along with the numerous foreign countries who were with them. . . . There was no high officer with me, no charioteer, no army-soldier, no shield-bearer. But my army and my chariotry melted away before them, none could withstand them, to fight with them. . . .

As he bravely and singlehandedly fought the enemy—so he claims!—Ramesses II says that at the same he was praying fervently to the god Amun for aid:

> I call to you, my father Amun,
> I am among a host of strangers;
> All countries are arrayed against me,

I am alone, there's none with me.
My numerous troops have deserted me,
Not one of my chariotry looks for me;
I keep on shouting for them,
But none of them heeds my call.
I know Amun helps me more than a million troops,
More than a hundred thousand charioteers,
More than ten thousand brothers and sons
Who are united as one heart . . .
I found Amun came then I called to him,
He gave me his hand and I rejoiced.
He called from behind as if from nearby:
"Forward, I am with you,
I, your father, my hand is with you,
I prevail over a hundred thousand men,
I am lord of victory, lover of valour!"

This is almost certainly wild exaggeration. Most scholars today would doubt that there ever were 2,500 chariots massed against Ramesses; he was certainly never left by his soldiers alone on the battlefield; and the majority of his infantry had not deserted him, they had just failed to arrive in time to fight this unexpected battle.

When Muwatallish's troops crossed back over the Orontes River, the battle was over and both sides retired to lick their wounds and to ponder the repercussions of a fight neither could truly claim to have won. In effect, Egypt failed to regain Qadesh, and Ramesses had to reconsider seriously any further expansion into western Asia.

Ramesses led several other military expeditions into western Asia during the next decade. In the eighth year of his reign, he successfully regained parts of Syria. In year 10, he managed to take Qadesh but hold it only briefly: the Hittites regained control almost immediately after the Egyptian troops withdrew. In part because their military campaigns were all so indecisive—and so costly—Ramesses II and Muwatallish's successor, Hatusilis III, signed a treaty in year 21 of the pharaoh's reign. Copies of the document have been found written in cuneiform on clay tablets at the Hittite capital. The Egyptian version, said to have been written on a tablet of silver, is known to us from two hieroglyphic stelae, one erected at Karnak, the other in the Ramesseum. The treaty recalls the battle at Qadesh, then lays out terms for a permanent peace: "The Great Ruler of Hatti shall never trespass against the land of Egypt, to take anything from it. And Usimare Setepenre, the Great Ruler of Egypt, shall never trespass against the land [of Hatti, to take anything fr]om it." Additional terms dealt with the extradition of criminals and the creation of a mutual defense pact if either Egypt or Hatti were attacked by a third party. The treaty was then witnessed by "thousands of gods male and female belonging to the land of Egypt," and by deities of Hatti. The list of the witnesses, a long and precious one, included: "the gods . . . the goddesses . . . the mountains and the rivers of the land of Egypt; the Sky, the Earth, the great Sea, the winds, the clouds."

THE EXODUS

When the news that KV 5 was possibly the burial place of Ramesses II's firstborn son hit the front pages in 1995, most reporters immediately focused on whether Amun-her-khepeshef was the firstborn son of the pharaoh mentioned in the Bible. The relevant text is Exodus 11, as quoted here from the Revised Standard Version:

The Lord said to Moses, "Yet one plague more I will bring upon Pharaoh and upon Egypt; afterwards he will let you go hence; when he lets you go, he will drive you away completely. Speak now in the hearing of the people, that they ask, every man of his neighbor and every woman of her neighbor, jewelry of silver and of gold." . . .

And Moses said, "Thus says the Lord: About midnight I will go forth in the midst of Egypt; and all the firstborn in the land of Egypt shall die, from the firstborn of Pharaoh who sits upon his throne, even to the firstborn of the maidservant who is behind the mill; and all the firstborn of the cattle. And there shall be a great cry throughout all the land of Egypt, such as there has never been, nor ever shall be again. But against any of the people of Israel, either man or beast, not a dog shall growl; that you may know that the Lord makes a distinction between the Egyptians and Israel. . . .

Moses and Aaron did all these wonders before Pharaoh; and the Lord hardened Pharaoh's heart, and he did not let the people of Israel go out of his land. . . .

God passed over the firstborn sons of the Israelites and, the Bible continues, Pharaoh finally relented and allowed Moses to lead the Hebrews out of Egypt and into the great and terrible wilderness of Sinai. This story has become one of the basic foundations of Judaic tradition. But is Ramesses II the pharaoh referred to here, and is Amun-her-khepeshef his firstborn son? Did the Exodus really happen?

If Amun-her-khepeshef, Amun-her-wenemef, and Seth-her-khepeshef were one and the same, then the chronology of the royal family suggested by Farouk Gomaa is probably correct. Gomaa believes that Amen-her-khepeshef was the heir apparent until his death in the fortieth year of his father's reign, when his half brother Ramesses Junior assumed that title. This means that Amun-her-khepeshef lived until he was at least fifty years old.

It is therefore likely that Amun-her-khepeshef was born shortly after the marriage of Ramesses II and Nefertari. Presumably, he was the royal couple's firstborn son, not just the first son to survive into childhood. If a son had been born to the royal couple before Amun-her-khepeshef, he must have died at an extremely early age, perhaps at birth, because otherwise his name would have appeared in the procession lists. This would also be true if a son older than Amun-her-khepeshef was born to Ramesses II's principal other wives. Therefore, for Amun-her-khepeshef to have had an older brother, Ramesses had to have fathered a son by a minor wife or a concubine. Such a child would not have been eligible to inherit the throne and would never have been named in any list of royal offspring, but his existence is possible. Of course, this is guesswork and not a shred of evidence exists for it. Amun-her-khepeshef was the firstborn son of Ramesses II and a *principal* wife, but we cannot be sure that he was "the firstborn son of Pharaoh."

It is also difficult to determine whether Ramesses II was the pharaoh of the Exodus or whether some other king ruled at that time. The Bible mentions no Egyptian names; it simply refers to "Pharaoh." Determining the date of the Exodus is nearly impossible: comparing chronological markers in Egypt with those in other ancient Near Eastern cultures is notoriously unreliable. Some historians and theologians have argued that Merenptah, Ramesses II's thirteenth son and successor, is a more likely candidate for the pharaoh of the Exodus; recently, several Egyptologists have suggested that it was Queen Hatshepsut. They push the date of the Exodus back by over a century and a half because they theorize that the volcanic eruption of Thera—the Mediterranean island of Santorini—could explain the parting of the Sea of Reeds (or the Red Sea, as some translations of Exodus describe it, probably erroneously). However, there is no proof for any of these theories.

A major problem is that no reference to the Exodus exists in any sources except in the Hebrew Bible and the Koran. The absence of references in Egyptian texts is understandable: why would the Egyptians record for posterity so terrible and humiliating an event? It would be better to excise the story of the plagues of Egypt and the Exodus from the country's collective memory.

Many scholars now believe that the Exodus is a story like that of Camelot. It is a folktale, a mythologized conflation of several earlier Egyptian events, and there are several good reasons to agree with this opinion. The first, of course, is the lack of any reference to the Exodus in Egyptian sources. American Biblical scholar William Dever notes the significance of this:

> It is well known that nowhere in Egyptian literature, in history, or in the archaeological record is there a reference or artifact that would indicate that the "proto-Israelites" were ever in Egypt. We confront virtual silence on the Egyptian side. The one text we do have, the famous Victory Stele of Merneptah, c. 1207 B.C.E., recognizes a people [sic] denoted 'Israel,' not in Egypt but rather in Canaan, and the text evidently knows nothing else about them. How could that be if these newly established "Israelites" in Canaan were former Hebrew slaves, recently escaped from Pharaoh and his armies in the eastern delta?

Cornell University historian James Weinstein elaborates: "There is no archaeological evidence for an exodus such as is described in the Bible in any period within the second millennium BCE. Perhaps there was a migration of Semites out of Egypt in the late 13th or early 12th century BCE, but if such an event did take place, the number of people involved was so small that no trace is likely to be identified. . . ." And Professor Israel Finkelstein believes that the total Israelite population in the twelfth century BCE was only about twenty thousand, certainly not the millions some supporters of the Exodus story have maintained.

Several Egyptologists point out that the biblical accounts of Exodus describe an Egypt more recent than the New Kingdom. It is a story unwittingly set by its authors in an Egypt of the sixth and seventh centuries BCE, an Egypt they had apparently never visited, and whose geographical names and cultural attributes they learned about secondhand.

The distinguished Canadian Egyptologist Donald Redford explains where this folktale might have come from: ". . . the Exodus was part and parcel of an array of 'origin' stories to which the Hebrews fell heir upon their settlement of the land, and which, lacking traditions of their own, they appropriated from the earlier culture they were copying." Redford refers here to the accounts in several ancient Egyptian and Near Eastern traditions of the so-called Hyksos invasion of Egypt after about 1640 BCE and the subsequent expulsion of these western Asiatic pastoralists in about 1570 BCE. This event, which is well documented, was the story that the Exodus was based upon. Jan Assmann, a highly respected authority on Egyptology and ancient religion and the author of a masterful study, *Moses the Egyptian*, agrees and also notes that much of the Exodus story owes its origins to later Egyptian and foreign views of the reign of Akhenaton and the so-called Amarna Heresy. Elsewhere, he concludes, "Egypt's role in the Exodus story is not historical but mythical: it helps define the very identity of those who tell the story."

As dramatic as it might be, the search for evidence that the Exodus really occurred, that Ramesses II was Egypt's pharaoh at the time, and that Amun-her-khepeshef was his firstborn son who was killed leads to a deadend: There is no point in trying to determine whether Amun-her-khopeshef was the firstborn son of Pharaoh killed by God's awful tenth plague, because no extrabiblical evidence supports the story of the ten plagues or a resulting Exodus. Or if an Exodus did actually occur, there is no proof that Ramesses II was pharaoh at the time. Or if Ramesses II *was* pharaoh at the time, there is no proof that Amun-her-khepeshef was the very first male child he had ever fathered. Or if Amun-her-khepeshef was the pharaoh's very firstborn son, there is as yet no proof that his body is one of those uncovered in the pit in chamber 2 of KV 5. Finally, if one of those bodies we found does turn out to be Amun-her-khepeshef's, it is hard to imagine what evidence we could find to prove that his death resulted from an unusual act of divine punishment and not a normal end to his life.

MUMMIES OF THE SONS

In autumn 1997 and spring 1998, we devoted a great deal of time to the painstaking clearance of the pit in chamber 2. The work began to pay dividends early one morning at the first week's end when we found parts of an adult male skeleton lying in debris about a meter below the floor of the chamber. We didn't see any traces of mummified tissue adhering to the bones, but the bones were stained, a typical feature of mummified remains, and fragments of tissue and linen wrappings were lying in the debris not ten centimeters away. Of course, we couldn't tell if the bones were the remains of one of Ramesses II's sons, but our workmen talked all morning about how exciting it would be if it were true. I warned them that the confused and fragmentary state of everything we had found in the pit meant that the bones might also have come from a later burial, or even that they had been washed into KV 5 by floods, but nothing seemed to diminish their enthusiasm.

"You know," one workman said, "Egyptian mummies are stuffed with gold. Even if we can see only bones now, there will be gold, too."

"I will be on television. My mother will be so proud if she sees me on television!"

As we continued clearing the pit, moving from the western end back towards the center, we uncovered the complete and mummified foreleg of a young cow that lay directly over even more traces of human bone. Haunches of beef were among the most prized grave goods, and this was almost certainly one of the food offerings brought to the tomb by priests for the burial of one of Ramesses II's sons.

A few days later, we began to expose a second skull, lying at the westernmost end of the pit, and an hour later we found a third. By the end of the day, there were tantalizing hints that a complete human skeleton (including a fourth skull) also lay in the pit. As we walked down to our truck at the end of work, I discussed plans for the next day's work with Ahmed. The skeletons required special care, and while I would prefer that Ahmed do the cleaning, I assigned the task to Sayed. Ahmed went to supervise the work in corridor 16.

Excavating the skeletons was extremely difficult: the bones were soft, easily crushed, and the fragments were embedded in a cement-like matrix of limestone chips and mud. That meant that we had to work with dental picks and artist's brushes—and great patience—carefully loosening the debris, then gently brushing or blowing it away from the skeleton. Some of the bones were in such bad shape that every few minutes we had to apply a thin solution of adhesive to keep them from disintegrating. This was unfortunate: obviously, we had to preserve the bones, but any adhesive we applied to a bone made that bone ineligible for chemical or biological testing.

This kind of meticulous work is awkward in the best conditions. Sayed and I squatted on the balls of our feet in a tiny space, only twenty centimeters wide, between the bones and the side of the pit. We had to use one hand to brace ourselves against the wall while we picked and brushed the skeleton with the other. It was difficult to clean the bones even cursorily in such a pose, but we had to do so before they could be photographed. Every piece of bone seemed to offer a troublesome problem, and it often took Sayed five or ten minutes to expose, clean, and stabilize a single square centimeter of the skeleton. It was slow going and exhausting. Every five minutes, we had to stop and stretch our cramped legs; every half hour one of the other workmen helped us out of the pit so that we could hobble about and restore our blocked circulation.

I wanted to clean the skeletons carefully and leave them *in situ* so that Francis could photograph them before they were removed and we could proceed to the next layer of bones and objects. The pit and its contents had the potential of being major finds, so I had Francis set up a tripod and camera directly over the pit so that, as we dug down through the fill, exposing more and more of the bones, he could take identically aligned photographs at regular intervals during the work. A technique such as this documents the clearing of the pit layer by layer and provides a step-by-step series of photographs.

Before leaving to pay a call on the inspectors in the Antiquities office, I repeated to the workmen my instructions not to touch the bones with their bare hands. Only Sayed and I are allowed near the bones, and we always wear gloves and are careful not to touch them with anything but a clean trowel and brush. It is essential to avoid contaminating the material. Even before we found the pit, I was hopeful that we would find human tissue in KV 5 that we could use to perform DNA analyses and other tests.

DNA tests could show that the four bodies are closely enough related to be brothers or half brothers. But there is a question about the reliability of testing mummies. Most scientists still doubt that DNA tests can achieve an acceptable degree of accuracy. No tests have yet yielded results acceptable to the majority of scientists. We will run DNA tests on the four skulls in KV 5, but I am not sure that any firm conclusions will come from them.

However, there is another test we can make. In 1972, James Harris, an orthodontist from the University of Michigan, and I X-rayed the royal mummies in the Egyptian Museum in Cairo. We wanted to learn about the health of the pharaohs, to determine their age at death, and to trace the physical similarities among them. We took meticulously aligned X rays of their heads, then, on computer, drew outlines of their skulls, precisely locating 177 anatomical points. Comparing measurements between these points on one skull with those on another, Jim Harris could argue that skull "A," was more similar to skull "D" than it was to skull "C," thereby showing degrees of similarity within groups of mummies.

Such statistical comparisons demonstrated that some of the royal mummies in the museum had been mislabeled by ancient priests when they moved the bodies from their original tombs to protect them from thieves. For example, the mummy labeled Seti II (Twentieth Dynasty) is more likely to be that of Thutmosis II (Eighteenth Dynasty), because it shows far greater craniofacial similarity to the Thutmosid series of pharaohs than to pharaohs of later times. This reattribution is supported by the age at which our pathologists said this mummified man had died. His age at death fits the historical data for Thutmosis II much more accurately than that for Seti II.

Craniofacial comparisons between the four skulls in KV 5 should show that they share a common genetic background: all four would have had the same father (Ramesses II), but ancient documents identify two as sons of Nefertari, two as sons of Isisnofret. We can also statistically compare the four skulls with the skulls of Seti I, Ramesses II, and Merenptah, their grandfather, father, and brother, respectively. If the craniofacial statistics show them to be closely related individuals, the chances are excellent that they are four of the sons of Ramesses II.

The overriding question, of course, is how these human bones were tossed into the pit. I doubt that the articulated skeleton was originally interred here—the body is jammed up against the western end of the pit. It also lies on top of several limestone pieces that probably washed into the tomb long after the last son was interred in the tomb. The three skulls must certainly have come from somewhere else, too. I have a theory about where, but at this point that's all it remains, a theory.

Let us imagine that ancient thieves entered KV 5 and removed the sealing blocks from the pit in chamber 2, pawed through its contents, and stole some of the objects that had been placed inside. We haven't yet determined what this pit was originally intended for, but a scene painted on the wall above it—the wall that Lotfy Khaled had to stabilize before we could proceed with our digging—shows a box containing four canopic jars. Such a box was probably placed in this pit; we may have found a piece of it last season in the fill of chamber 2. Most likely, a human mummy was buried here as well—the pit was certainly large enough to accommodate one, and the traces of painted plaster on its walls are consistent with a burial vault. The mummy must have lain in a wooden coffin because the pit is too narrow for a stone sarcophagus, and we have found traces of wood at the bottom of the pit.

Hastily, the ancient thieves probably hacked through the coffin and the mummy's wrappings, searching for gold jewelry and amulets.

Later, tomb robbers continued exploring the many chambers in KV 5, taking whatever treasures lay deep inside. Somewhere in the tomb, they discovered the burials of at least three more mummies. They dragged these bodies back into chambers 1 and 2, where light streaming through the front door made it easier for them to see as they ripped through the mummies, hacking heads from torsos, tossing skulls into the pit, punching holes through the wrappings, ripping out the amulets that had been placed there. Then they left mummified body parts scattered across the floor of chamber 2. Over the next several centuries, flood debris washed the body parts back into the tomb and buried the skulls in the pit with debris.

Just before shutting down for the 1997 season, we had removed three of the skulls from the pit in chamber 2. They were assigned catalog numbers in order from top to bottom, east to west. Number One is an extremely robust skull with large, rugged muscle attachments, and is certainly that of an adult male. The skull is very dolichocephalic—meaning that it is very long in relation to its width. There are at least four cervical vertebrae still attached to the cranium. The teeth are large and only moderately worn. There is a healed scar on the frontal bone just above the right eye similar to wounds made by a sword or ax—the kind of wound inflicted during a military battle. The blow would certainly have broken the skin and caused heavy bleeding, but the wound shows signs of having begun to heal and therefore was not fatal.

Skull number two, although also male, is more delicate. The jaw is small and the muscle attachments suggest someone of lithe build, not as muscular an individual as number one. Two or three neck vertebrae are still attached to the skull. The teeth are small and fairly heavily worn. Skull number three is very much like number two, but it is very badly broken and banged about. Its teeth are small and worn.

Skull number four, which is part of the fully articulated skeleton lying near the bottom of the pit, is similar to skull number one, and there is no doubt that it is of an adult male, around fifty years old. Its teeth are in beautiful condition and, in fact, of all the thousands of ancient Egyptian mummies and skeletons I have examined, I remember none with such nearly perfect teeth.

We removed the three skulls, but left the fourth skull and its skeleton in the pit. At some point we will have him moved in order to be X-rayed, but for now, as Ahmed said when we had finished cleaning in the pit, "We should let him sleep."

14

ENGINEERING AND TERRORISM

WE returned to KV 5 in the autumn of 1997, this time not to clear more chambers, but to begin some of the extensive engineering work in chamber 3 that will eventually allow us to clear it as well. I am still convinced that this pillared hall will offer up some of the most important clues yet to the purpose and history of KV 5, and I am anxious to strengthen its ceiling, stabilize its pillars, and expose its decorated walls and artifact-strewn floor. This work is going to take considerable time and money. If it were only an engineering project, we could probably complete it in a few weeks. But any clearance of the debris in chamber 3 must be done in an archaeologically sound manner, and that means several months of work. I have had mining engineers from Parsons-Brinckerhoff and a French team of structural engineers examine the chamber, and John Abel, from the Colorado School of Mines has designed a system of ceiling supports and pillar repairs.

THE terrorist attack at Deir el-Bahari in November 1997 that killed fifty-eight Egyptians and tourists shocked everyone in Luxor. We were working outside KV 5 when it happened. Susan

was sorting pottery next to the tomb entrance; Francis was photographing on the hillside above KV 7; I was on the hill above KV
5 watching our workmen clean and fill natural fractures in the
bedrock with cement. Thousands of tourists were in the valley, and
we could hear tour guides talking in a dozen languages telling their
groups about the sons of Ramesses II. At about 8:45 A.M., Ahmed
and I heard what sounded like gunshots and screams coming from
over the hill.

"What on earth was that?" I asked. The noises and screams continued for a few moments, stopped, then started again.

Mohammed was alarmed. "Someone is shooting." He ran down
the hill toward the inspector's office. "I'll telephone and see what
is happening," he shouted back. Ahmed pointed toward the
entrance to the valley. Two unarmed antiquities site guards were
running up the road. They looked scared and from their walkie-
talkies we could hear the voices of men shouting and obviously in
panic.

"They're killing tourists! They killed some workmen! O God! O
God!" The guards ran through thick crowds of tourists toward the
inspector's office.

"We must get off the hillside, Doctor!" Ahmed turned and
shouted to the workmen. "Everyone get inside the tomb!"

As we made our way down the hillside toward the tomb,
Mohammed returned from the inspector's office. He was pale and
seemed to be in shock. He leaned against the pottery-sorting table
and began to cry. "Terrorists are killing people at Deir el-Bahari.
They say many tourists are dead, and they have killed some
guards. The terrorists are still killing and someone says they are
coming here. Please, put everyone in the tomb, Doctor. God curse
these murderers!" He repeatedly slammed a clenched fist into his
hand as the tears streamed down his face.

Susan walked down the steps into KV 5, and Mohammed ran
across the path to help Francis carry his photographic equipment
down the hill. Hundreds of tourists were still milling about,
unaware of the situation, but gradually a few site guards, presum-

ably on somebody's orders, began steering them down the road to the rest house. There was no panic, not even hurried footsteps, and as some tour groups headed out of the valley, other groups continued to come in, oblivious to what was happening.

Unasked, our eight workmen had formed a line around the entrance to KV 5 and our pottery table, forming a human barrier. One of them, a powerfully built worker who holds many body-building awards, paced in front of the line, telling any passersby who looked in our direction to keep moving, not to stop anywhere near us. In furious tones, Mohammed said, "By God, I will kill anyone who threatens us with my bare hands." I believe he truly would have. As the minutes went by, we received reports that several terrorists had been killed by villagers, who chased them and kicked them to death.

Gunshots and screams and shouts could still be heard, but over the next hour they became increasingly less frequent. Twenty riderless donkeys clipped through the valley, abandoned by a group of tourists who had retreated to the rest house. Ahmed and I stood outside the tomb entrance, listening to one of the guards' walkie-talkies. Hysterical voices continued to track the path of fleeing terrorists, tearfully giving body counts, and we heard that several terrorists had come to the Temple of Hatshepsut at Deir el-Bahari dressed as policemen. The walkie-talkie reports described people not only shot but nearly decapitated. Some victims had had their throats slashed or had been disemboweled. These stories—which later proved true—grew increasingly sickening and terrifying.

All of us were in a state of shock. It was more than an hour before any armed policemen finally appeared in the valley, and even then only two teenaged recruits and a lieutenant arrived in a beat-up pickup truck. Francis and I stood outside the tomb.

"How do we know those policemen are really cops and not terrorists?" I asked.

Francis and I both moved several steps nearer the tomb. Susan had gone into chamber 4, our storeroom, and was sorting through bags of pottery. She said, "At times like this I want to be busy, not stand about worrying. It does no good."

About two hours later, we were told that we could leave the valley. By then, the several thousand tourists who had been standing at the rest house had been herded onto buses and driven back to the river to board boats across to Luxor. One of the rumors spreading around was that two or three of the terrorists had still not been captured, but none appeared to be heading toward the valley.

We drove out with the French team that had been working in the tomb of Ramesses II, because there were no taxis to be had and our car was back at the hotel. It seemed inadvisable to walk over the mountain.

Dr. Michael Jesudason was with us. He is an emergency-room physician who spends a month each year helping Susan record our pottery finds. He asked to be dropped at the clinic at Ta'arif to help treat the wounded, but when we got there we were told that the victims had already been taken to the hospital in Luxor. We found a taxi outside the clinic and returned to the Amoun Hotel. Except for a large number of villagers standing outside the clinic's walls awaiting news of the wounded guards, the West Bank was empty. There were no buses, taxis, private cars, or police to be seen except at the traffic station, where half a dozen policemen in flak jackets milled about with automatic weapons in their hands, peering into passing vehicles and occasionally stopping them and asking the driver for identification.

Back at the hotel, we turned on the BBC and listened in silence to the news reports and the mounting death toll. It was still only 6:00 A.M. on America's East Coast, but I crossed the river and telephoned our children to let them know that we were safe before they heard the gruesome reports and worried.

The next morning, our workman Nubie came by to report that his younger brother had been at Deir el-Bahari during the massacre. He had chased after one of the terrorists, catching him by his belt and hanging on to him while crying out for help. The terrorist turned and shot him in the groin, but Nubie's brother still refused to let go. Finally, the terrorist broke free, and Nubie's brother fell to the ground, weak and bleeding. The terrorist tried to run up the mountainside, but he had twisted an ankle and wasn't able to make it. One of his gang came back to him and shot him in the head, apparently unwilling to leave anyone alive whom the Egyptian police could interrogate. The terrorist ignored Nubie's brother, apparently thinking him dead. Local villagers ran up the hill after Nubie's brother, and four of them stopped and carefully lifted and carried him down the hill to the parking lot, where they commandeered a car and drove him to the clinic. Others stayed behind on the hillside and vented their anger by kicking and spitting on the corpse of the terrorist.

Nubie's brother was visited in hospital the next afternoon by Egyptian security men, who gave him a handshake, praised his bravery, handed him five hundred Egyptian pounds, and arranged to fly him to Cairo to have the bullet that had lodged near his intestines removed.

This whole affair was tragic not only for the tourists and their families, but for the people of Luxor, whose constant refrain, "No Egyptian could do such a thing, it must be a foreigner," gave way to shock and tears when they realized that the incident had been the work of their countrymen.

Two days later, a group of about a thousand West Bank men paraded from the temple of Seti I to Deir el-Bahari, chanting, "Death to terrorists," trying to convince news reporters—and themselves—that such a horror would never happen again. They carried banners: "Terrorist Not Egypt," "Egypt Love You," "Here You Never Be Stranger," "We Are Very Sorry."

Tourists began leaving Luxor in droves, and hotels were being deluged with cancellations. What was expected to be the best tourist season ever—some hotels were overbooked at 110 percent occupancy through New Year's Day—turned into a debacle. By the end of the week, most hotels had only 8 percent occupancy, and some had simply shut their doors and laid off their staff. It was a rough time for the locals, who depend almost exclusively on tourism for their livelihood. The press says that the terrorists wanted to bring down the Egyptian government by bringing about economic chaos. The government will survive, but economic disaster has indeed hit Luxor and to its inhabitants, the future looks bleak.

Two of our workmen, Mohammed and Said, left us at the hospital on the day of the massacre and walked back to the temple at Deir el-Bahari, where they volunteered to help the police remove bodies. Mohammed described the carnage he had witnessed, saying that only a sense of duty kept him there.

"This is my country, Doctor, and I had to help. The tourists came here as our guests and we failed to keep them safe. This is wrong!" He began to cry. "I hope God will kill all terrorists!"

The day after the "incident" (as the slaughter now is being called in Luxor), I went to Deir el-Bahari to deliver a note to one of the inspectors there. The grounds in front of the temple had been cleaned, but in its porticos, eight laborers from the Antiquities Department were scraping gore from the decorated walls and trying to remove bloodstains with abrasive stones. One workman was using a knife to gouge out bullets embedded in the brightly painted plaster. As they worked, the men seemed almost to be in a trance; their movements were jerky, their work sloppy and random. A few tourists walked past, and I wondered why the EAO had not closed Deir el-Bahari for a few days so that the cleanup could be done properly and the inspectors could be spared the embarrassment of being photographed as they worked.

We also went back to work in KV 5 the day after the incident. It seemed best to preserve some semblance of normalcy. The mood of the men was subdued, and they talked quietly, discussing who among their friends had been killed and how families were coping or relating what they had seen on television about the world's reaction to the events. All of the men were furious at the government for having been so ill-prepared for such an attack; for the arrogant attitude of a police force that now showed itself to be incompetent;

for the cowardice of several guards who failed to join villagers who were chasing the terrorists; for the economic ruin the incident brought to Thebes; for the humiliation of Egypt in the eyes of the world.

"The police know nothing!" said one workman. "They only swagger and demand free cups of tea and bribes—and for what? They are not trained and they are lazy! They are stupid people! We can take better care of ourselves without them. They do not help, they only make problems for us!" He spat on the ground. "*That* is what I think of the police!"

We stayed on in Thebes for two more weeks and continued work in KV 5. Then it was time to return to Cairo. Having spent two months in the tomb, we acquired so much material that it will take at least three or four months to analyze and prepare it for publication. Drawings of plaster fragments must be compared with the decoration in other tombs if we are to reconstruct the complete wall scenes they came from. We have artifacts to study and pottery to reconstruct and date; soil, plaster, paint, and mineral samples to analyze; human and animal bones to identify and test.

WE returned to the Valley of the Kings in January 1998. Susan and I had spent Christmas and New Year's sailing the Nile from Aswan to Abu Simbel, visiting temples we had not seen since the 1960s—Beit el-Wali, Amada, Derr, Wadi es-Sebua, Abu Simbel. These were the fortunate few that had been moved to high ground before Lake Nasser came into being. We photographed scenes that Ramesses II had carved on their walls showing long processions of his sons and daughters, and checked the records of his battles at Qadesh and in Nubia.

Amun-her-khepeshef was in many of the scenes, standing in his war chariot, climbing a scaling ladder to breach an enemy fortification or marching at the head of a procession of sons, dressed in an elaborately pleated gown and carrying a bouquet of flowers. Whenever I saw him, I thought of the human remains in KV 5.

Was one of them he? In real life, did Amun-her-khepeshef look like the figures carved on these temple walls? When we returned to Cairo, I contacted several anthropologists and forensic pathologists in America. I suggested to Susan that we should find someone to make a computer reconstruction of the skeleton's face, put flesh on bone, and see what Amun-her-khepeshef might have looked like. Such reconstructions are now made with computers rather than plaster casts and modeling clay. They produce images similar to those one might see on a Wanted poster, not portraits, but they might prove interesting.

In the meantime, we spent most of spring 1998 doing engineering work in the tomb. We hired steelworkers and welders to erect steel pillars and I-beams in chambers 1, 2, and 3, following the carefully designed support system laid out for us by John Abel. Each morning, I stood in a chamber, John's written instructions in my hand, and watched as our quarrymen pried blocks of stone, some of them weighing half a ton or more, away from the ceiling. The noise when they fell reverberated through the tomb chambers. It was safer to remove loose blocks than to try to support them, but the process was nerve-racking.

Once the loose blocks were removed, we installed supports and beams. First in chamber 2, then in 1 and 3, our workmen held screw jacks in position as steel cross-beams were fitted and wedges driven between the beams and the ceiling. Then the jacks were leveled and tightened, and the workmen moved away quickly as the beams and cross-members were welded into position and the tomb chamber filled with showers of sparks and the acrid smell of smoke. Thanks to this engineering work, KV 5 is becoming the safest, most stable tomb in the Valley of the Kings.

We had deliberately left debris around the pillars in chamber 3 to give them extra strength until the engineering work necessary to support them could be performed. Now, we were ready to install the supports and beams, and we began clearing around the first pillar beyond the doorway into the chamber. About eight feet below the ceiling, in the debris adjacent to the pillar, Ahmed found what he thought at first was a piece of roughly cut alabaster. He called me over, and together we began removing the debris that encased it. Gradually, we exposed a curved surface that looked like the lip of a large stone container. Half an hour later, we lifted the stone from the debris. The piece was about the size of a soccer ball. One surface had been carved with two male figures, each with blue-painted skin and a red kilt. The figures, the curved surface, and the carved lip clearly identified it as a fragment of an alabaster sarcophagus lid. My American colleague Edwin Brock, who has spent several years studying the royal sarcophagi in the Valley of the Kings and who was also working in the valley, visited us later in the day, and I asked him to examine the fragment.

"It's part of a sarcophagus lid," he said, "but it's unlike any I've seen before. It's certainly Nineteenth Dynasty in style." He paused and looked at the decorated surface. "The two male figures are interesting. They're both the same size, but the head of the first looks higher than the head of the second. That could mean they're climbing steps. Now, there are figures of 'denizens of the Netherworld' climbing steps in scenes that accompany 'the Book of Gates.' " The "Book of Gates" is one of the "Books of the Dead" that describes the journey of the sun each night through the Netherworld. Copies of "The Book of Gates" are frequently found carved or painted on royal tomb walls.

"There's a fine copy of 'The Book of Gates' on the alabaster sarcophagus of Seti I in the Soane Museum in London," Ted continued. "But I've never seen figures as large as these. Either it's a very large sarcophagus or only a part of 'The Book of Gates' is included here."

"Could it have been carved for one of Ramesses's sons?" I asked.

"That's very possible."

This was exciting. The fragment was one more clue that KV 5 had been used as the burial place of the royal sons, and it reaffirmed my conviction that, somewhere down the tomb's many corridors, we will eventually come to burial chambers. They were probably robbed by ancient thieves, but the increasing likelihood that they exist gives us additional reason to continue with the clearing of KV 5.

After we removed the sarcophagus fragment, the workmen continued digging down to floor level. Last season, we had already discovered that when the floor along the front wall of chamber 3 had been finished off by Ramesses II's quarrymen and the chamber walls decorated, then the floor level was dug another seventy centimeters (twenty-seven inches) lower. Now, we found that there was a third construction stage: after the floor was cut and then lowered, it had been raised back to its original level by dumping thousands of pieces of limestone in the front of the room and covering them over with a thick layer of hard, white plaster, well made and nicely applied. Across the plaster floor were scattered hundreds of potsherds, many of the smallest ones lying in clusters as if a larger sherd had been crushed under the feet of ancient visitors. There were also small pieces of faience and alabaster canopic jars and chunks of decorated plaster from the adjacent pillars and walls. Beneath the plastered floor, however, the limestone filling was clean, free of dirt, sand, or artifacts.

Raising the floor to its original height was apparently a project of importance to the ancient Egyptians, but it makes no sense to me. Its explanation—and, indeed, the explanation for much of KV 5's strange plan—may lie in the center of chamber 3. I am increasingly anxious to complete the badly needed structural engineering here so we can clear the debris in order to trace the room's complicated history. For example, there are sixteen pillars in chamber 3. We know that fourteen of them were cut from the living rock, but two others, in the center of the room, were built, at least in part, of hewn blocks. Remember that the principal axis of the first chambers of KV 5 was shifted about three meters north in chamber 3 before continuing down corridor 7. Could building the two pillars have been delayed because they would have been in the way? Perhaps a large object—a sarcophagus, for example—was dragged down the axis of chambers 1, 2, and the beginning of chamber 3, then moved north before being pulled further into corridor 7 or chamber 5 or 6. Ahmed and I wondered aloud if there was another passageway beneath the center of chamber 3.

There are still basic questions about this tomb that can be answered only if we continue to dig and meticulously analyze the data. For example, what was the purpose of each of its many chambers? That can be learned only studying the contents of every room and the traces of decoration on every wall. Perhaps determining the pattern of flooding in the tomb might help, too. If it can be determined in which direction the floodwaters moved through the tomb's corridors, we might be able to distinguish objects that were washed into a chamber from objects placed there by ancient priests. We will have to spend hours in Egyptological libraries trying to find any scenes similar to those in KV 5 if we hope to reconstruct the pottery fragments we have found. Susan, of course, has hundreds of hours of drawing and pottery analysis to look forward to; Francis has elaborate photographic surveys to process; Walton has months of work at the computer, generating maps and plans of KV; Brendhan has to translate all of these new data into a user-friendly format for our web site so we can make them available to colleagues as rapidly as possible. The time we spend away from the excavation is even more hectic than time spent in Thebes.

Of course, there is still a great deal of fieldwork left, too. Our studies of the Valley of the Kings are almost finished, but there are years of work ahead for us in KV 5, even though we do not plan to excavate the tomb completely. That would be bad archaeology. Every generation of Egyptologists asks different questions of its data and data are a finite resource. We will leave parts of KV 5 undug so that archaeologists of the future, armed with new questions and new excavation techniques, can seek new answers to old questions and to others we haven't even dreamed of.

In the meantime, there is plenty to keep us busy: the tomb probably contains more than 150 corridors and chambers, and we have cleared fewer than 7 percent of them. Studies of the fragmentary artifacts will take several years, the wall decoration even longer.

But I am convinced that when we have finished, KV 5 will be the best-documented and best-protected tomb in the Valley of the Kings and its former occupants, the sons of Ramesses II, will have given us more information about their lives and their society than we have today. I have no problem waking each morning in Luxor: every day is filled with the most exciting and rewarding work I could ever hope for. I am constantly grateful that I had teachers in my hometown willing to encourage an eight-year-old boy who dreamed of Egypt.

EPILOGUE

ON our last night in Thebes, at the end of the 1998 spring season, Susan and I sat on the balcony of the Amoun Hotel, making lists of the supplies we needed next season and watching the sun set behind groves of palm trees and fields of sugarcane. Sun birds were taking a final flight among the branches of a tamarisk tree before settling in for the night. As we stood watching the sunset, we looked over the balcony. Below us, a tiny girl, about six years old, walked past the hotel. She wore a tattered red dress, blue plastic shoes, and an orange ribbon in her unkempt hair, and with shrill cries and a large stick prodded four huge camels down the dirt path to her family home. Ordinarily, these camels would have been ridden by tourists who had spent an hour "going native" on the West Bank, riding through the fields and drinking cups of sweet tea in the desert. They would have paid twenty dollars for the adventure. Today, the camels had been tied in a field to graze, and no tourists came to ride them. The effects of the incident at Deir el-Bahari are still being felt in Luxor, and the poorest people are being hurt the most.

Susan and I talked about the changing character of the West Bank and about what we would do when we returned to Cairo tomorrow. I had computer work to see to with Brendhan and Walton, fund-raising letters to send out, a mound of data to pore over, and a lecture tour in the States to prepare for. I told Big Ahmed that we would return to Thebes in June. Summers are hot in Luxor—typically over 110 degrees Fahrenheit in the afternoon—but inside KV 5 it's a nearly constant 75 degrees year round, and the work is relatively pleasant, although we gulp five or six liters of water per person per day.

As the last rays of the sun disappeared, Nubie called from the courtyard below.

"Doctor! Hello, Doctor! Can I come up, Doctor? I have some news."

"Of course, Nubie," I called back. "Come and have tea."

Nubie climbed the flight of stairs to our balcony and sat at the table. "Zeinab had our new baby last night! I am the father of a new daughter!" He looked at Susan. "We named her Jasmine, but whenever you are here in el-Gezira we will always call her 'Susan' in your honor."

"Nubie, that's wonderful! Thank you!" Susan beamed and shook Nubie's outstretched hand. "Please tell Zeinab that I will visit her in the morning, before we leave. We are so happy for you!"

"Thank you, thank you. I am very happy. This is very good. Thank you."

Ahmed and the staff of the hotel heard our laughter and quickly came up to offer congratulations. Everyone shook hands and hugged and kissed, drank tea, offered the usual wishes for good luck and good health, then jokingly asked about the baby: did she resemble Zeinab (lucky baby, they said) or did she look like Nubie (poor thing!)? The group laughed, and one of the men went to fetch a radio so we could have music while we drank our tea.

Ahmed turned to me. "It is good, Doctor. There are problems, but then we remember that we have family and friends and sometimes God blesses us even more with babies. And He has blessed us with many wonderful things in KV 5." He paused.

"I have been thinking, Doctor. Could we bring more men and work faster in chamber three next season? I want to look at the floor of the room. In the middle. I am sure there is something very interesting there. Next season, *insha'Allah,* God willing, I think that Ramesses will tell us where his sons were buried."

He looked at me and smiled. "*Ilhamdulillah!* Thanks be to God! KV 5 is very exciting, Doctor. Don't you think so?"

APPENDIX

TIME LINE of Ancient Egyptian History

BCE 3100	Neolithic Cultures		
	Early Dynastic Period	Dynasty I	3100 – 2900 BCE
		Dynasty II	2900 – 2700 BCE
2700	Old Kingdom	Dynasty III Djoser, Sekhemkhet, Huni...	2700 – 2610 BCE
		Dynasty IV Khufu, Khafre, Menkaure...	2610 – 2500 BCE
		Dynasty V Userkaf, Sahure, Niuserre, Unas...	2500 – 2345 BCE
		Dynasty VI Teti, Pepi I, Pepi II...	2345 – 2184 BCE
2184	1st Intermediate Period	Dynasties VII - X	2184 – 2040 BCE
2040	Middle Kingdom	Dynasty XI Intef I, Mentuhotep I, Mentuhotep II...	2040 – 1991 BCE
		Dynasty XII Amunemhet I, Senusret I, Amunemhet II...	1991 – 1782 BCE
1782	2nd Intermediate Period	Dynasties XIII – XVII	1782 – 1570 BCE
1570	New Kingdom	Dynasty XVIII Thutmosis III, Hatshepsut, Akhenaton, Tutankhamun...	1570 – 1293 BCE
		Dynasty XIX Seti I, Ramesses II, Merenptah...	1293 – 1185 BCE
		Dynasty XX Ramesses III, Ramesses IX, Ramesses XI...	1185 – 1070 BCE
1070	3rd Intermediate Period	Dynasties XXI – XXVI	1070 – 525 BCE
525	Late Period	Dynasties XXVII – XXXI	525 – 332 BCE
332	Græco-Roman Period	Macedonian Kings Alexander the Great, Philip Arrhidæus...	332 – 305 BCE
		Ptolemaic Dynasty Ptolemy I, Ptolemy III, Cleopatra VIII...	305 – 30 BCE
AD 395		Roman Emperors Augustus, Trajan, Septimius Severus...	30 BCE – 395 AD

TIME LINE of The New Kingdom

BCE 1570			
	Dynasty XVIII	Ahmose	1570 – 1546 BCE
		Amunhotep I	1546 – 1524 BCE
		Thutmosis I	1524 – 1518 BCE
		Thutmosis II	1518 – 1504 BCE
		Thutmosis III	1504 – 1450 BCE
		Hatshepsut	1498 – 1483 BCE
		Amunhotep II	1450 – 1419 BCE
		Thutmosis IV	1419 – 1386 BCE
		Amunhotep III	1386 – 1349 BCE
		Amunhotep IV (Akhenaton)	1349 – 1334 BCE
		Smenkhkare	1334 BCE
		Tutankhamun	1334 – 1325 BCE
		Ay	1325 – 1321 BCE
1293		Horemheb	1321 – 1293 BCE
	Dynasty XIX	Ramesses I	1293 – 1291 BCE
		Seti I	1291 – 1278 BCE
		Ramesses II	1278 – 1212 BCE
		Merenptah	1212 – 1202 BCE
		Amunmesses	1202 – 1199 BCE
		Seti II	1199 – 1193 BCE
		Siptah	1193 – 1187 BCE
1185		Twosret	1187 – 1185 BCE
	Dynasty XX	Setnakhte	1185 – 1182 BCE
		Ramesses III	1182 – 1151 BCE
		Ramesses IV	1151 – 1145 BCE
		Ramesses V	1145 – 1141 BCE
		Ramesses VI	1141 – 1133 BCE
		Ramesses VII	1133 – 1126 BCE
		Ramesses VIII	1126 BCE
		Ramesses IX	1126 – 1108 BCE
		Ramesses X	1108 – 1098 BCE
1070		Ramesses XI	1098 – 1070 BCE

NOTES

Page

6 "It was . . . sunshine." Amelia B. Edwards, *A Thousand Miles Up the Nile*. London: Longman, 1877, pp. 414–415.

6 "His and hers." Kenneth Kitchen, *Pharaoh Triumphant: The Life and Times of Ramesses II, King of Egypt*. Warminster, Eng.: Aris and Phillipps, 1983, p. 66.

7 "On every . . . he trod." Edwards, op. cit., p. 432.

44 "Nothing that . . . Vatican Library." Arthur Stanley, *Sinai and Palestine in Connection with Their History*. London: Murray, 1856.

46 "Please manufacture . . . stolen." Ostracon Deir el-Medineh 251, translated in Edward F. Wente, *Letters from Ancient Egypt*. Atlanta: Scholars Press, 1990, p. 141.

46 "[The mayor] . . . pay heed!" Ostracon Berlin 11238, ibid., pp. 134–135.

49 "a narrow . . . the rock." Richard Pococke, *Travels in Upper and Lower Egypt*, vol II. Edinburgh: 1805, pp. 34–35

54 "the story . . . buried there." Claude Sicard, *Oeuvres*, II: *Relations et mémoires imprimés* (=*Bibliothèque d'Etudes*, 84). Cairo: Institut français d'archéologie orientale, 1982, pp. 264–265.

54 "there are signs . . . just finish'd." Pococke, op. cit.

56 "I, Dioskorammon . . . bewildering!" Quoted in George Hart, *Egyptian Myths*. Austin: University of Texas Press, 1990, p. 8.

59 "in parts . . . rubbish." Quoted in Elizabeth Thomas, *The Royal Necropoleis of Thebes*. Princeton: privately printed, 1966, p. 75.

59 "he was obliged . . . lights." Ibid.

61 "King's Daughter . . . Hatshepsut." Sarcophagus inscription, quoted in Thomas, op. cit., p. 196.

64–65 "has paid . . . any other." Giovanni Belzoni, *Narrative of the Operations and Recent Discoveries* . . . London: Murray, 1820, p. 231.

65 "about noon . . . magnificent tomb." Ibid.

68 "Sir, I have . . . a purpose." Quoted in Donald Ridley, "Champollion in the Tomb of Seti I: An Unpublished Letter," *Chronique d'égypte* 66, 31 (1991): 23.

68–69 "Rest assured . . . to sell." Quoted in Stanley Mayes, *The Great Belzoni*. London: Walker, 1959, p. 293.

69 "The limestone . . . and candles." Howard Carter, "Report on General Work Done in the Southern Inspectorate," *Annales du service des antiquités égyptiennes* 4 (1903): 43.

70 "a complete . . . decoration." Erik Hornung, "Studies in the Decoration of the Tomb of Seti I." In Richard Wilkinson, ed., *Valley of the Sun Kings: New Explorations in the Tombs of the Pharaohs*. Tuscon: University of Arizona Egyptian Expedition, 1995, p. 70.

71–72 "I gave it . . . day before." Quoted in Mayes, op. cit., p. 182.

73 "The sarcophagus . . . was there." Belzoni, op. cit., pp. 236–237.

73 "an inclined . . . 150 feet." Quoted in Thomas, op. cit., p. 150.

77 "attempt to . . . the god." Henri Frankfort, *The Cenotaph of Seti I at Abydos* (= Memoires of the Egypt Exploration Society, 39). London; 1932.

78 "not having . . . hundred figures." Belzoni, op. cit., p. 237.

90 "In the brain . . . venereal complaints." In the unpublished diaries of James Burton, British Museum Library.

90–91 "My friend . . . for sale." Ibid.

92 "This tomb . . . sarcophagus stood." Ibid.

92 "Situated quite . . . or order." Edward Lane, unpublished manuscripts, GI notebook (1). Quoted in Thomas, op. cit., p. 150.

97 "Now, Ushihe . . . my superior." Turin Papyrus, quoted in Kent R. Weeks, "The Theban Mapping Project and Work in KV 5." In Nicholas Reeves, ed., *After Tutankhamun: Research and Excavation in the Royal Necropolis of Thebes.* London: KPI, 1992, p. 102.

100 "Ramesses Mery-Amon . . . before Osiris." I am grateful to Marjorie Aronow for confirming these titles and those of sons in the following quotes.

118 "turned from . . . shed blood." Gaston Maspero, quoted in Alison Roberts, *Hathor Rising: The Serpent Power of Ancient Egypt.* Devon, Eng.: Northgate, 1995, p. 12.

146 "representation . . . a story." G. A. Gaballa, *Narrative in Egyptian Art.* Mainz, Germany: von Zabern, 1976, p. 5.

148 "Whether . . . Kàrnak hypostyle." James Henry Breasted, *A History of Egypt.* New York: Scribner's, 1937, pp. 418–419.

148–149 "So uncertain . . . New Kingdom." William J. Murnane, "The Kingship of the Nineteenth Dynasty: A Study in the Resilience of an Institution." In David O'Connor and David Silverman, eds., *Ancient Egyptian Kingship.* Leiden, Netherlands: Brill, 1995, p. 214.

149 "Everything has . . . the army." Great Dedicatory Inscription of Ramesses II, Temple of Seti I at Abydos. In Kenneth Kitchen, *Ramesside Inscriptions.* Oxford, Eng.: Blackwell's, 1979. (Hieroglyphic text, I: 328; translation, I: 167–168.)

150 "When my . . . for [me . . .]." Ibid., pp. 168—169.

151 "some new . . . of nature." Henri Frankfort, *Kingship and the Gods: A Study of Near Eastern Religion as the Integration of Society and Nature.* Chicago: University of Chicago Press, 1948, p. 102.

151 "The Falcon . . . of Amun." Kitchen, *Pharaoh Triumphant,* op. cit., p. 43.

160 "The historical . . . description." Stanley Weintraub, *Victoria.* New York: Dutton, 1987, p. 636.

164 "The princes . . . no seed." Donald Redford, *Egypt, Canaan and Israel in Ancient Times.* Cairo: American University in Cairo Press, 1992, pp. 71–72.

188 "many turn stupid." W.M.F. Petrie, *Ten Years Digging in Egypt, 1881–1891.* London: Religious Tract Society, 1891, p. 167.

198 "I see . . . for ever." Pyramid Text 170, translated by Raymond

Faulkner, *The Ancient Egyptian Pyramid Texts*. Oxford: Oxford University Press, 1969, p. 270.

199 "like a . . . cannot interpret." Elizabeth Thomas, "Cairo Ostracon J. 2460." In *Studies in Honor of George Hughes* (= *Studies in Ancient Oriental Civilizations,* 39). Chicago: University of Chicago Press, 1976, pp. 109–216.

200 "From *(tr(t)yt* . . . 445 cubits." Ibid.

205 "Monitoring has . . . the tomb." John McDonald, *The Tomb of Nefertari, House of Eternity*. Santa Monica, Calif.: Getty Conservation Institute, 1996, p. 44.

207 "greatly favoured . . . her voice." Inscription in Luxor Temple, translated in Kitchen, *Ramesside Inscriptions,* op. cit., vol. I, p. 553.

210 "by situation . . . Ramesses II." Thomas, *The Royal Necropoleis,* op. cit., p. 150.

214 "He made (it) . . . his majesty." Stela translated in Arielle Kozloff, Betsy Bryan, Lawrence Berman, and Elizabeth Delange, *Egypt's Dazzling Sun*. Cleveland: Cleveland Museum of Art, 1992, p. 91.

218 "family ties . . . political scene." Nicolas Grimal, *History of Ancient Egypt*. Oxford: Blackwell's, 1992, p. 221.

221 "It was . . . son of Amen." Kheruef inscription quoted in Kozloff et al., op cit., p. 40.

221 "Luxor Temple . . . onwards." Lanny Bell, "Luxor Temple and the Cult of the Royal Ka," *Journal of Near Eastern Studies* 44 (1985), p. 280.

222 "out of good . . . the stars." Kozloff et al., op. cit., p. 83.

223 "researched (in) . . . to alight." Kitchen, *Ramesside Inscriptions,* op. cit., vol. II, pp. 165–166.

223 "the divine . . . royal *ka*. Bell, op. cit., pp. 251–252.

223 "actually *becomes* . . . ceremony." Ibid.

224 "rejuvenation . . . *Sed*-festival." W. Raymond Johnson, "The Dazzling Sun Disk: Iconographic Evidence That Amenhotep III Reigned as the Aten Personified," *KMT* (Summer 1991), p. 22.

225 "the presence . . . on earth." Ibid.

226 "Thus, we find . . . (Aten)." Kozloff et al., op. cit., pp. 110–111.

227 "the ritual . . . of rule." Johnson, op cit., p. 60.

227 "Re-Horakhty . . . sun disk." Ibid.

227 "Amenhotep's construction . . . of Ra." Kozloff et al., op cit., p. 111.

232 "the son . . . for him." James P. Allen, "The Religion of Amarna." In Dorothea Arnold, ed., *The Royal Women of Amarna*. New York: Metropolitan Museum of Art, 1996, p. 127, f. 12.

251 "If he . . . mercy." Farouk Gomaa, *Khaemwese, Sohn Ramses II und Hoherpriester von Memphis* (= *Ägyptologische Abhandlungen*, 27). Wiesbaden, Germany: 1973:

251 "Ramesses II . . . the temple." Ibid.

255–256 "The King's Son . . . Son, Khaemwese." Memphite statue inscription in Gomaa, op cit.

256 "Your beloved . . . Khaemwese." Memphite column inscription, ibid.

256 "His Majesty . . . personnel." Inscriptions on the Old Kingdom pyramid of Unas and the Sun temple of Niuserre. In Kitchen, *Ramesside Inscriptions,* op cit., p. 567.

257 "So greatly . . . aforetime." Ibid.

257 "black and . . . the tongue." Herodotus, quoted in *The Apis Embalming Ritual: P. Vindob. 3873* (= *Orientalia Lovaniensia Analecta,* 50). Leuven, Belgium: Leuven University Press, 1993, p. 60.

260 "unscrupulous . . . antiquities." Ibid., p. 1.

260–261 "He begins . . . upwards." Ibid., p. 60.

261 "On this . . . incense." Kitchen, *Ramesside Inscriptions,* op. cit., p. 202.

263–264 "The *Sem*-priest . . . [such works] . . ." Ibid., pp. 569–570.

265 "Year 30 . . . justified." Gebel es-Silsileh inscription, ibid., pp. 208–209.

265 "Father Amun . . . your goodness." Ibid., p. 597.

268 "Chief . . . far-flung." Ibid.

269 "Ramses II doth . . . general." John A. Wilson, *The Culture of Ancient Egypt*. Chicago: University of Chicago Press, 1956.

271 "Then said . . . Majesty was . . . " Kitchen, *Ramesside Insciptions,* op. cit., p. 597.

271–272 "Then said . . . Old Qadesh." Kitchen, *Pharaoh Triumphant,* op cit., p. 15.

273 "His Majesty . . . with them." Ibid.

273–274 "I call . . . lover of valour!" Miriam Lichtheim, *Ancient Egyptian Literature,* II: *The New Kingdom.* Berkeley: University of California Press, 1976, pp. 65–66.

275 "The Great Ruler . . . the clouds." Kitchen, *Ramesside Inscriptions,* op. cit., pp. 81–84.

278 "It is well known . . . delta?" William Dever, "Is There Any Archaeological Evidence for the Exodus?" In E. S. Fredrichs and L. H. Lesko, eds., *Exodus: The Egyptian Evidence.* Winona Lake, Indiana: Eisenbrauns, 1997, pp. 81–84.

278 "There is no . . . identified." James Weinstein, "Exodus and Archaeological Reality." In ibid., p. 98.

278-279 "the Exodus . . . copying." Redford, op. cit., p. 422.

279 "Egypt's role . . . the story." Jan Assmann, *Moses the Egyptian: The Memory of Egypt in Western Monotheism.* London: Cambridge University Press, 1997, p. 41.

ACKNOWLEDGMENTS

I owe debts of gratitude to the people mentioned in the text and to a number of other friends and colleagues.

In Egypt, the members of the Supreme Council for Antiquities, and especially Dr. Abd el Halim Nur ed-Din, Dr. Gaballah Ali Gaballah, and Dr. Zahi Hawass, have been very supportive of our work. In Luxor, Dr. Mohammed el-Sughayyer, Dr. Mohammed Nasr, Dr. Sabry Abdel Aziz, Chief Inspector Ibrahim Soliman, and Inspectors Ahmed Ezz and Fathy Yaseen made that work possible. Our local workmen, headed by Ahmed Mahmoud Hassan and Nubie Abdel Basset, are among the finest people one could ever want to work with.

Also in Egypt, I want to thank my colleagues at the American University in Cairo, including Chairman of the Board Frank Vandiver, President Donald McDonald, Provost Andrew Kerek, Dean of Humanities Cynthia Nelson, and architects Marston Morgan and Ashraf Salloum for allowing me time for extensive fieldwork and research and for helping to establish our office in Cairo.

The people in my office, as usual, demonstrated talent, enthusiasm, hard work, and skill in assembling the photographs and drawings for this book and for all of the other projects we are working on. Francis Dzikowski is the finest photographer I've ever worked with. And, put simply, our architect and computer designer, Walton Chan, is brilliant. Architectural associate Samar Zaki is performing wonders, translating cryptic field notes into isometric tomb drawings. Brendhan Hight, webmaster of www.kv5.com, has published our data in a timely, attractive, and meaningful format that already has won countless awards for excellence. Conservator Lotfy Khaled ensures that the walls of KV 5 will continue to impress for centuries to come. Interns Marcie Handler and Melissa Zabecki have worked diligently, tracking down obscure references and checking facts for our database. Egyptologist Edwin Brock oversees those databases with knowledge and skill.

There have been scores of expedition members over the years, all of whom have contributed to the success of our work and whose names can be found in our annual reports. I would especially like to thank long-term past members Frank Ho, Gaston Chan, Bruce Lightbody, Richard Smith, Michael Jesudason, Marjorie Aronow, Barbara Greene, and Dr. Salima Ikram.

Dr. Catharine Roehrig and Mr. David Goodman have been with the TMP nearly from the beginning. It would be no overstatement to say that the project was able to proceed only because of their foresight and dedication.

The Theban Mapping Project is supported by several foundations whose concern for the protection of Egypt's monuments is clearly demonstrated by their encouragement of our work, not only in KV 5 but in Thebes and Egypt generally. To the Amoco Foundation, the Mobil Foundation, Pfizer Pharmaceutical, the Seaver Foundation, Santa Fe International, and their administrators go my sincere thanks. To the National Geographic Society I owe a debt of gratitude not only for financial support but for constant advice and encouragement. I especially would like to thank Society staff members Bill Allen, John Echave, Andy van Duym, George Stewart, and Margaret Sears for their help.

Many private individuals have contributed to the Theban Mapping Project: all are listed on www.kv5.com, and all know from my regular letters that we consider them project stalwarts. Without them, our work would simply stop. Special thanks go to Michael, Lock, Jerry, Martha and Loulou, whose modesty precludes more elaborate credit. Thanks, too, to Ilse Howe for aid and shelter.

To Bruce Ludwig go heartfelt thanks for constant and unwavering support of the project. Not only has Bruce contributed to its funding, either directly or by encouraging others to do so, but he has been generous with his time and advice and has helped to ensure that the TMP made it over the rough spots. There would be no TMP today were it not for Bruce's continued support.

W. Raymond Johnson, John Swanson, Edwin Brock, and Jill Kamel read parts of earlier drafts of the manuscript and offered sound advice. I am also pleased to acknowledge the encouragement and editorial help of Owen Laster (at William Morris), Henry Ferris, Joan Amico, and copyeditor Sonia Greenbaum (at William Morrow), and Ion Trewin (at Weidenfeld and Nicholson).

Susan Weeks has filled the roles of wife, mother, artist, epigrapher, ceramicist, cook, and camp organizer throughout the TMP's history, and she has performed every one of them superbly. Her talent and her patience deserve much more credit than these simple lines can offer. I am in awe—and in love.

INDEX

Page numbers in *italics* refer to illustrations.